THE
GOAT
SLEEPS
IN THE KITCHEN

The True Story of an Amazing Woman; Maria Insalaco Reina

D1479315

Joe Reina

ISBN 978-1-63630-230-0 (Paperback)
ISBN 978-1-63630-231-7 (Hardcover)
ISBN 978-1-63630-232-4 (Digital)

Covenant Books, Inc.
11661 Hwy 707
Murrells Inlet, SC 29576
www.covenantbooks.com

FOREWORD

When Joe Reina told me, he was writing a book, my first reaction was "Really, when do you have time?" But as Joe moved closer to his version of retirement, I realized he did have some time and when he said the book would be about family (which he calls the clan) and centering around the life of his mother, Maria Insalaco Reina, it made perfect sense.

Joe and I met by chance almost twenty years ago when his office building and my photography studio were around the corner from each other on Randolph and Washington Streets in Chicago. Two fellows originally from Saint Louis became friends. Over the years we would get together for lunch or he would stop in the studio to talk about one of my projects, or a business deal he had in the works. We shared ideas about books, economics, politics, current world events. But we always seemed to circle back to family, history, and business. At the time I had no idea he would write a book that combines those elements in the story of "The Goat Sleeps in The Kitchen." Through the chapters we see how his mother instilled in him, and the entire family the basics of entrepreneurship, and the will to seize a chance when others do not recognize the possibilities. Her keen mind and resolute spirit, when odds were clearly against her, were combined with fairness and always integrity.

Because Joe sets the scenes in detailed historical context the reader can appreciate the resilience of a diverse family that faced adversity together as a family supporting each other and following Mrs. Reina's vision for their successful future. She had the courage to leave a small village in Sicily for an uncertain life in America. "The Goat Sleeps in The Kitchen" is a story of a proud family legacy and is a fascinating read!

David Phillips

Maria Insalaco Reina
1893-1991

DEDICATION

Thank you to Virginia Reina Maniscalco and Josie Reina Mocca for being my secondary mothers, they gave me their undying love, and never gave up on me.

ACKNOWLEDGEMENT

The long-awaited writing of this story became a reality with help of some exceptionally good friends, family members, and associates. Some that knew my mother and some that had heard of her from me, and others, about her. They encouraged me from the start to tell the story, and they were there in the early days when I began writing, pushing me to "just write!" I was told "most books about early twentieth century people were primarily about men." At the top of the list is my cousin Hugh Ingrasci, he helped me develop my style, and especially helped form the early stages of the story. Paul Juettner, my good friend and attorney, guided and encouraged me. He set up guidelines to assure I would not fall into any legal traps, and read the entire manuscript, then asked questions to insure I had not made any legal errors.

Early on, the first author I interviewed was Adrian Windsor, she shared great advice about what to do, and what to expect, and because of that I became driven to get the story told. There is no way to thank my dear friend and photographer David Phillips, who took small photos, some that dated to the '20s and were in bad condition, and he miraculously brought them back to life. I spent hours with him as he readied over a hundred photos for publication. Patricia Benesh, the owner of Author's Assistant, helped me take a bunch of chapters to manuscript, patiently, yielding to my demands of her undivided attention. She got the message early, that I am not the most patient person in the world! Without her this book would have been written but would have been a long drawn out bunch of words. Thanks to my niece Susan Reina Gerke for allowing me to use her story, "Turkey and Dressing Optional", which not only described the feasts of Joe and Josie Mocca's thanksgiving dinners, but truly describes the "festas" the clan enjoyed! I will be eternally grateful to Michelle Holmes at Covenant Book Publishers for her help at every level of taking the manuscript to print, editing, page design, cover design, the guidance from her has been incredible.

And then there is my wife Laurie, who has the patience of Jobe in dealing with me. I was confused when I began writing, and she went online and sent me "how to" articles about writing which really helped alleviate the confusion. She tolerated my frustration in those early days and kept me from throwing in the towel. She gave me the idea of using a timeline to tie into the original outline prepared with my sisters and helped me with suggestions on various chapters. Finally, she took the chapters and did the grammar and spelling corrections and put them in some semblance of order.

As has always been the case in every business venture we entered, she has been the "wind beneath my sails", and has handled my Sicilian emotions, like the trooper she is.

PROLOGUE

This book is based on a true story about an amazing early twentieth century woman. She stood out in a crowd of very good friends and relatives from the same small town in central Sicily called Casteltermini. She found herself in a forced marriage and endured more traumas in the first few years of the relationship than most women go through in a lifetime.

This is the story of a significant but little-known segment of a twentieth-century diaspora. It was not a societal dislocation after a forced exile like the Israelites scattering after their Babylonian captivity but a mass exodus from Europe by some "huddled masses yearning to be free." This oppressed group fled the dire poverty of Sicily and southern Italy—a subsistence lifestyle that subsidized the owners of the coal mining industry and early American factories. For roughly sixty years, 1860 to 1920, Sicilians and Italians fled their bleak living conditions, the hope of earning a humane, livable wage for themselves and their children.

At that time, the US population was largely split, a great many living on farms and in rural areas, while the factories were springing up in the cities creating a need for laborers. Many Americans were reluctant to work in them because in most cases, the machinery was dangerous and lacking safety features.

The work was tedious, labor intensive, nine to ten hours a day, six days a week, for very low wages, and the factory owners were vigorously seeking help from Europe. This ushered in the immigration, especially so in the later part of the nineteenth century.

The situation was different in the coal mining industry; the mines were usually in small unheard of towns with little or sparse housing. It forced the coal mining companies to make accommodations, building crude, barely livable houses and company stores to service the miner's families.

There was no electricity available, no sewage system, the houses usually had outhouses, no indoor plumbing, wells were dug for water in the center of town and had to be fetched for use in the house. Living conditions were horrible all because the price of coal was cheap, and the miners were taken advantage of.

The mines were more dangerous than the factories; the miners had to go down as far as thirty to forty feet. The air was thin, and breathing was difficult, ultimately causing severe lung problems from the coal dust. The miners spent ten hours a day in the mines. The most dangerous problem, however, were mine collapses and explosions caused by the use of dynamite that the miners used when it was too difficult to excavate with picks and shovels.

The workers worked very long hours, and were pushed to dig and load as much as ten tons a day. They lived in boarding houses under unbelievable conditions. They had not heard of this living situation in their former country, but once they were there, they had no choice but to hope for the best. And then there was the ultimate problem of the mine drying up, and the miners would have to move to the next coal mining town to seek employment.

The story begins in a small town in Sicily named Casteltermini. It takes place in the early part of the twentieth century, the interrelationships of a clan of families—some that were related—their struggles, hard work, successes, failures, and dedication to achieve a better lifestyle. They came with barely the clothes on their back, for the most part, they were uneducated, Catholic, did not use birth control, had many kids, and rose above the rough and horrible conditions of the times.

They came looking for work and were willing to do what the average American in their respective age groups refused to lower themselves to do. The Americans were better educated and wanted better, higher-paying jobs.

In this particular period, many ended up in the coal mines in Southern Illinois, and quite a few arrived in St. Louis, Missouri, where there were plenty of hard-labor, intense jobs. There they found work in the clay mines. The clay was being used to make brick. The Howard Brick Company employed 90 percent Italians and Sicilians. They also worked in the factories, such as Banner Iron Works, which had the same percentage of both groups.

They were mostly congregated in a small area in south St. Louis called Fairmont Heights, better known as the "Hill." It was a ten-square-block neighborhood of which 95 percent of the people were Italians and Sicilians.

The story revolves around the *clan*—the Reinas, Insalacos, Castellanos, Rumbolos, Cunettos, Burruanos, and their offspring. The succeeding generation groups that emerged were better educated, more professional, doctors, dentists, druggists, lawyers, teachers, professors, accountants, as well as small and large business owners. There was one common denominator; they all inherited the hard-work ethic from their parents.

This amazing woman, Maria Insalaco Reina, was married to a lackluster, strong-tempered, hardworking, tough, fearless, uneducated man who never had steady work his entire life. She endured a series of traumas—miscarriages and still births—each time berated by her husband for not delivering a healthy child.

She refused to be the typical stay-at-home housewife, who would raise a bunch of kids, cook, and perform the usual everyday household chores. She refused to live a paltry lifestyle, she refused to accept the status quo of a below-poverty life in the early days after her arrival in America, and she refused to accept the role of most women of her day.

And having a second-grade education was no barrier; she didn't use the fact she lacked schooling as an excuse, for she had great "street sense." She was determined to rise above the obstacles thrown at her at every level to create a better life for her family. Starting at age twelve and until she died, her immediate family was her life.

She questioned her lowly status as a woman, and as far as she was concerned, it was up to her to do something about it. "Who says a woman can't own a business? And who says a woman can't own real estate? And why should a woman settle for one half the pay a man

THE GOAT SLEEPS IN THE KITCHEN

makes for doing the same work?" She was fifty years ahead of the role played by women at the time.

She passed her work ethics, her entrepreneurial skills, and her determination to get ahead onto her children.

This story is also about one of her children, whose nine lives as a successful businessman began at age twelve, working in a grocery store.

Maria Insalaco Reina was my mother!

THE CLAN

The Reinas: Carmelo and Maria Insalaco, Virginia (1916), Carlo (1918), Giuseppina "Josie" (1920), Ignazio "Jim" (1923), Joseph (1927), and Joe (1936).

The Castellanos: Carmelo and Giusippina D'Angelo, Frank, Lilly, Jimmy, Joseph, and Carmella.

The Castellanos: Giuseppe and Anna (Annuzia), Frank, Jimmy, Rose, and Caroline.

The Burruanos: Giuseppe and Rosa Insalco, Giovanna "Jennie" (1921), Salvatore (1927), and Giuseppina "Josie" (1932).

The Ingrascis: John and Rosa Insalaco and Carmelo "Hugh".

The Cunettos: Jake and Carmella Insalco, Vince, Giuseppe "Joe", Lena, and Lilly.

The Rumbolo's: Giuseppe (Pepe) and Santa, Sam, Carlo, and John.

CHAPTER 1

The Kidnap Casteltermini

Sicily 1909

Maria picked up the pace as she walked to the bakery with her loaves of bread to be baked. She sensed someone was closing in on her.

"Good morning, Maria. I have been watching you from time to time going to the bakery to have them bake your bread, and I have decided to marry you. How old are you now?"

"I know who you are, and you are not marrying me, Carmelo. I need to take care of my family. Please leave me alone."

"Are you going to tell me how old you are?"

"No, please let me pass."

One evening, a short time later, Maria was outside disposing of the dinner pasta water when Carmelo's two sisters-in-laws threw a shawl over her head and kidnapped her. They took her to Luigi Reina's house (Carmelo's brother) to convince her to marry Carmelo. Unless she agreed, they would keep her all night and ruin her reputation. After all, this was a tiny town in early twentieth-century Sicily!

Maria said, "You can keep me here for the next ten years. I am not marrying him."

At which time, they informed her there could be severe harm to her father, Ignazio, if she didn't give in. "You and your family will be orphans. Do you want that?"

This threat hit home with Maria, who was mature beyond her sixteen years. She had been caring for her family since her mother, Giuseppina, passed away four years ago of pneumonia. She was well aware that the Reina family were well-known and connected to what was then a well-organized group controlling crime throughout Sicily. That was the word on the street, and while it was never proven, the fear was there. The Reina clan was never to be crossed. Through the night, they wore her down until she finally agreed to marry the Scoundrel!

Maria Insalaco was a beautiful blond, blue-eyed fifteen-year-old young lady when Carmelo Reina started pursuing her. It was the summer of 1909 in Casteltermini, Sicily. Her mother, Giuseppina, had died suddenly at age thirty-one. Maria was twelve. Her father, Ignazio, worked in a coal mine in Alabama, sending money home each month so that the family of five could survive. There were no jobs in the small towns in Sicily, and as had so many, he had gone off to America to find work. Ignazio worked for $0.10 an hour, ten hours a day, six days a week. He lived in a boarding house, paying $1.50 a week for room and board. The town was owned by the coal mining company; this was the case in most coal mining towns.

There was nothing to do in town, so he saved just about everything he earned. The shock of his wife's passing came three months after she passed, for there were no means of reaching him, except by mail. All he could do was write to the family and drown in his sorrow.

Maria had two sisters, Carmela and Rosa, and a baby brother Ignazio. She had already been helping her mother by the time she was ten; thus, she knew how to make bread and pasta. She was born on November 25, 1893. Carmella was two years older, Rosa was five years younger, and Ignazio was four. Maria only had a second-grade education.

She would take the loaves of bread to the bakery up the street every three or four days for them to bake it since there was no oven in the stovetop at the house. It was here that Carmelo began his quest, at times stalking her. She was leery of him, for his family's reputation was notorious. His older brother was very tough and ruled the family with an iron hand and was believed to be involved in illegal activities.

She would check out the street before leaving the house all the time to be sure Carmelo was not in the area.

Carmelo was born October 9, 1885, and was eight years older than Maria. He had four brothers, Giuseppe, Luigi, Cologero, and Salvatore, and he worked when there was work in the sulfur mine. His reputation as somewhat of a lady's man was well-known. Everyone in the neighborhood knew he had a very nasty temper. Maria's friends had warned her to be careful around him.

Casteltermini was a very small town in the middle of nowhere in central Sicily. There was no industry, and the only jobs were at the nearby sulfur mine. There were the usual stores, grocery, bakery, barbershop, livery stable, and even a nice restaurant in town. Since many foreign countries in its three-thousand-year history had occupied the island, some areas in the smaller towns still spoke different dialects. So much so that it was difficult to understand people from one town to the next.

This was Sicily of 1909, an island that had been part of the unification of Italy in 1861 by General Garibaldi. The people of Italy looked down on the island. The Greeks and the Carthaginians were there first about three thousand years before Christ was born. Then the Romans took the island since they needed wheat to feed their armies, and they could, thereby, get two crops a year. Rome conquered the island about two hundred years before Christ. But the French, Austria, Spanish, and the Moors, over the centuries, also ruled the island. Needless to say, all of these cultures influenced the people, the architecture, and the language. The brutal fact remains that occupied Sicily was raped; the people were maligned; and when the invaders settled, the natives ended up very poor with little or no industry. By the start of the twentieth century, its economy was a disaster.

The Wedding to Carmelo

The wedding happened on a beautiful sunny day in June 1910. Maria wore a simple white dress; her friend, Giusippina D'Angelo, had sewn it for her. She had very little to do with the preparations. Luigi's best friend hosted the reception in his beautiful garden where landscapers had worked for days to prepare it. The air was scented from lilac bushes that were in full bloom. Not a cloud was seen in the solid blue sky.

Luigi had the affair catered by the only nice restaurant in town. The food was lavish. He spared no expense; two pasta dishes were served and fresh homegrown vegetables. Wild rabbit was roasted on site, and the dinner ended with a ripe tomato salad. At both ends of the table were two large bowls of fresh fruit and several cheeses. The local baker made a beautiful cake and donated it out of respect for Maria. And compliments of the host, the homemade wine was reputed to be the best in town!

Luigi and his other brothers, like Carmelo, were about the same size, short and stocky, and with very dark complexions. Their skin color left no doubt that somewhere along the line, their ancestry and bloodlines were Moorish. While the name Reina sounds Hispanic, the origin is Arabic!

The wedding guests were mostly friends of the Reinas. Maria's family and some few friends were at two tables and segregated themselves from the rest of the crowd. There was little discussion between them because of the coerced marriage arrangement. A very handsome, nicely dressed guitarist played softly songs of the past, classic favorites of the Reina family. Maria had little or nothing to say during any of the activities, and throughout most of the day, she was stoic and rarely smiled. The same mood prevailed among her guests since they knew the wedding was a forced affair.

Carmelo drank too much of the homemade wine as usual and danced with and flirted with many of the local young girls. Maria refused to dance with him, explaining, "I don't know how to dance." She was dreading the thought of sleeping with Carmelo. There was plenty of homemade wine consumed, and not much attention was paid to the small group sitting with the bride. When Carmelo and Maria got home, he passed out the minute he hit the bed to Maria's delight. She laid in bed, unable to sleep; all she could think about was what she believed to be a dismal future.

Maria knew from day one of meeting him that Carmelo deserved the name Scoundrel. It was only a matter of time that Maria found herself pregnant, and she visited a midwife, Angelina Severino. The nearest doctor was in a nearby town, eight kilometers away.

"Maria you are probably three months pregnant, so the baby will be here next April. Come to see me once a month, but sooner if you start having any problems. Be careful and do not lift anything heavy! You will know when it is time. Water will break, as your sign, and as soon as that happens, send for me no matter what time of day it is."

Maria informed Carmelo about the pregnancy, and he was excited and asked, "Maria, speak to the midwife to see if she can tell if you are having a boy." He was persistent in his demand and feared his wrath if she had a girl instead.

On the morning of April 5, Maria experienced serious pain. She assumed it was time and sent Carmelo to get Angelina for the delivery. Angelina delivered twins; both were stillborn. There were no drugs to ease Maria's pain of losing two babies in a matter of hours nor any to help with the mental anguish of carrying them for nine months only to realize they were gone in a matter of minutes! Angelina sat with Maria for a while and held her hand and tried to comfort her.

"Maria, you are young and very healthy, and you have plenty of time in your life to have a family, don't be sad." But Maria was more concerned about Carmelo's response when he learned about the death of the babies.

Sadly, this was a small town located thirty kilometers from the next big city, Agrigento; hence, there was no hospital, and even if there had been a doctor in the town, most people were poor and could not afford one even for childbirth.

Her fears were justified; the Scoundrel scolded her, screamed that it was her fault that she failed to bear him a healthy heir. "We will keep trying until you bear me a son!"

A few months later Maria informed Carmelo, she was with child again, but she miscarried shortly thereafter. Once again, six months later, the midwife informed Maria she was going to have another baby. Maria lived in anguish during the nine months of the pregnancy for fear of losing the baby. A baby boy arrived and was baptized, but seven months later, her next trauma, he got an infection of some kind and died. Again, Maria was the victim of Carmelo's anger. He became relentless about wanting a child and showed no mercy for what she was experiencing. Somehow, she endured trauma number three!

The Getaway

At a wedding party one evening in 1913, Carmelo was his usual self, consuming too much homemade wine. He was on the stage also known as the old man in the first *Godfather* movie, singing the "Butcher Boy" song and was loving every minute of the attention he was getting. Maria again was concerned about his getting drunk and how his temperament changed for the worse. Before long, he was on the dance floor with the daughter of a family friend, and as always, he was dancing a little too close. The woman's older brother, Pietro, was keeping an eye on the Scoundrel's advances, and within minutes, the brother and Carmelo were arguing on the dance floor. Soon they were asked to take it outside by the father of the bride who approached them.

"If you two are going to fight, go outside. Don't ruin my daughter's wedding." The room was dark, there was no electricity, and it was lit by candlelight. No one really noticed them leaving; few had seen the argument.

Now Carmelo was slightly built and only five feet and five inches. The other man was taller and heavier, and he struck first. It was then that a life-changing event took place. Carmelo was challenged by Pietro with a knife. But little did Pietro know that the Scoundrel had his trusty Sicilian switchblade! Carmelo stabbed his opponent three times, and the man, moaning, fell to the ground. Carmelo walked calmly back into the wedding party, grabbed Maria, went immediately to his brother, Luigi's, house, and told him what had happened.

Bear in mind at this point, the incident happened in a town with no hospital, no doctor readily available, and Agrigento, thirty kilometers away over a dirt road. The only means of transportation to get there was by horse and buggy; it was late at night. Carmelo's victim was certainly doomed, and early the next morning, Carmelo and Luigi left for Agrigento, assuming the man was dead! Luigi had to rescue his brother from the law.

"Carmelo, we have to get you out of the country! You will be staying with my friend, Salvatore Vacarro, until a ship arrives, and we will get you to America. I'll notify our brother, Giuseppe, all the information he needs to meet you when you arrive."

Giuseppe was working in a coal mine in Whiteash, Illinois, as Carmelo was aware.

"But, Luigi, I do not speak English. How am I going to communicate?"

"I will work things out with the captain of the ship. Don't worry about it," replied Luigi.

They next visited a friend with the right connections and, within a matter of hours, created papers with a new identity for Carmelo with his new name, Carmelo Castellano. There was a man in Casteltermini with the same name.

Consider for a moment that Carmelo had no education, and he could not even sign his name. He had gone to work as a five-year-old in the sulfur mine near the town. He was temporarily staying with the Vacarros sleeping on the floor, for they had no guest room. The weather was hot and muggy, and he was miserable. Mrs. Vacarro was nowhere near the cook that Maria was, but Luigi had told Carmelo, "These people are good friends of mine. Do not cause any problems. They will notify you when a ship arrives to take you to America."

The departure day finally arrived; thus, the captain was properly bribed, and Carmelo was allowed to board without the preliminary procedures for entry. He was ushered to the steerage section of the ship and was told to remain there as the captain's assistant explained, "You need to keep a low profile. Do not talk to many people. Do you understand? We will come to get you when we reach America."

Here Carmelo nodded and did as he was told.

Because he could not speak a word of English, Carmelo remained below deck when the ship arrived in New York harbor, and the Americans began cleaning the area. Then the captain's assistant came to get him. He bypassed Ellis Island, earned via the bribe given to the captain, and he was elated to finally be off the ship to get some fresh air. His only luggage was a small leather bag, and he had worn the same clothes for twelve weeks. The stench of his body odor was beyond description.

Escorted secretly off the ship by the captain's assistant, Carmelo was taken to a nearby tavern and met by his brother, Giuseppe, and a Polish coal miner who spoke English.

Giuseppe greeted his baby brother with open arms, "*Buona sera*, Carmelo, welcome to America. We have been waiting here two days, and we have a hotel room. Let's go there so you can take a bath, and then we will get some dinner. I have made arrangements for you to work with us at the Whiteash coal mine, and you can stay with us in the same house. Everything is going to be fine, and later when things settle down at home, you can send for Maria."

Carmelo was so exhausted; he barely heard a word Giuseppe said. The next morning, they boarded a train for St Louis, Missouri, and ended up on the "Hill," the Italian/Sicilian neighborhood. They met up with some old friends from Casteltermini, who, in turn, got them to a coal mining town in southern Illinois called Whiteash.

No consideration was given to Maria. How was she to survive? This was not the ordinary woman of the times. It was the start of her traumatic survival, life with the Scoundrel, the first of a series of setbacks, forever toughing of her via a lesson in learning to deal with utter disaster! She moved quickly back with her family. By now, her father had luckily returned, and he was working in the sulfur mine when there was work.

Ignazio welcomed her back with open arms as did her siblings. There was no timeline for how long she would be with them. She was relieved to be rid of the Scoundrel. She could breathe again. But she knew it was not the end of dealing with the misery she had endured in the short time they were married.

CHAPTER 2

America
The Castellano Identity

Whiteash, Illinois
The coal miner, 1913

Carmelo went to work for the Marion Coal Company in Whiteash, Illinois, a small town in southern Illinois founded by the company owner, Charles A. Gent, in 1903. It was not much of a town. Its main street was named after the mine. There were no other businesses in town, and its meager housing was mostly owned by the coal company. There was a post office, and that was it, no shops or services.

Carmelo moved into a small three-room house with two bedrooms and a tiny room with a table where the group ate and a stove for heating. A coal miner and his wife were running it as a boarding house. The kitchen was a lean-to outside where the wife cooked all year in heat, cold, rain, or snow. And, of course, it had the proverbial outhouse. Water was available in the town center from a well a block and a half away!

The Scoundrel slept in a room with his brother, Giuseppe, and the other miner who came to get him in New York, all three in one bed. The man and woman who ran the house occupied the other bedroom. There was no indoor plumbing, no electricity, and, needless to say, nothing in the way of entertainment. Same for the town, there was nothing to do except to work, eat, and sleep.

Carmelo went to work for $0.10 an hour, ten hours a day, six days a week, and paid the lady who ran the house $2 a week for room and board. By the time he finished dinner, he was so exhausted he went to bed. He started saving money to send for Maria since he had nowhere to spend it. Carmelo hated the weather. It was late February, cold, windy, occasional snow, and rain, which made the walk to the mine difficult. The mine was damp and cold, nothing compared to the beautiful weather in Casteltermini.

He was constantly complaining to his brother, saying, "What are we doing here? Many of our *paesani* are working the mines in Alabama!"

Giuseppe reminded him, "Carmelo, you should have thought of that before you stabbed that guy!"

Meals were sparse. Breakfast was a piece of bread, sometimes stale, and a cup of black coffee. There was no milk, for lack of refrigeration. Lunch consisted of a piece of stale bread and a hunk of cheese and an occasional apple. There was no grocery store nor any other kind of store. This was a workman's town. Period! Schools were unknown in most coal mining villages. A man would come once a week from Johnson City, Illinois, which was 2.8 miles away by horse and wagon to deliver groceries and take the order for the next week. Everybody in town was at his mercy regarding what he could find to fill their orders. The average grocery list consisted of canned vegetables, bread, onions, potatoes, and pasta, with very little in the way of fruits and fresh vegetables.

Carmelo struggled with the workload and harsh demands of the supervisor. He was pushed like the rest of the miners to load as much as ten tons of coal a day. It was obvious the supervisor, who was a mainlander Italian, disliked the Sicilian miners. On numerous occasions, Carmelo argued with the supervisor and reached for his knife. Luckily Giuseppe was there to remind him why he was there—the wedding stabbing.

The rest of the year went by quickly, and soon Carmelo was in a hopeful rhythm, savoring the day when he could send for Maria. That fact alone was the driving force that kept him going. Life was boring; there was to be a reunion day, and her arrival would be that special day! The bright sunny days of spring and early summer in Whiteash made life a little better, and the Scoundrel stopped complaining to his brother, but it was short-lived. The one-hundred-degree days of summer arrived, and the humidity made it worse. There was only one window in the eating area of the house, none in the bedroom where he slept. The miners were deprived of a good night's sleep. The trio rarely took a bath; the stench was only bearable by each other.

1915

The man and wife running the shanty house made a sudden announcement that they were moving, and Carmelo informed them, Maria was on the way from Casteltermini. At Carmelo's request a few months earlier, the Polish miner living with them had sent a note to Maria to come to America.

Because Carmelo could not speak English, the husband and wife went with him to the mining office to inform them that the Reinas would be assuming the monthly house rent. He signed an agreement with an X to have the rent taken from his check, hence, the term, "You owe your soul to the company store." The rent for the house was $9 a month.

Maria arrived in New York aboard the Italian ship, *Palermo*, on Friday, June 18, 1915, after a grueling twelve weeks at sea, but the trip for Maria from Casteltermini had been a nightmare! First by horse and wagon to Palermo, a rough five hours, then four weeks with friends of the Reinas, waiting for the ship's arrival.

Once again, Luigi came through and had made arrangements for her stay in Palermo. She was very uncomfortable staying with strangers—and pretty much stayed to herself—sleeping in a tiny room, and eating very little. It was hot and humid. She slept on the third floor with no window, which made sleeping very difficult. As it was the case in those days, there was no indoor bathroom. Maria used a bedpan which she would empty outside in the outhouse, after descending three flights of stairs every morning. It was a disgusting privy, and it was rarely cleaned. She took to cleaning it every other day, for which she received no gratitude. She did make bread on occasion and offered to cook, but the lady of the house had an attitude about a strange, pretty girl staying there. Her husband was always very nice and pleasant towards Maria, of course he was doing it out of respect for Luigi.

Finally, the day came to go to the dock and prepare to board the ocean-going ship. As was customary in those days, Luigi had his contacts in *Palermo* bribe the captain, who shared the money with his two aids, and Maria bypassed the thirty-one questions that were required by all passengers before they boarded. She was escorted to her berth, given a blanket and a pillow, plus a metal plate and fork and knife for eating. The regular fare was $30, but Luigi had paid $60, which included the bribe to the captain. This was a special accommodation for Maria, which included train fare from Ellis Island to St. Louis and bus fare to Whiteash where Carmelo and his brother, Giuseppe, lived. Maria had no idea what she was in for, but she was on her way.

Maria travels steerage

The accommodations for steerage passengers were horrendous, cramped, and overcrowded. The food consisted of mediocre soups, stale bread, boiled potatoes, and sometimes tough, boiled meat. For Maria, getting to the port in Palermo was a chore. A tag with directions to a destination written in very crude English was put around her neck on getting to a New York train station and later by bus to Whiteash. Her brother-in-law's connections there were the key.

The sailing immigrants needed $25 before boarding, and sometimes it could take weeks for a ship to arrive. She should have also had to endure a medical exam that was required, but this too she averted. Steerage passengers were required to be processed at Ellis Island, and it was a nightmare. She was not told about this, nor was she told of the twelve to fourteen weeks needed to get to New York. People were often seasick through the entire trip, and many died during the voyage. They very rarely were allowed to go above board for fresh air. Toilet facilities were horrible, people constantly getting nausea, and they were hardly ever washed or cleaned; thus, the stench was constant. The same was true for bathing; there were no facilities on most ships to bathe themselves.

People wore the same clothes for weeks. On most ships, there was simply no way to launder them. It was an emotionally and mentally disturbing experience. There was also no sense of urgency at Ellis Island, and the inspection lines were long and tedious.

Once off the ship, they had to proceed to a waiting area to be processed. A tag was attached to Maria, and she was put on a boat with no protection from the elements. Then she was sent to Ellis Island. After the arduous trip, her patience was put to another test. She was examined head to toe and had to bathe in groups and was sprayed with a solution to rid her of any bugs or lice. Once the long examination was over, there were no other problems, so she was sent to the final interview and asked many questions, mostly about her health.

Maria did not speak English, and her Sicilian dialect made it difficult for the Italian translator to understand her, but somehow, perhaps her beauty, blue eyes, and charming smile got her through it. However, if there was the slightest sign of a problem, these aliens were detained. They were released once the doctors were comfortable with it, and this could take as long as a month.

Once they had answered all the necessary questions, they proceeded to another area. They could exchange here their foreign money for dollars, and they could be taken by boat to train terminals or to Manhattan. Most were given a meal and sent on their way with little or no idea on how to get to the next or even a final destination, but Maria avoided much of this and soon found herself on the train to St. Louis, directed by fellow travelers.

When she reached the big city, a very nice conductor read the tag pinned to her dress and surprised her by speaking Italian, and though it was in a different dialect, she understood him.

"I am supposed to meet some people on the Hill. Do you know where it is?"

"Yes, as a matter of fact, I live there! Do you have their name and address?"

She reached into her purse and pulled out a name, Jake Cunetto, and an address.

"I know him. He has a barbershop. Let me finish my paperwork, and I will take you to his house."

A few minutes later, they boarded a bus across the street from the train station and headed for the Hill. It was a bright sunny day. Maria was grateful, for she had no heavy coat.

The conductor walked with her from the bus stop. It was two blocks to the Cunetto home, and they knocked on the door. Maria's cousin, Carmella Insalaco, who had just married Jake Cunetto, almost went into shock when she saw Maria. Both embraced in tears; it was a grand reunion. Carmella invited her in after she had thanked the conductor, and they entered a very nice home. It was a delight to be somewhere clean after weeks of grimy travels. They sat in the kitchen, and Carmella made an espresso for Maria while Maria unfolded the story about the stabbing and the escape of Carmelo to Whiteash.

"We had heard there was a problem, and what I don't understand, Maria, is why you came here. You should have left him. He is not good for you. You had a chance to be rid of him!"

"Carmella, you know about his family, and that my father is still in Casteltermini, taking care of my brother and sisters, and I don't want anything to happen to them. I can't offend Luigi Reina."

"Well, Maria, when was the last time you ate? I'm going to make some pasta for us for lunch."

"No, Carmella, please, I'm fine. Don't go to any trouble. I need to hurry and get to the bus station to get to Whiteash."

"Maria, you just completed a long trip, relax. Let's eat. Later, after you take a nap and when Jake gets home, we will figure out how to get you to Whiteash."

They had a nice lunch, and Maria reluctantly agreed to take a nap. She was so exhausted she fell asleep the minute her head hit the pillow.

Soon Jake Cunetto came home, and when Maria heard the door close and heard voices, she woke up, and Jake greeted her with a hug and welcomed her by making her an offer.

"Maria, stay with us until Sunday, and we will take the bus with you to Whiteash. I do not want you to make the trip alone."

She eagerly agreed, especially after he had described the sleazy town. She needed a rest after the trip from Sicily, her long time at sea, the ordeal at Ellis Island, and the train ride to St. Louis.

On Sunday, they boarded the bus for the short ride to Whiteash and then walked and found the house where Carmelo and his brother were staying. Maria, Carmella, and Jake were shocked at the place's squalor. They could not believe how awful it was! Before they even knocked on the door, Carmella looked at Maria and sadly shook her head.

The house was an old wooden frame shack, sitting on stilts, and had never been painted. It leaned a little to the left. There was one small window and a beat-up old stove outside sitting under a make-shift small awning and a wooden shelf next to it. There were a few dirty pots and pans on the shelf. It truly was disgusting. The stench from the nearby outhouse was offensive even from a great distance.

They knocked on the door and were greeted by Giuseppe who immediately called out for Carmelo. He was sleeping! The shock was even more disappointing when they looked around the small eating area. Jake looked at Maria with pity, and Carmella grabbed her cousin and held her until Carmelo came out of the bedroom. Maria was embarrassed, for she knew what her cousin and Jake were thinking.

Carmelo entered the room. There was no warm and wild embrace. In fact, he didn't even offer his wife a hug. He just shook Jake's hand. He barely noticed Carmella, which was hard to understand since she had the Insalaco good looks and was beautiful—hard to ignore. Carmelo turned to Maria and showed her the small bedroom they were to occupy.

He said, "Drop your bag here. Why don't we cook some pasta for the Cunettos?"

Jake made a quick excuse to negate the suggestion, so he and his wife could leave.

Jake said, "Thank you, Carmelo, but we promised some of our friends we would be at their home for dinner tonight, and we need to get to the bus stop to get the last bus. It departs in thirty minutes."

All he wanted was to get out of that house. It was filthy. There was no way he would eat anything there. Maria thanked the Cunettos and hugged her cousin, and both shed a few tears as they said goodbye.

Maria wasted no time getting settled. She sent Giuseppe to get some water and told Carmelo to heat up the stoves, both the inside one for heat and the cooking one outside. Then she cleaned, scrubbed the floor, and washed all the pots and pans and dishes. Later she stripped the beds and washed the sheets in boiling hot water and hung them outside to dry. The hot sun dried them, and for the first time in weeks, they smelled fresh enough to sleep on.

The groceries had been delivered the day before, and she took an onion and some garlic and a can of tomato sauce and made a pot of *sugo* (homemade marinara sauce) and cooked pasta for dinner. It was the first good food the brothers had had since they first arrived in Whiteash.

Maria took charge. Her first change, upgrading the grocery list. The very first Saturday there, she informed the man with the groceries, "I want flour and eggs so I can make my own bread and pasta. Bring me whatever fresh vegetables you can find and see if you can get me a female goat!"

The following Saturday, the peddler, Mr. Parisi, delivered the new groceries and the goat. Thus, she began the changes in the Reina lifestyle and that of the miners. The goat was named Nunzio, named after Carmelo's goat in Casteltermini. Maria's instincts had kicked in and her mind was working overtime with regard to all the things she could do with the milk. One of the first things she made was cheese. The goat became a major part of the family's food source.

Dinners were much better. For early in the week, they began having meals which consisted of homemade pasta, vegetables, and great homemade bread. She made lunches for the miners from that same bread using it for sandwiches she made with eggplant, mixed with other vegetables, and the cheese that she made. Breakfast consisted of two-day old bread and coffee with milk from the goat. On Saturdays, she washed the coal miners' filthy clothes and used the water from the laundry to scrub the heretofore filthy wood floor in the house. It was a new day in Whiteash! Ah, the goat! Fresh milk and cheese!

The weather turned beautiful. It was October, and outside of an occasional fall shower, the days were warm, cool nights, and cooking outside was not as bad as it first appeared when she arrived. But she dreaded the coming winter, keeping warm inside and cooking outside.

There were quite a few *paesani* from Casteltermini living in Whiteash, even a few of her friends. On occasion, Carmelo would invite some of them for dinner on Sundays, so they did have a limited social life. At Carmelo's insistence, it didn't take long for Maria to get pregnant, which was the last thing she needed. She figured the child's arrival would be sometime in July 1916. She sought information about a midwife and had made a friend, Stella Mancuso, who was from Casteltermini. Stella knew of a midwife Maria could trust.

The family, 1916

Winter arrived sooner than usual as did the snow. Carmelo brought the goat into the house every night, and it slept in the kitchen where the group ate. As expected, the goat would urinate and sometimes defecate on the floor—one more situation Maria had to deal with. Maria longed for the earlier warm fall days, and cooking outside became a chore. Being pregnant didn't make it any easier.

"Carmelo, why are we here in this god-awful town? We should be in the south. There are coal mines in Alabama, and many of our relatives are there!"

"Stop complaining right now, you have to have a baby. Let's see if you can get through this pregnancy and have a healthy child."

He was totally uncaring of her situation and the horror of living in Whiteash. On a hot humid morning, July 28, Maria woke up suffering from the heat and pain, so she had Carmelo go get the mid-wife, who hurriedly brought water to the lean to and boiled it and prepared for the birth. She sent Carmelo and Giuseppe and the other miner to visit with friends to get them out of the way. Maria was in labor all day and into the evening. The baby was born in the house late that night. There was no hospital in Whiteash. Rosalia Ferrara, the midwife, delivered the baby, fortunately with no complications. Maria purposely named the baby Virginia after Carmelo's mother because she didn't want any grief from him for having a girl.

The baby proved to be a lot more than Maria was prepared for. She had to sleep in the small room where Maria and Carmelo slept. Her midmorning cries to be fed or to have her diaper changed was very irritating to Carmelo. Maria had made baby clothes and makeshift diapers from flour sacks she'd bleached. She was nursing and decided this feeding system was not going to work. It was tough enough having a new baby, but two miners lived in the next room. The worst part was dealing with the Scoundrel's temper tantrums. His behavior had made her more miserable than the nine months of her pregnancy. She took the baby to Stella's house and told her of the dilemma. Stella suggested she find a small used bed that would fit up against the wall in the small kitchen where they ate every night. She called for help from Pepe Rumbolo and his wife, Santa, her friends from Casteltermini who had arrived in Whiteash. Pepe worked at the mine. Within a week, he brought a bed to Maria. He had paid $2 for it. Knowing she didn't have very much money, he told her to forget any payment, and she could pay him later. But she insisted on paying him.

The year 1916 was flying by. The July and August heat was brutal, especially in a house that had one window. Sleeping was intol-erable, but the worst was cooking outside, especially when it rained. Maria wondering what she did to deserve this. She vowed to find a better way. This was not what she expected, considering the stories she had heard about opportunities in America.

Finally fall arrived, and the weather became more tolerable, especially since Virginia was a really good baby. She was easy to care for and slept through the night, making Maria's life a lot easier. But

Maria was already thinking of the hardships winter would bring. Sometimes the cold and snow made cooking outside the lean-to impossible. The inclement weather would often delay the arrival of the groceries, for the road was impassable. There seemed to be no end to the miserable life in Whiteash, and she started pressuring Carmelo to make a change, but it went in one ear and out the other for her muleheaded husband.

In mid-1917, Maria found herself pregnant again, and she estimated the baby would be due sometime late February or early March of 1918. She informed Carmelo of the news and how this was going to present a problem with regard to sleeping arrangements, the miners, and the young children. She was fearful of her next suggestion; the miners needed to go, and as she expected, the Scoundrel went off the deep end into rage.

"How are we going to live? Are you crazy? We need the income!"

She let him rant, and then she said, "I will take in sewing, and I will figure it out. Let me worry about it."

She soon put the word out. She wanted to buy a used sewing machine, and one day, Stella told her about a neighbor moving back to Italy who had one. She wanted $15 for it. Maria still had the $25 from when she left Casteltermini, so she bought the sewing machine. She told Carmelo it was a gift. Otherwise, she would have had to disclose she had money, and he would take it from her.

March 17, 1918, arrived as a cold nasty windy morning. Maria was in her pre-labor pain and told Carmelo to get Rosalia. It was snowing all day, and Rosalia arrived minutes later and started making the trips to the well for water. It was difficult trudging through the wet snow, but such was life in Whiteash. People endured the hardships and rarely complained, for they had no choice.

Rosalia had plenty of hot water and was well prepared for the baby's arrival. The miners and Carmelo went to the home of a miner to get them away from the house. At eight thirty in the evening, Carlo Reina arrived, a beautiful healthy baby boy. Maria was overjoyed and thanked Rosalia for helping deliver her new son. He arrived with no complications. Maria paid Rosalia with the usual two loaves of her homemade bread and two bags of her pasta. Maria had been fearful after losing her first three, and this preyed on her mind the entire nine months of her pregnancy. She was now happy that she had a beautiful healthy little boy.

She had informed the miners they would have to move the end of February. As she had planned, they found another place to board and moved the previous morning. She had bought a twin bed for Virginia, who was almost two now, walking and talking up a storm. Carlo slept with her in the room formerly occupied by the miners. Things were a lot more peaceful this time around.

Maria saw that Carmelo was overcome with joy at the sight of his first son. She had escaped his macho wrath! The winter was the worst yet since her arrival, and it seemed to snow endlessly for two days. Then the temperature would drop to a few degrees above zero, then it would warm up for a few days, and then the snow would come again.

Carmelo was constantly getting sick and, on occasion, would miss work and, of course, bring home less pay, causing Maria to dip into her savings.

"Carmelo, aren't you sick of this town? This house? Please, let's move to Marion. Soon our children will be ready for school. There is no school here!"

It was like talking to the wall. He was so callous; he didn't even respond.

Life continued to be boring and difficult for Maria, and her frustrations continued to get to her. She was constantly on Carmelo to get him to move to Marion, the next coal mining town a short distance away. The year 1918 came and went with little or no major events. But in late July of 1919, Maria realized once again that she was with child. She estimated the next baby was coming sometime in February. She went to see Rosalia and said, "I think I may be pregnant again."

"Maria, when are you going to stop?" came the reply.

Maria laughed. "Next time you see my old man, tell him that!"

On a miserably cold morning on February 26, 1920, Maria sent Carmelo to get Rosalia Ferrara before he left for work. The midwife arrived within a few minutes, prepared to deliver the next child. She began the runs to the well for water and prepared for the delivery. Virginia and Carlo were taking their afternoon naps.

Maria did not go into labor until early the next morning. The weather was horrible; it was a typical February day and became worse as the evening progressed. The cold wind blew right through the wood-framed house. There was no insulation!

"I am worried, Rosalia. I have never had this problem!"

"Don't be concerned, Maria. It will happen. Have you selected any names?"

She tried to get Maria's mind off the subject. Maria's dealing with the inadequate lifestyle—cramped in a three-room house, doing all the cooking outside via the lean-to kitchen amid the heat, rain, and humidity in the summer—was more than anyone should endure. The cold and snow in the winter, the demands from Carmelo, and two kids were too much to ask of anyone.

Yet somehow knowing she had no choice, she dealt with it because she was determined to make a life change. If nothing else, it was her dream to look forward to—hope to escape. Maria had insisted Carmelo to stay with their friends, the Rumbolos, but after dinner, he decided to return home, where he spent the night. Maria did not want him in the bedroom where she was being attended to by the midwife. But for the first time he heard the moaning and groaning in the next room, he feared the worst, that perhaps something serious was happening to Maria.

By eight thirty, the kids were asleep, and later he, too, fell asleep in the room with the children. Maria told him to sleep in the room with them and take care of them and to be sure to put plenty of coal in the stove.

"We can't afford to let the stove burn out!"

The baby arrived early the next morning. Maria named her Giuseppina after her mother. She prayed to God and hoped this was the last. Three children and six births were enough. This pregnancy was the worst.

While living in Whiteash, neither Maria nor Carmelo spoke a word of English. Maria was a bright woman with very little education, and her incredible street sense helped her overcome her disadvantages. The fact that there was no school in Whiteash that the kids could attend was constantly used as Maria's bone of contention to get Carmelo to move to Marion. Their kids were speaking only the old Sicilian dialect and had never spoken a word of English. All this had to change, and she tried to force Carmelo to make it happen.

The coal mine

In May of 1920, a short time after Baby Giuseppina's arrival, the mine's ore petered out, and this triggered what was to become the first of a series of moves for the Reinas. They packed what furniture they had and prepared for the move to Marion, Illinois, a nearby coal mining town. It was less than three miles away, a short distance by today's standards but very difficult on a dirt road, especially in bad weather.

Nonetheless, the family had no choice but to move. Maria called on Pepe Rumbolo, who was leaving too because the mine was closing, and he helped them with the move, which took two arduous trips. It was a painfully rough ride over that dirt road. Giuseppina was three months old, and Maria was still nursing her. Maria had packed plenty of food for the trip, and fortunately it was a nice cool day, and they arrived late that afternoon. Three kids, two adults, and the goat. Always the goat!

The Scoundrel's brother, Giuseppe, was established in Marion, working for the Southern Illinois Coal Company, earning $0.15 an hour. He told his boss that Carmelo was a real hard worker with three kids and could load ten tons a day. Thus, a job was waiting for the Scoundrel when they arrived at the new locale. There had been a serious explosion at this strip mine located halfway between Marion and Herrin. It happened on May 31, 1920. Several miners had been killed, and many others were injured. The company needed minors, and Carmelo got hired. Giuseppe had made arrangements for them to stay with friends from Casteltermini who lived in Marion.

Carmela Insalaco (Maria's 1st cousin) &
Jake Cunetto wedding, 1915

CHAPTER 3

The Move to Marion

Marion, Illinois
The coal miner, 1920

Maria was delighted to finally be out of Whiteash and the miserable house after five years! They were in another coal company-owned house, and it was much better than the one they vacated. But her business mind was bringing the thought of having the family's own home.

Marion was founded in 1839 and sat on approximately twenty acres. It was named after a revolutionary war hero by the name of General Francis Marion. The population in 1920 was slightly over ten thousand and was a much nicer town than Whiteash. It had the usual things a town of that size had in 1920, schools and stores of all kinds. It became a real awakening and pleasant surprise for the Reinas.

Carmelo was back digging coal now for $0.15 an hour, ten hours a day for six days, and $9.00 a week. But the cost of living and supporting three kids was just not cutting it, as was the case with most families in those days. The coal mining towns with lack of steady work and financial matters caused tremendous stress!

Maria was doing everything she could to make ends meet. She started buying fifty-pound sacks of flour, and after using the contents for her bread and pasta, she boiled them and bleached the sacks to remove the printing to make clothes for the kids, using the sewing machine she had purchased.

Carmelo was not helping matters; he was buying homemade wine for $0.50 a gallon and consuming it in less than a week, sometimes having his coal mining friends over to the house for pasta and Maria's bread and sharing the wine. After they left, Maria would give him grief about it. Needless to say, he would give her grief right back. It was here that she started standing up to him!

By this time, Maria was reading anything she could get her hands on, and she started borrowing books from neighbors and friends. She was so grateful her second-grade teacher pushed her to read! Later when her children started school, she stressed to them the importance of reading using Carmelo's inability to do so as a lesson.

There were many miners working with the Scoundrel from Casteltermini, and a small group always visited each other. Maria would sit around at night and entertain their friends with stories, even read them *The Count of Monte Christo*. She borrowed a book on wine making using raisins and informed Carmelo that it might be a good idea to sell the wine to the miners.

She said to him, "Speak to the men and see if there is interest, and I will order a few cases of raisins, and we will make some wine and see what happens."

Thus, it began her career as an entrepreneur, a time and place to figure out a way to better the lifestyle of her family, always the family. Never ever was there any consideration for herself. It was the Sicilian way, making sure your kids would be better off than the path laid before you. Prohibition had started in 1920, and it paved the way for making money aside from the extreme hard labor by Carmelo.

The wine business was going great. Carmelo was making it with her on weekends. They had purchased two twenty-five-gallon barrels to allow fermentation and storage. He dug a hole to hide them in the shed where the dogs and the goat slept in the spring and summer. Much to the dismay of the children, all the animals were sleeping in the kitchen in the winter! The stench was pitiful. More often than not, they urinated on the floor, and Virginia had to clean up the mess. The two hunting dogs were useful in Carmelo's Sunday hunting trips for rabbits. Maria used the rabbits as a source of meat, since there was no money to buy meat to feed a family of five. She'd fry them in olive oil and then drop them in the tomato sauce and slowly cook them until tender. It became a Sunday treat.

Marion, 1920

The year 1920 ushered in the roaring twenties. Women were given the right to vote; it was the beginning of the women's movement. The economy was very strong, and the stock market was wild. One could buy stocks with 10 percent down! The word reached immigrants about how to get rich in America by investing in its future, but it was a dream for most.

About this time, a miner by the name of John L. Lewis was coming to power with the unions, and he favored the coal miners as a ripe plum to pick and began organizing them. Lewis was born in Cleveland, Ohio, to immigrant parents and grew up with a definite impression of what it was like to be poor, the hardships those people endured, and how hard they had to work to survive. At age seventeen, he went to work in Lucas, Ohio. He attended the United Mine Workers convention in 1906 and became affiliated with them and was assigned to organize coal miners in Pennsylvania, Ohio, and Illinois. He did an outstanding job and worked his way up the ladder and later became president at a very young age.

In 1920, he called for a nationwide strike, and over three hundred thousand miners were idled, including Carmelo and those of the "clan."

The strike was short-lived. President Wilson got congress to issue an injunction, and Lewis called off the strike. He told the miners, "We have to do what the president has ordered. We can't fight the government, but I promise to fight the coal companies." Over the years, he was successful in getting higher wages, pensions, and relief for the families with regard to health issues caused by years of exposure to the coal dust, including those that caused "black" lung disease.

Maria was overwhelmed. She could not understand what was going on. How were they going to live with no money coming in? This was insane! Coal was used for fuel at just about every level of life, for trains, stoves, and furnaces to heat buildings, hospitals, and retail operations, even the White House! Fear of the strike's economic impact along with hardships since no coal was being mined caused President Woodrow Wilson to obtain the injunction, forcing the end of the strike. The miners went back to work.

The Volstead Act

The wine business was easing the financial burden and making life easier, for the family was no longer depending on Carmelo's income. Maria was saving for the rainy days of the past.

Prohibition of manufacturing and selling alcohol was voted in by congress in 1918. It had no serious effect on the economy. Minnesota congressman Andrew Volstead was a member of the judiciary committee who helped pass it through congress. But it was vetoed by President Woodrow Wilson. However, the law took effect in 1920 after congress overruled him. It became the National Prohibition Act and the eighteenth amendment to the constitution. It had a major effect on the economy, for all the bars and night clubs had to close. Restaurants could no longer serve alcoholic beverages, thus, severely reducing their profits and causing tremendous job loss. Many closed as a result of the lost income.

It ushered in the illegal gangs selling beer and booze, bringing it into the US from Canada and Mexico. The gangs became very organized; they hired bright lawyers and financial people to run their businesses. This was especially true in the major cities. They were stronger and tougher than the authorities trying to police them, to say nothing of the fact they paid off the cops, the judges, and bribed higher up leaders. They were very successful in spite of the federal government spending millions trying to enforce the new law.

Big time gang leaders surfaced in every major city; New York and Chicago were the most famous. In Chicago, Al Capone shared the city and most the state and some of the surrounding states with three other mobsters. It didn't take long for the three to battle each other for control of the city, the suburbs, and the surrounding states—Missouri, Iowa, and Indiana.

Soon, because of America's insane wish to drink and party, the clubs reopened in new locations and were called speakeasies. They were operated more or less as private clubs. The operators had to know you or you couldn't get through the door, and they got away with doing business because the authorities were paid off! Speakeasies were located in never before seen places, locations, using fronts of legitimate businesses with the speakeasy in the rear. They operated in warehouses in industrial complexes and, in some cases, some of the old establishments were reopened as private clubs after police and top officials were bribed and given membership.

People were drawn to the crazy new establishment for entertainment and were drinking more than ever. This caused many problems. They drank too much and had many auto accidents. There was an increase in fights between the gangs and shootings in the bars and in the street! The general morality of the country slipped to all-time lows. In small towns, there were always a few bootleggers, as they were called, many doing business with the miners!

1921

Maria had saved some of the money from the Whiteash boarders, but she never disclosed it to the Scoundrel, nor was he aware of how much she had hidden from the wine sales. She was tired of living in company-owned houses. They were barely habitable, no electricity, no modern conveniences, no indoor plumbing. Having visited other people's homes with these amenities, she was determined to own her own home. Up until this point, the family had never had indoor plumbing, and all the kids slept in one room. The houses had the usual two bedrooms, kitchen, and a small room for dining, and the room where she and Carmelo slept.

Without Carmelo's knowledge, she started speaking to a realtor, Pietro Giordano. Jimmy D'Angelo had introduced her to him. Pietro was the son of a *paesano* whose family had migrated to Southern Illinois in 1905, and he had graduated high school in Marion. He spoke Maria's exact dialect. Pietro showed her several homes, mostly owned by the coal company. Most were beat-up and not in very good condition and needed a lot of work.

Maria was doing this without Carmelo's knowledge. While Virginia was in school, Maria hauled the kids around from house to house. She knew Carmelo would protest, but she was not concerned. She knew how to handle him and had made up her mind. She was going to buy a house.

Pietro came to see her one day and said, "Maria, I think I have found the right house for you."

She dressed the kids, and off they went. The weather was warm and almost as if by design, a perfect day to walk. The streets of Marion were filled with people strolling to shop and visit friends. For a change, Maria was happy and was looking forward to seeing this house, and perhaps the weather was an omen.

When they arrived at the house, Pietro said to her before they knocked on the door, "Maria, please let me do the talking. These people are asking a lot more than they will take. The house has been on the market for over a year, and they are desperate."

Maria loved the place; it had three bedrooms, a living room, and a nice kitchen. The nice coal stove had four areas on top to cook on, a small wooden icebox and an oven with no controls. But at least it had an oven for her to bake her bread. It even had a small pantry. The people selling the house were moving from Marion to Italy and were willing to sell some of the furniture at a very low price. Maria went into the bedrooms and noticed they had really nice brass beds and what appeared to be very comfortable mattresses. She asked if the beds were for sale. She received the answer she was hoping for—yes, $50 for all the beds!

The place was a dream compared to the shack they were living in and heaven compared to the three rooms they had lived in in Whiteash.

Maria took Pietro aside. "How much are they asking for the house?"

He said, "They are asking $5,000, but I think you can get it for $3,000!"

"Let me discuss this with my husband, and I will get back to you."

Maria had no idea how she was going to pay for this.

She went to see Jimmy D'Angelo about buying the house and the possibility of getting a loan.

He said, "Don't be concerned, Maria. I know people at the bank, and I will take you there and make the introduction."

She asked, "How does that work, Jimmy? I am going to have to discuss it with Carmelo."

She was confronted with the problem of discussing this with the Scoundrel. It was time to step up and speak her piece.

That night, after the kids were asleep, she brought up the idea of purchasing the house, and as could be expected a major argument proceeded.

She pleaded, "It is not a good idea to have three kids sleeping together in a tiny bedroom. You go to work and are gone ten hours a day. Then you come home exhausted, eat at six thirty, drink your wine, and by seven thirty, you are asleep six days a week! So you don't care about the rest of us!"

He was like a maniac, screaming at her. "Don't you realize the mine can dry up at any time, and we may have to move again. Do you want to be stuck with a payment and have to move? And what if you can't sell the house?"

She decided to drop it at this time. The baby started crying, and she had to comfort her. But she was determined to get her way. There was no way she was going to let him talk her out of this.

Maria continued her pursuit of the house. She met with Jimmy D'Angelo while the kids were in school, and Jimmy explained about loans and the financial responsibility of mortgage payments. He took her to the South Marion State Bank and explained to the loan officer she spoke very little English, that her husband was a hard worker, and that they could afford the monthly payment.

They discussed the price of $3,000! The bank officer told her she would need 10 percent down.

She said, "I can put $900 cash down!"

The banker was astounded that she had that kind of money.

He said, "In that case, your payment will be $14.50 a month."

She said it would be no problem.

But it was a problem. She was paying $9 a month for the current residence and already scheming on some kind of supplemental income. For even though Carmelo was now making $0.15 an hour, $9 a week, it was not enough to pay the weekly expenses and support a family of five. He was working hard loading ten tons of coal a day with no real future for making any more than his current pay. One thing about him was he never missed a day of work, as long as there was work, but often there were days when he arrived at the mine and was told, "No work today." He had a strong back and an incredible work ethic; something Maria never really acknowledged about him.

The First Home

Maria got her way. Carmelo finally got tired of her complaining about the terrible living conditions and agreed to take a look at the house. After seeing it, he gave in. She knew this was the beginning of her independence.

One day, when Carmelo was laid off, the Reinas and Jimmy D'Angelo went to the South Marion State Bank to sign the loan papers for the house. The loan officer spoke a little Italian, but it was a different dialect, so the Reinas kept asking Jimmy to explain. He assured them it was fine and allowed the loan officer to proceed. When it came time to sign the documents, they were presented to Carmelo first, and he asked Jimmy, *"Ma che cosa vuole?"*

Jimmy explained to the loan officer, "Carmelo does not know how to sign his name."

Maria was really ashamed, but the loan officer had been there before with Italian, Sicilian, Polish, and Greek immigrants, and he knew Maria was an honest and sincere woman. He was banking on her reputation to make the mortgage payment, to say nothing of the fact she was putting $900 down on the house. He looked at Carmelo and took a piece of scratch paper and made an X and told him to just make an X.

The loan officer directed them to another desk where a handsome young man was sitting with some people and asked the three of them to have a seat.

"Mr. Donatello will be with you to explain about the insurance shortly."

Maria had a quizzical look on her face, looked at Jimmy, and said, *"Ma che e insurance?"*

Jimmy put his index finger to his lips and said, *"Non dire nulla, fammi parlare"* (Let me do the talking).

Jimmy D'Angelo explained about insurance to them. Maria was a little baffled, for he had not mentioned anything about insurance in the earlier visit to the bank. Once again, he assured them, "This is necessary and mandatory in case there is ever any serious damage to the house such as a fire—God forbid—the insurance company would pay to repair the damage." He also said, "The house is constructed of wood, and if it would burn to the ground, the company would pay the loan at the bank."

Soon Mr. Donatello was finished with the other clients and asked the trio to sit. He began explaining to them about the bank's policy regarding insurance and was talking and looking directly at Maria. He was great looking, tall, and well dressed and could not take his eyes off of her.

Carmelo was offended by this. There was no doubt Donatello was enamored by the beautiful, blond, blue-eyed woman sitting across from him, and Carmelo—always the suspicious one—knew what Donatello was thinking. Carmelo's eyes were daggers aimed at the salesman's eyes.

Donatello sensed Carmelo's concern and momentarily looked at him and then directed the next part of the discussion at Jimmy. He too had noticed Carmelo's stare. He knew all too well about Carmelo's temper and reputation, for even though he was only five foot five, he was no one to mess with.

Pepe Rumbolo had told Jimmy, "When it comes to Carmelo, *stai atento* [be careful] around him. Most the minors were scared to death of him. He was that tough."

Jimmy now took charge of the discussion. He explained he had already discussed the insurance information to the Reinas and asked what the charge was. Donatello knew Jimmy and cut to the chase and told them the cost was $60 a year for the insurance.

Maria said she would have to come back and pay it, knowing and sensing Carmelo was about to explode. He later admonished her about this, assuming she knew about it and had planned to hide it from him. They left, and on the walk back to the house, she invited Jimmy in for an espresso. He declined, then she asked, "How much do we owe you?"

He told her, "Nothing, Maria, please, we are *paesani*."

When they walked into the house, Carmelo started to rant about the insurance, but Maria was ready for him, and she looked him right in the eye with her "Reina look" and told him in a tough and loud voice, "I knew nothing about the insurance. I was just as surprised as you were about it!"

The house

The house was a dream. The girls had their own bedroom as did Carlo. Still no indoor plumbing, a small but efficient kitchen, and water had to be brought in from a well down the street. There was a room to dine in that also served as living room. The kids could not believe it, but the Scoundrel would not show any emotion. He just could not believe Maria had pulled this off.

The family was really doing well in the new house. Maria cooked great meals, and the kids made new friends in the neighborhood. It was a very exciting time for the Reinas.

Of course, the Scoundrel was showing off his new home to his close friends by inviting them for pasta on an occasional Sunday, once again to the chagrin of Maria, for she did the cooking and cleaning of the mess. She resented the fact that Carmelo was showing off the house as if it was his accomplishment, but in her heart, she knew the truth.

The year 1921 was a good year, and everyone was healthy. The kids were speaking English a lot and trying to teach Maria words and some grammar. But the financial struggle never seemed to end.

One day, a salesman by the name of Carlo Matranga knocked on the door, the son of some people she knew from Casteltermini who had settled in Marion. He had graduated from high school and was well liked in the area. He had been a star soccer player for Marion High School.

"Good morning, Mrs. Reina, how are you?"

"Come in, Carlo, what can I do for you? Would you like a cup of coffee? How are your parents?"

"I am fine, Mrs. Reina, so are my parents. I don't care for coffee. I want to show you something."

"What's that book you are carrying?"

"Mrs. Reina, this is an incredible health book written by a group of doctors. It belongs in every home in America. Do you have time to look at it? If not, I can come back at a later time."

"No, sit down, let me see it."

At this time, Maria was most interested in discovering anything she could read regarding health and keeping the family healthy. She started thumbing through the book. It was eight inches thick with photos on almost every page describing the various possible health issues. Carlo was doing an excellent job of explaining things. Even though Maria's reading was getting better, there were medical terms she did not understand and pronounce. She wanted that book, so after a little over an hour, she asked the price.

Carlo said, "It is $25, Mrs. Reina, but you can buy it for $5 down, and $5 a month for four months."

She bought the book but did not tell Carmelo, it did not matter because he could not read. She did not even show it to him. He would have had a fit if she had told him she paid $25 for a book, he would have screamed at her, "I have to work three weeks for $25!"

By late May, the summer heat and humidity in Southern Illinois had arrived, and it was miserable. The entire family was suffering, and it had become impossible to sleep. The kids were constantly getting into fights, and it was trying Carmelo's patience, and he, in turn, would be irritable with Maria. It took every bit of mental strength to deal with all of it. The only good news was Carmelo was still working ten hours a day and six days a week, and the nights were short. Maria stopped bothering him about his wine drinking at dinnertime, for he would fall asleep almost immediately after dinner and quit trying to have sex. Hence, she didn't get pregnant that year.

She received an incredible letter from her sister, Rosa, from Sicily, informing her that she and her husband, Giuseppe Burruano, were coming to America along with their infant daughter, Giovanna "Jennie." They were expected sometime in June. Maria sent a return letter explaining what to anticipate, including the Ellis Island experience, the trip from Ellis to the train station, and the trip to St. Louis, then the Greyhound bus trip to Marion.

She had Virginia write a letter of explanation in English for Rosa to present to the authorities to get the family to the train station and the bus ride. She even explained the approximate cost of everything to avoid Rosa getting cheated. Knowing Rosa did not have much money, Maria sent money with the letter. Maria was always giving despite her concern about her own financial security.

The year 1921 brought the worst winter the family had seen since the arrival in 1915, and the kids were sick a lot. On numerous occasions, Maria consulted the book, for it was expensive to take them to the doctor. A visit was $2 to say nothing of the long trek to the doctor's office, especially in the inclement weather. When the kids had head colds, she would boil water, creating steam, put the pot in their bedroom, and rub their chests with Vicks VapoRub.

She made great *zuppa d' verdure* (vegetable soup), sometimes spending $1 for a chicken from which she created several meals. This was normally a treat at special holidays.

The rendezvous with the Castellano's

Maria had heard from Pepe Rumbolo that the Castellano's were living in Marion. Giuseppina "D'Angelo" Castellano was one of Maria's best friends from Casteltermini, and she had not seen her since she left. It had been a long five years. She had married Carmelo

Castellano shortly after Maria left Casteltermini in 1915. The Castellanos had five children by now, Lilly, Frank, Jimmy, Joe, and the baby, Carmella. They were an incredible, well-mannered bunch of kids. There was no denying that they were brothers and sisters, for they had the face of their mother. Giuseppina was a beautiful lady, and both she and Carmelo were as gentle and kind as any two married people could be. Later as their children grew, they all inherited the same kind, warm, gentle personalities!

Maria and Giuseppina's hug lasted what seemed like an eternity. It was a moment the two would never forget. They parted with tears in both eyes, and they promised they would never be apart for the rest of their lives. This was to be the beginning of a similar relationship between their children, ironically the ages of the kids were very close. Virginia and Lilly were the same age, Carlo and Jimmy the same. Joe was two years younger than Jimmy. The babies Carmella and Giuseppina were practically the same. Frank was the oldest.

Thus, the journey of the clan, the Reinas and Castellanos, commenced, and later the tie-ins between them—the Cunettos, the Insalacos, the Rumbolos, and the Burruanos, all from Casteltermini—were united.

Carmelo Castellano, Giuseppina's husband, had a brother living in Marion. His name was Giuseppe. His wife was Anna (Annuzia). They had five children, Frank, Carolina, Rose, Jimmy, and Josephine. They, too, were part of the clan. It is important to note at this time, many of these children later intermarried.

It was not too long after the Reinas arrived that the family get-togethers with the people from Casteltermini were forming their own little section of Marion. The feasts were awesome. They would get together once a month, switching from house to house. Everyone contributed something, homemade bread made by Maria, along with her homemade pasta, great meatballs (a rare treat rarely prepared by Maria), on occasion, ravioli, heretofore never seen by Maria's family.

On occasion, Pepe Rumbolo would grill a couple of chickens—again, a treat. A whole chicken was $1. His wife, Santa, made colossal salads and great vegetables and one of the main treats, wild cardoons. This was a root weed that usually grew in deserted areas and had the taste of artichoke hearts. It had to be boiled first, then it was stringy like celery. So after boiling, Santa would slowly string it, for if left undone, it made the cardoon tough to chew. Next, it was dipped in an egg wash, breaded with *mudica*—a combination of breadcrumbs, green onions, and graded cheese—and then deep-fried in olive oil. There was always a couple of plates with a mountain of cardoons at each end of the table. The uncooked weed brought to Santa from two of the men, who had spent a couple of Sundays, their only day off, scouring the areas collecting it.

By this time, Rosa and Giuseppe Burruano were in Marion, and he always had the connection for buying good homemade wine. These were memories that the kids would cherish throughout their lives. Even though they were not related, they became lifelong friends and, in later life, would always introduce each other as cousins.

Giuseppe and Rosa Burruano

Rosa was born October 8, 1898. She was five years younger than Maria, and she idolized her older sister. The truth of the matter was Maria cared for her baby sister almost from the day she was born. She got an early lesson in caring for babies. She watched her mother nurse her, she learned all she needed to know about motherhood, and it prepared her for what it would be like to become a mom.

Rosa met Giuseppe Burruano at a wedding in Casteltermini in 1914 when she was sixteen. She was an absolutely beautiful young lady. Like her sister, Maria, Rosa, too, was blond and blue-eyed and had an hourglass figure, which by tradition of the day, well camouflaged in a loose-fitting dress.

Giuseppe's family were real good friends with the Insalaco's, and even though he was fifteen at the time, he knew he was going to marry Rosa. The Burruanos were related to the Insalacos; in fact, Giuseppe was Rosa's cousin.

The following weekend, his father, Vincenzo, visited Ignazio. "Buongiorno. Ignazio, I am here to share my joy about my son's interest in Rosa. Would you allow him to start seeing your beautiful daughter?"

Ignazio replied with a warm smile on his face, "For me, Vincenzo, there is no one in this world I would rather see her be with. I am honored." He was delighted to know that the son of one of his closest boyhood friends wanted to be with his beautiful daughter.

Giuseppe and his mom and dad came calling on the Insalaco family the following weekend and brought some very small gifts, the traditional thing in those days. The formal announcement was made that Giuseppe would start courting Rosa; of course, they would be chaperoned by an adult from each family.

Giuseppe was great-looking, tall, handsome, and had a great smile and a suave personality to go with the looks. She on the other hand was very quiet and shy and did not possess an overwhelming personality, but her demeanor and looks far overshadowed any negative concerns as far as Giuseppe was concerned.

Giuseppe paid a visit to Ignazio. "Buongiorno, Signore Insalaco, I would like to speak to you about Rosa."

Ignazio smiled and said, "Giuseppe, I am sure I know why you are here, and in the future, since you will become my son-in-law, you can start now by calling me Ignazio!"

Later that evening, Giuseppe called on Rosa and asked her to take a brief walk and proposed. He told her about the meeting with her father, and they laughed. Rosa accepted, and they set a date for March 16, 1919.

The wedding party was held in the garden of the home of Antonio Amari's house. Antonio was the local baker and had a very nice home and backyard. He supplied the cake, bread, and wine for the two families. Weddings were by design held at homes of close friends. There were no banquet halls. Food was prepared by both families. Sometimes close friends brought food substituted for gifts. It was a perfect warm sunny day, and all the friends and families enjoyed the food, in spite of the fact it was very simple. Good food, nice families, a nice guitarist, and a beautiful young couple. The newlyweds moved into the house with Giuseppe's parents, and Rosa started helping with cooking, the house cleaning, and household chores. Within a couple of months, she learned she was pregnant with her first child.

Giuseppe was laid off at the sulfur mine soon after learning his bride was with child. There were no jobs in Casteltermini or in any of the surrounding towns, and Vincenzo advised them to go to America. Rosa delivered the baby on February 7, 1920, a healthy girl, and named her Giovanna "Jennie." Giuseppe almost immediately set everything in motion for them to leave for America. Rosa was given some money from Ignazio and the same from Giuseppe's father, and within a month, they departed for the great hope as so many young Sicilians had at the time.

Unlike most immigrants from Sicily, at this time, Giuseppe had finished what would be equivalent to sixth grade in Casteltermini. He could read and write, but the language barrier forced him to go to work in the coal mine. Carmelo had vouched for him. However, it was not long before his Sicilian dialect helped him get promoted to assistant supervisor in the mine. This also helped him learn some English by communicating with the other supervisors, which later would give him an edge against other immigrants in his employment in succeeding years. The price of the ticket for the trip was $30 per person for third class and no charge for the baby. They survived the twelve-week trip to America after the usual stress at Ellis Island and arrived in Marion and were greeted warmly by the Reinas.

Giuseppina and Carmelo Castellano, about 1914

CHAPTER 4

The Great Shed Raid

Marion, Illinois, 1922

Just about the time Maria and Carmelo were starting to accumulate a few dollars, as is always the case, someone spoke to the authorities about their wine business. One Saturday morning, Maria answered a knock at their front door. It was the police.

Maria allowed them to enter the house. The language barrier presented a problem, so she called Virginia to translate, who was smart enough to pretend she didn't really understand.

"Young lady, we are here to search for the wine your father is making. Where is it?"

She replied in Sicilian and broken English, "*Non capisco*, I no understand."

The officers bullied their way through the small kitchen and, after walking around the house, found nothing. They exited the back door and headed for the shed, where the dogs and the goat slept, only to be confronted by the barking dogs! Carmelo was right at them with no fear, his hand on the knife he always carried in his pocket.

But one of the officers pulled his pistol and pointed it at the dogs and said, "Either you get those dogs away from us or I will shoot them!"

Carmelo pleaded with the cop, his Sicilian temper somehow controlled. He stood between the two cops and put his hands up and walked over and pulled the dogs aside. The cops entered the shed and started moving the hay covering the wine barrels, lifted the boards, and discovered them. They lifted them one at time. It was easy because one was empty and the other half full. They immediately dumped the wine in a field next door and arrested Carmelo.

Maria was beside herself, fearful of the fact Carmelo would miss work on Monday and lose his job. She went to seek help from Pepe Rumbolo who worked in the mine. He said he would contact Jimmy D'Angelo, who was well connected with the authorities.

Carmelo spent the night in jail, and on Sunday, Maria visited him and brought food. Once again, Virginia acted as translator with the police. Maria explained Pepe Rumbolo was involved.

Carmelo was due to appear in court Monday at 8:00 a.m. As fate would have it, he was not aware of this. On Sunday evening, Pepe Rumbolo and Jimmy knocked at Maria's door. While Jimmy was not an attorney, he knew his way around Marion. He really was knowledgeable about legal things.

"Maria, relax, I will take care of this. I will be at the police station first thing in the morning and handle the problem. I need $300 in cash for the police and the judge." He explained the money was his badge. Maria went to her bedroom and came up with the money. He guaranteed Carmelo would be home for dinner Monday night. Maria asked Pepe Rumbolo to inform the boss at the coal mine that Carmelo was ill and would be back at work on Tuesday.

Carmelo never appeared in court and was released early Monday morning. Of the money, $200 went to the judge, and $100 went to the two cops, who also never appeared in court.

Ah the badge, better known as the payoff, Maria's first lesson on how to solve disasters, the "green badge." What a great country America!

When Virginia started school, she couldn't speak English. She came home the first day and shared her experiences and started crying. "We need to speak English in this house."

The Scoundrel yelled at her, "And how do you propose we learn? You learn in school and start teaching your mother and your brother and sister."

She began doing that, and Maria and Carlo learned. Carmelo refused to participate.

Things were not always rosy. The weather was cold and nasty that winter as there was only one stove in the house. Homes built in those days did not have the luxury of insulation. If by chance the stove died in the middle of the night which happened on occasion, it would wreak havoc in the household. Carmelo's short fuse would show up, and the kids often got sick, causing Maria to continue her vow to move to St. Louis.

Once again, she would retort to the Scoundrel, "Let's get out of here," only to be reminded of his fear of being caught by the authorities and forced to be extradited to Sicily.

He said, "Do you want to see me be tried for the death of the man I stabbed?" Little did he know the man had lived.

At this point, neither Maria nor Carmelo were aware the man was alive. There was no correspondence from Carmelo's family. He could not read. He was an alien the entire time he lived in the US. He also would comment on the fact that he only knew how to do one thing—use his back to dig.

The summers were not any better than the winters as far as living conditions. The temperature on many days reached one hundred degrees, and the humidity was always near the same, 100 percent! There were few windows in the house, and the kids never got a good night's sleep. They often woke up in the middle of the night in a deep sweat. The same for Maria and Carmelo, and needless to say, he was in a bad mood when he got up to go to work.

The kids stayed in their room until they knew he was gone to avoid listening to his rants. Then they descended on Maria and hugged her. Even though they were young, they knew what kind of woman she was and what she was dealing with regarding the Scoundrel. After the hugs, she would prepare their breakfast, which never changed, two-day-old bread cut into small cubes with coffee and goat milk and a small amount of sugar spilled over the mix. Later as adults, they continued, the stale bread at times, the bread was substituted with cornflakes.

About this time, the mine started to peter out, and there were days where Carmelo was told no work the next day. And this was having an effect on the wine business. The miners were not getting steady work, money was tight, so sales were slipping. Maria was getting concerned about their future.

Prohibition was wreaking havoc in the larger cities, and illegal booze was having a major problem for the federal government and local governments to control. In fact, there was no control. There were now more illegal drinking establishments than before it was enacted. Maria and Carmelo were having a serious discussion about financial matters; both were concerned about the situation in general. This was a very desperate time, trying to make ends meet, especially true with the condition at the mine. People were actually leaving town and returning to their countries of origin.

This was not an option for the Reinas as there were no jobs in Sicily, for sure none in Casteltermini! They decided to write a letter to Luigi, who knew a lot of people in the United States and was connected to a somewhat international group in Chicago and St. Louis. The connection was through those whom had left Casteltermini and Palermo! They were seeking a connection to make additional money to compensate for the days Carmelo would miss work.

The Scoundrel talked about a guy who was selling whisky to the miners and other people in town with alcohol from St. Louis. His name was Salvatore Pontarelli, and he was making a lot of money.

Little did they know, Luigi knew the players in St. Louis, who were controlled by the "big boss" in Chicago. His name was Al Capone. Carmelo invited Salvatore to the house on Sunday for some pasta and introduced him to Maria.

Salvatore wasted no time and came right at her. "Maria, would you be willing to make a trip at least once a week to St. Louis, which is a short train ride, and meet up with my friends who are making alcohol from sugar and various ingredients? He purposely withheld the other ingredients. You would return the same day with a five gallon can of alcohol. We will pay the $0.50 round trip train ticket, plus $5 for your trouble."

Maria didn't hesitate for a minute. "Salvatore, thank you. The answer is yes. When can I start?"

Let's bear in mind that these were desperate times. She had three kids to feed and a house payment to make. She was dealing with Carmelo's irregular work schedule, and while she was a smart woman, she didn't know or realize the laws pertaining to prohibition, especially transporting illegal alcohol across state lines. Nor did she believe she was doing anything wrong, for she was not selling it! They agreed to make a sample trip to St. Louis the very next day.

The following morning was a bright and sunny day. Maria got Virginia off to school, and took the kids to her sister Rosa's house. She walked the short distance to the train station and boarded the train for St. Louis with Salvatore. He was dressed like he was going to a wedding, nice suit, and tie, wearing a very expensive dress hat. She knew this guy was connected to some kind of group or gang, and she became concerned as to what she was getting into. But she had no fear as she remembered Carmelo's arrest from the great shed raid and Jimmy D'Angelo's "badge." She was well aware of how the system worked to free him.

Salvatore noticed she was in deep thought, and he knew she was concerned, so he decided to calm her.

He said, "Maria, have no fear. The people I am dealing with have the police under control in St. Louis, and we are perfectly safe. We will be back in Marion in plenty of time for you to cook dinner for your family. There is a train that leaves at three thirty, and we will be on that train. I want you to follow this same train ride next week and every time I ask you to make the trip. You will be met at the station by my friend, Giovanni Martino, or one of his friends you are going to meet this morning. They will take you somewhere to get the five gallon can and bring you back to the station, and you will board the train, and I will meet you later at your house to pick it up and pay you the $5.50. They will always take you to a different location near the train station to hand you the container."

They arrived at the train station, and the two of them got into an automobile, a Ford Model T, and while there were a few cars in Marion, Maria had never ridden in one. This was unbelievable. She could not wait to tell her friends about it. She arrived at the grocery store owned by Signore Giovanni Martino and was shocked at the inventory. Every conceivable Italian and Sicilian delicacy was displayed, and she was astounded at what an experience it would be living in St. Louis and what it would be like to own a store like it. She was ushered into a secret back room, where there were four other men seated around a table. They all rose to meet her. All four were Sicilian, all from a town called Pallozo Andriano that she had heard of it but never had visited.

The first thing they told her was not to discuss this with anyone—*no one*—and the fear of God entered her mind at this point. She got the message. Giovanni served espresso and the best biscotti she had ever tasted, even better than the ones she made on special occasions.

Giovanni spoke first and explained the routine, "Maria, we will know what train you will be on, and one us of will meet you. You will be taken to a special place, different each time, and then returned with the can to the station in time to make the return."

"I understand. I see no problem, Signore Martino."

The meeting lasted less than ten minutes. He then asked if she needed anything from the store.

She said, "May I just look around? I didn't bring any money."

Giovanni said, "Go ahead take what you want, and you can pay me on the next trip."

She gathered mostly some spices, some canned Marzano tomatoes from Napoli, canned artichoke hearts, a nice piece of Parmigiano cheese.

Giovanni put them in a sack and said, "This is on us. Welcome to our group."

As they exited, Salvatore told her they had some time before they were to depart, and he asked Giovanni to do a tour of the area, which had the official name, Fairmount Heights, but was referred to as Hill. She was told there are no *Americani* living on the Hill, *Tutti Siciliani, e Italiani!* (all Sicilians and Italians). She did not tell them she had family there, nor that she knew Jake Cunetto.

Maria said to herself, *One day, I am going to live here, and I am going to have a store like Giovanni's, if it is the last thing I do on this earth.*

Maria and Salvatore returned from the visit to St. Louis on the three thirty train and she made mental notes on each detail so she would not make any mistakes. There was little discussion; both were in deep thought. They carried a five gallon can with them; it had a logo on the side that read, "Lucca Olive Oil." It was a well-designed logo, and no one even gave them a second look. They seemed like a nice couple who had made a trip to the city to do some shopping. A lot had to do with the way Salvatore was dressed. That, of course, was by design, and Maria had her shopping bag with the things she got at the store.

The following Monday, Salvatore was at her door and asked her to make her maiden trip to St. Louis on Friday.

He asked, "Maria, are you sure you can handle this with no problems?"

She said, "I am confident but concerned about the can. Will it be the same one with the olive oil label on the outside?" He assured her it would. "One more thing, I cannot remember all the names of the men I met."

He wrote them down on a piece of paper for her, Dominick Feretti, Pete Salamone, and Francesco Pellitari. This was a matter of respect, for they were the capos, the leaders of the gang. She assured Salvatore she could accomplish the task and asked a favor.

"Salvatore, from now on, please come to see me on Sundays when my old man is home. I don't want the neighbors to think something is going on with a strange man coming to my home while he is at work."

Salvatore immediately began his admiration and respect for this woman and said to himself, *This woman has coglione (balls)!*

On Friday morning, Maria took the kids to Rosa's and asked, "Watch my kids. Do not ask any questions. I will be back by four. Please feed them lunch and have them take a nap." She dropped Virginia off at school, then she went to the train station, and boarded the train for her maiden voyage and the next venture. Another step away from depending on Carmelo and the coal mines.

As had been the case on the previous trip, Giovanni met her at the Tower Grove Station and drove her to his store on the Hill. She went in and spoke briefly to the men. She offered to pay for the previous bag of groceries, but Giovanni refused the money.

She said, "But I want to buy a few things, and unless you take the money, I will take the can and leave."

Giovanni's respect was easily visible. Here, too, the group began to show tremendous respect for Maria. Bear in mind, this was a woman in 1922, and in those days, the woman's role was to stay home and have babies, cook, clean the house, raise the kids. Period. Here they were getting her involved in an illegal business. But this was not one of those women!

Once again, she marveled at the selection of fine Italian foods, not Sicilian. She had never seen product like this in Casteltermini. There were canned sardines and tuna, all kinds of canned vegetables, fruits, tomato paste, tomato sauce, peeled canned tomatoes, semolina flour which she knew made great pasta, fresh vegetables, including Sicilian eggplant. Many varieties of spices and at least ten kinds of cheese, including fresh ricotta. She had heard of it but never seen or tasted it.

Giovanni asked Maria, "I want you to taste some of the cheeses."

She tried them and selected the ricotta and the Pecorino; she bought a little of each. When she finished her purchases, Giovanni totaled it on a brown paper bag and told her she owed $2.90. She was shocked, for the bag was full. She didn't realize what he had done until she was back on the train. He gave her half the stuff at no charge! This was the beginning of a warm long mutually respectful relationship with this mild-mannered man!

The weather was delightful, warm, and sunny, a perfect day to walk. She really wished she could visit her family and the few friends she knew living on the Hill, but then she would have to explain what she was doing there! She had some time to kill before she had to be at the train station, so she asked Giovanni if he would take her to St. Ambrose Church, and she paid a visit while he waited in the car. She had never seen such a beautiful church in her life. She didn't realize until he dropped her off at the train station, that the can had no logo. It was a plain tin can, and she began to panic, fearful some policeman would see her get on the train or when reaching Marion. Her concerns were for naught; she saw no police. Perhaps it was the bag of groceries; that threw off any suspicion by strangers. This was an attractive lady walking in and out of the stations and strolling down the street with a bag of groceries and a five-gallon can. It appeared very normal. And that was exactly the plan by the gang. Who was going to suspect a woman hauling alcohol in 1922 America?

The following Sunday, Salvatore dropped by the house to pick up the can.

"I want you to make the run the following three Fridays."

She agreed, but not before telling him about the can with no logo. She was a little aggressive in her voice. He was both amused and respectful and said, "We are having trouble getting enough of the Lucca cans. Come up with a way to hide the outer surface of the cans for the coming trips." He paid her the $5.50 and left.

That week, she went to the local grocery store to see if they, by chance, had an empty potato sack, which was made of burlap, and they gave her one at no charge. She took it home and made a perfectly shaped cover for the can, including a top to cover it, and used two zippers on the top to seal it.

Sometime in August 1922, as Maria was stepping down from that train on one of her now weekly trips from St. Louis with the five-gallon can of alcohol and her usual bag of groceries, she felt that pain she had felt a number of times, and she knew she was with child. It took her but a few minutes to figure out this baby should arrive sometime late February or early March next year.

While there was a doctor in Marion, Maria told Rosalia Ferrara, the midwife, of the coming birth. Rosalia responded saying, "Why spend money for a doctor?" Besides, he was a man, and the last thing she wanted was for a man to see her naked. For that matter, Carmelo had never seen her naked!

When she arrived at Rosa's to pick up the kids, she informed her of the coming child, and that she had already started praying to God to make this the last. Four was enough. She was more eager than ever to accumulate money and save for what she knew was coming. The mine was starting to dry up, and she knew it was only a matter of time before they were going to relocate. Perhaps this time, Carmelo would listen to her and opt to move to St. Louis.

Carmelo was already aware of the status of the mine, as for some weeks, he was only getting three or four days of work. Maria was more grateful than ever for the weekly $5 she was earning for her travels back and forth to St. Louis. That night at dinner, Carmelo gave her more bad news.

"I have been laid off the rest of the week."

Maria wasted no time. "You only got two days this week. It's time, we need to move to St. Louis!"

"And what do you propose I do there? There are no coal mines!"

The children were all at the dinner table and took in every word. They were always concerned about the family's financial conditions, and that marked them. And it got worse as the years rolled on, and they grew older. Maria made no bones about keeping them aware of those conditions. The hard times marked them for the rest of their lives. They were well aware of what happened to her at a young age when her mother passed away.

On her next visit to drop the kids off, Rosa informed Maria that she and Giuseppe were moving to St. Louis, and that he had been traveling there on days when he was not working to find a job. This really shook Maria up. Who could she trust to leave her kids with for her weekly trips to St. Louis, to say nothing of having to explain why she was doing it every week? Again, she would be separated from her baby sister, and that was more concerning than all the above.

A few weeks later, Rosa's baby girl, Giovanna "Jennie," got sick, and the doctor in Marion told Rosa and Giuseppe that there was nothing he could do. He suggested they take her to the hospital in Herrin. They contacted Pepe Rumbolo, and he went to the local livery stable and rented a horse and wagon and they went to the hospital.

It was a grueling 9.6-mile trip over a dirt road, there was no cover on the rig, and the sun beat down on them all day. Fortunately, Maria had made sandwiches for them, and she put a gallon of water in their hands before they left.

The first two hours were not so bad because they left at seven in the morning. Rosa was in deep thought; all she could think about was what the doctor had told her. "There is nothing more I can do."

They arrived around noon. The baby was admitted, and immediately a very nice doctor, who spoke Italian, was summoned.

After the examination, he informed them, "I am very sorry to inform you your baby has fluid in her lungs. Her little heart is not strong enough to pump it out. There is nothing I can do!"

Rosa was beside herself. Giovanna was less than two years old. She was a baby when the Burruano's left Casteltermini, and Rosa could not understand why God was taking her baby. She swore to herself she should never have left Casteltermini. Perhaps her baby would still be healthy. Rosa spent the night in the room with the baby.

Pepe knew people in the town where he and Giuseppe could be fed and spend the night. Giuseppe ironically was thinking the same. What did they get themselves into? Why did they come to this country? He was digging coal, he hated it, and while he was making more than the regular miners, the mine was starting to dry up, and he was not getting a full week's work. The income was barely enough to put food on the table.

The next day, they all departed for Marion and suffered from the miserable heat and humidity. All Rosa and Giuseppe could think about was their baby, who was crying almost the entire trip.

Perhaps the move to St. Louis would bring better luck, and Giuseppe vowed to get Rosa pregnant soon. He figured she would bounce back from this trauma as soon as she realized she was with child. Maria was aware of the fact that they were hurting, and every Friday, she would share some of the food she purchased at Martino's, and there were no questions asked. When they returned from Herrin, Giuseppe tried to pay for the horse and wagon, but once again, Pepe Rumbolo stepped up and refused payment, especially considering what he just witnessed at the hospital! This was a man with a heart of gold, supporting his *paesani*.

Baby Giovanna passed away on Tuesday July 12, 1923, and was buried in Marion. It was a sad day. Maria had insisted the families to go to her house to be together. The Rumbolos, Castellanos, and many friends from Casteltermini showed up. Maria had been up most the night before making bread and pasta from the semolina she bought at Martino's. She even had some cardoon, and as usual, Giuseppe Burruano brought some good wine. While it was a festive event food wise, the silence, as everyone ate, was typical of the times. Rosa could not wait until it was over; all she wanted to do was go home and grieve. She could not wait to leave Marion and get to St. Louis.

The birth of Ignazio (James Francesco), 1923

Maria went into labor late afternoon the fourteenth of March. She knew this was to be the day. She sent Virginia down the street to get Rosalia Ferrara, the midwife, who knew enough from experience to bring plenty of towels, rags, pots, and a change of clothes, just in case it was to be a long night. As it turned out, she was right. The labor lasted over twelve hours and into the night. Maria had suggested to Carmelo to make some pasta for the kids and get them to bed when he got home from work. She retired to their bedroom and lay in bed. Rosalia comforted her with warm towels. It was a cold nasty winter night, and snow had started falling late in the afternoon.

Carmelo was trying to keep the kids quite, considering what was going on in the next room, but they were hungry and crying, and his impatience was starting to get to him.

Update: Considering what was going on in the next room, Carmelo tried to keep the kids quiet. They were hungry and crying and he had no patience left. He boiled a pot of pasta, sauteed olive oil and garlic in a pan, and fed the three of them. By eight, all of them went to bed in the other bedrooms. Meanwhile, Maria was in agony. This by far, was the worst delivery of them all, and she swore there would be no more kids. She was determined to give Carmelo the word! The midwife fell asleep with her head on the side of the bed, and around three thirty in the morning, Maria awakened her. Baby Ignazio arrived shortly thereafter, but delivery was very difficult. Rosalia cleaned the healthy baby boy, and Maria nursed him, and he fell asleep soon after he was fed.

Rosalia stayed and made coffee for Carmelo the next morning and made his lunch for him to take to work. Maria tried to get up to help feed the kids, but she was too weak. Rosalia stayed all day and attended to her and the family. She stayed until Carmelo came home from work and prepared dinner for him and the children, a gesture Maria never forgot. Every time she made bread and/or pasta, she sent one of the kids to Rosalia's house with the rewards for her efforts.

Maria had already made the decision to have Santa and Pepe Rumbolo be the godparents for Ignazio, who was named after her father. He would never see his namesake. This was a forgone conclusion, and Carmelo had no part in the decision. He knew Santa was one of Maria's closest friends since they were little girls in Casteltermini, and he respected Pepe Rumbolo for helping him escape problems when the police raided the house regarding the wine business.

At that time, being selected to be godparents was both an honor and a responsibility. It was accepting the role of adopting the child until it reached majority in the event of the death of both parents. It was especially serious because people were dying much younger. The average life expectancy in the United States in 1900 was in the early forties, younger in small towns in Sicily. It was not ceremonial. The Rumbolos accepted, and for the first time, a Reina baby was baptized in Marion. It was a joyous April day. Maria cooked up a storm, and all the clan from Casteltermini showed up with enough food for the festivities to feed the whole town of Marion!

CHAPTER 5

The Explosion

Marion, Illinois, 1923

The mine in Marion was starting to dry up. The mine company noticed that the coal coming out was subgrade, not as pure as before. Complaints were coming in from the companies selling the coal, and the company was discounting the invoices in order to collect. They sent an engineer and a geologist down to the current dig area. It was suggested they dynamite the walls on both sides, hopefully exposing a new vein for samples of a better grade.

Giuseppe, Carmelo's brother, had been working at the company for five years. He left Whiteash the year Carlo was born and had worked his way up the ladder at the mine. He was making $0.20 an hour. His job was supervising the crews and ensuring they made their daily quotas. Acting as a go-between with the Sicilian workers and the bosses who spoke a different dialect, he had picked up their Italian dialect. He was in charge of setting the wicks on the dynamite sticks and making sure the miners down in the mine were out of harm's way. It was a slow process. He could not use too much dynamite at one time for fear of collapsing the mine. This had happened recently in Marion at another mine where several people died and many miners were seriously hurt, some never to dig coal again.

John L. Lewis, the president of the United Mine Workers Association, came to Marion and raised a big "stink" over it, and it got national attention with the news media. He and his associates tried to organize the miners. He had an interview with the newspaper and spoke of the disasters all over the United States. But once again, he could not convince the miners as they feared that they would lose their jobs if they joined the union.

After the initial blasts, samples were brought to the company lab, but the quality showed no improvement. Once again, the miners working this section of the mine were laid off to the dismay of Maria. She had to dig into the money she had been saving to pay living expenses.

Pepe Rumbolo was in that group, as was Carmen Castellano and other *paesani* from Casteltermini, and there was no time line for their return. The engineer and the geologist were summoned again. This time, they continued to blast in the direction of one wall that they felt might be the next vein.

Giuseppe and the miners were called back and descended the thirty feet down to the area, where they would be needed to dig and clean the debris from the blasted wall. Giuseppe set up the sticks, and the miners stepped back. Unfortunately, he had too short a wick on two of them. The blast blew back coal and parts of the dynamite and injured several of the miners, including Pepe Rumbolo, Carmelo Castellano, along with six others. It was a miracle that no one was killed. It took two days to dig away the debris and get them out of the shaft to the hospital. Giuseppe Reina was also taken to the hospital, although he was not seriously hurt. He faked injury as he did not want to face his bosses for fear of being accused of negligence and possibly be arrested. He also feared retribution from the miners who were not hospitalized, concerned they would gang up on him and hurt him! He waited until the wee hours when everyone in the room was asleep and proceeded to the washroom, checked around to see if any nurses or doctors were around, put his pants and shoes on, and quietly dashed out the door. He went to the boarding house where he spent the night and left early the next morning for St.

Louis. The next week, he departed for New York and returned to Casteltermini.

Once they were feeling better, Pepe Rumbolo and Carmelo Castellano decided to move to St. Louis and settle on the Hill to reunite the families with the clan. It was a joyous reunion; the food feasts were epic! They were constantly invited for dinners every weekend for over a month. They were offered whatever they needed to get established by the *Societe d' Casteltermini*, a not for profit organization on the Hill. It initially served as a welcoming group for people from Casteltermini to the neighborhood and played a serious roll to help those in need, especially for financial assistance or when there was any kind of serious illness in a family. Jake Cunetto was the leader of the society.

Once again, Maria was saddened. She was going to be separated from her two best friends, Giuseppina Castellano and Santa Rumbolo. The only consolation was the hope of seeing them on her visits for the alcohol runs on Fridays. This was one more nail in the coffin for Maria as to the downside of living in the coal mining towns and depending on the mines to support the family

Maria continued her weekly runs to St. Louis in the coming months. The fact that her sister had moved to St. Louis presented a problem. She had no one to watch the kids, at least no one she could trust with her secret. She would drop Virginia off at school, catch the train, and return with the other three in the afternoon in time to pick Virginia up from School. The trips gave her the money needed to pay the bills and provided the income to offset Carmelo's lack of work. The mine was drying up with no relief in sight.

Maria's concern about what to do with the kids on subsequent trips to and from St. Louis was being short-lived. On her next trip, she followed the usual pattern. Only this time after she dropped Virginia off at school, she had no choice but to take the kids with her. Try to picture a young attractive woman with young children dressed nicely boarding a train in broad daylight with a bag full of groceries and a sack with the alcohol and heading for Marion on the return trip. Nothing looked unusual; in fact, she looked even less suspicious with the kids.

When they arrived in Marion, the baby started crying; it was feeding time. She knew he would cry until she started nursing him. That was not to be soon because as she stepped off the platform, two Marion police officers grabbed her and the five-gallon can immediately! Someone had told the authorities about the whole deal and her involvement with a group from St. Louis. That group was suspected of being involved with Capone's group from Chicago.

The police put all of them in the police car and took them to jail. Maria was brought to the sergeant. The kids were left with a lady in the office; Ignazio was in tears even worse now as they hauled Maria away. Giuseppina and Carlo were also crying.

The sergeant explained the seriousness of the crime and admonished Maria that she had the crossed state lines, which made the offense worse. He asked if she had a lawyer. She understood very little of what he said, and the sergeant told one of the cops to get Tomasino, a desk cop who spoke Italian. When Tomasino arrived, the sergeant told him to explain some of what he had already told her.

"Tell her we are going to have to formally arrest her."

Maria began to cry and explained, "I have three kids in the lobby, if you put me in jail, you have to put my kids in there with me."

The Italian cop looked at the sergeant for instructions, and apparently he had a soft spot in his heart.

He told Tomasino, "Get her out of here!"

Of course, they kept the five-gallon can of alcohol. It was worth $5,000 after dilution with cooked sugar water.

Maria was released and went home and made the decision to stop the weekly runs to St. Louis. But she was concerned about informing Salvatore about the arrest. He came Sunday as expected and had heard about the arrest and understood her decision. There was no problem. He paid her the $5.50, a gesture she never forgot.

The hernia

In early January 1925, Baby Ignazio was sleeping in a crib on a small table in the bedroom with Maria and Carmelo. Maria kept him close so that when he woke up for his feeding in the middle of the night, she would take him to the kitchen to breast feed him to avoid waking Carmelo. He was twenty months old and did not like people food. It had been a nasty, windy, miserable day, and that night, Maria told Carmelo, "Put extra coal in the stove. The last thing we need is for the stove to burn out in the wee hours of the morning."

Ignazio woke around twelve thirty and started crying. Maria hurriedly got him into the kitchen so as not to wake Carmelo and the kids sleeping in the next room. She thought this was unusual in that he usually slept until three or three thirty. She tried to feed him, but he kept turning away, and the crying got worse. He was squirming and kicking, and Maria realized he must be in pain. Was it possibly another tooth, a stomach ache, or colic? She was baffled.

She went to Josie and Virginia who both had heard the baby crying, and they too were getting concerned. This was highly unusual as he was a pleasant child, and there had been no problems with him of any kind. Maria asked Virginia to put something warm on and come to the kitchen. Maria handed the baby to Virginia, and he had calmed down a little. She threw more coal in the stove and thanked God that they were not in the last house that was owned by the coal company; it was built on stilts, and the wind gusts and drafts in the winter had made it impossible to heat.

Maria went to the drawer below the buffet and took out the heavy medical book she had purchased and started thumbing through it, looking at pictures until she reached the section about babies. She called Virginia over, who was almost nine, and read everything she could get her hands on. Maria summoned her to the table where she had the book open to the section on babies, and asked her to look for anything to do with a child crying incessantly. Virginia started turning the pages slowly and could not find anything.

At some point, Maria saw a section on hernias, and it showed a baby's penis and groin area, and Maria, embarrassed, sheepishly asked her what that was about. Virginia explained as best she could, translating it in Sicilian. "Mama, it looks like he has a hernia."

Maria took the blanket Ignazio was wrapped in, removed the homemade diaper, reached down, and felt a lump in his groin area. This scared her to death! Now what? Maria knew the hospital in Marion had just closed. It was owned by a couple of doctors. She was beside herself.

"I have to get to Herrin. It is a long way to go. Get dressed and later get Carlo up and make the sandwiches for the two of you for lunch."

The baby had cried himself to sleep. She put him in Virginia and Josie's room, and she and Virginia went to work in the kitchen, preparing the lunches and the breakfast.

The baby woke and started crying; he wanted to eat. Again, she wrapped him in his blanket and went to the kitchen to nurse him. Soon he fell asleep, and she put him back to bed. At about five, she got Carmelo up, told him of the problem, made coffee, and said, "I am going down to the livery stable to speak to Mike d'Amico about getting someone to take me to Herrin to the hospital." She explained the hernia in layman's terms as to the potential problem Virginia had explained and the need to get the child to a hospital for surgery immediately! She had never seen Carmelo so concerned. He sat dumb founded and said nothing.

Maria threw a heavy coat on and stepped into the terrible wet snow and made her way down the street to the livery stable. She knew Mike was there feeding the horses as he did every morning.

"Buongiorno, Mrs. Reina, what are you doing up so early in the morning?"

She explained the problem, "Mike, I need to get to Herrin as soon as possible. Do you know who could take us there?"

Mike said, "With the storm, it will be difficult to find someone. It is a long trip. It could take several hours. But let's go see Jim Scarpelli. Do you know him?"

She did not, but Maria knew by experience what the "green badge" could do, and she gave Mike the word. "Let's go knock on his door."

Mike pointed to a very nice coach that had a hood over the driver's seat to protect the driver against the elements.

"That's his coach." He told her it will be expensive. She gave him a look (the Reina look), and he never answered.

As they walked, Mike told Maria about Jim Scarpelli. He was from a small town in Tuscany, his mother and father were Italian, his wife was Jewish, and she wanted to raise their children in the Jewish faith. There were no Jews in the town and no synagogue, and because of that, she was constantly on his case to move to America. They migrated to Marion in 1924. They had heard a building had been purchased from the community center, later to be named a synagogue, and that's what brought them to Marion. Jim bought the coach and established his business that year. He rented horses from Mike when he needed them and stored his coach there. His Italian really helped his business, and the fact he had the nicest coach in town really was the key, along with the fact he kept his prices down.

Braving the wet snow and wind, they made it to Jim's house and knocked on the door.

"Come in Mike, hello my name is Jim Scarpelli." He offered coffee, and Mike introduced Maria. He began to explain the situation. Maria cut him off and started to tell her story with tears in her eyes.

Jim could not resist the deep blue eyes of this incredible woman, and the tears got him. He agreed to take her and the baby to Herrin. When Mike asked the price, he once again got the look from Maria and shut up. Maria didn't want to know the price, always thinking, always ready to barter, never to speak first. The person who speaks first always pays more in negotiating. She learned that with the boys on the Hill with regard to the alcohol runs. When she was buying groceries at Martino's, she watched Giovanni dealing with salesmen while she shopped. He never paid asking price for any merchandise!

"Allora Jim, undiamo?"

"Yes, Maria, I will need at least an hour to get the coach and horses set up. I will pick you up at your house, dress warm, bring blankets. It will be cold inside the coach."

Maria thanked Mike for his trouble and left, but on the way home, she made a mental note to drop off a couple loaves of bread to him next time she baked.

It was seven by the time she arrived back at the house. Carmelo had left for the mine. Virginia had already awakened Carlo and Giuseppina and cut up the two-day-old bread and served the usual coffee and milk and sprinkled a little sugar over it. She was nine going on ten. Maria had taught her how to make bread and pasta. She always helped with the cooking. The stories of Maria's mother dying when she was twelve were indelible in her mind, always the fear that something similar could happen to her mom, and she would have to take care of her siblings.

In that regard, Virginia was developing into quite the student in so many ways. Her teacher had taken her to the Marion Carnegie Public Library which had opened the year she was born, and Virginia was reading at least one book a week and discussing it at the dinner table every evening. She had become a voracious reader, and her teacher was encouraging her to read books on history, both world and American.

Ignazio had slept until Maria arrived, but the minute she walked in the door, he awoke crying and was in obvious pain. At Maria's breast, he quieted down.

Carlo and Virginia left for school as soon as Maria finished nursing the baby. She began getting things ready for the trip. She was smart enough to know she would be in Herrin for a few days and laid clothes for her and Ignazio on the bed. She had no luggage; she had made a large bag from burlap from a fifty-pound potato sack and sewed two handles double stitched together from a piece of the burlap. Then she made sandwiches for her and Jim.

She bundled up Giuseppina and the baby and walked down the street to the Mortarano's, *paesani* from Casteltermini, and told them what was going on and asked them to watch Giuseppina.

She told Mrs. Mortarano, "Please go to the house around four when the kids return from school. Bring them to your house until my husband gets home from work, usually at the same time." She went back to the house and loaded the stove with more coal and waited for Jim Scarpelli.

He arrived a few minutes with the beautiful coach and two horses, and as if the good Lord was looking down on them, the snow had almost stopped. He helped Maria into the coach. She could not believe the beautiful red velvet seat coverings. Once she was settled, Jim handed her the sleeping baby.

He said, "Maria, it normally takes a couple of hours to make the trip, but because of the snow on the dirt road, I have no idea how long it will take."

Jim knew where the hospital was; he had made the trip many times. They arrived at Herrin Hospital in less than three hours. Jim had pushed the horses to the limit!

Maria and the crying baby were admitted immediately, and the only doctor who spoke Italian was summoned. As soon as he arrived on the scene, Maria showed him the hernia, and he took her and the baby to the operating room and asked her to have a seat outside. He stopped by the desk and told the sitting nurse to get the other surgeon and two nurses to the operating room at once!

The operation took a little less than two hours, and the doctors emerged and told Maria her baby was fine. The operation was a success. Soon one of the nurses came out with Ignazio, who was still asleep. They had given him a shot to put him out so he would not suffer any pain during the operation. Maria was escorted to a nice private room, where she was to spend the next four nights.

Early one afternoon on the fifth day, the Italian doctor came to examine the baby, and he told Maria, "There are no complications. You may leave tomorrow."

Now the problem of the return. She knew a family by the name Bottini from Marion had moved to Herrin, and the husband, Pietro, worked at the coal mine. She walked the ten blocks to the mine, found a man who spoke Italian, and left a message for Pietro to come to the hospital when he finished his shift. When he arrived in the room, Maria told him of the dilemma.

"I need to get a message to Jim Scarpelli or Mike d'Amico. We need a ride back to Marion tomorrow morning." Pietro went to the local livery stable and told the owner who said he'd get the message to them.

At seven the next morning, Jim came knocking on Maria's door, and as soon as she saw him, her eyes watered. Once again, she felt God was looking down on her. It was not the first time and not the last! The sun was shining, and while it was brisk, there was no snow. The best news was the warm sun during the past few days had melted the snow, and the road was clear. She bundled up the baby who had been fed and was sleeping, boarded the coach, and in less than two hours, she was at the house.

She asked Jim, "*L' conto*, how much do I owe you?"

He looked at her and said, "Signora, this one is on me. You see, my real name is Ignazio, and as a child, I hated it. When we arrived at Ellis Island, the man at the desk could not pronounce it. He wrote Jim on my papers. I had a special feeling about that baby. Something told me to help."

Years later, Maria told young Ignazio the story.

Maria arrived to a freezing cold house and the entire family sick! The previous evening after dinner, Carmelo went out to feed his dogs. Somehow the gate to the shed had opened, probably caused by the strong winter wind, and the dogs and goat had run off. He immediately went in, got the kids bundled up, and they all went looking for the animals. It was a bitter cold, windy night, and the kids were not happy about it, but they were afraid of Carmelo and knew better than to argue with him. Besides, he trapped rabbits and hunted them with the dogs, and they loved the meat. After several hours, they located the animals and got them back to the house. But while they were away, the fire in the stove died out. It was cold and late, too late to build a new fire. He told the kids to put extra blankets on their beds and go to sleep. The next day, they were all feeling tired and aching, and everyone was sick. They were sleeping when Maria walked in the door. She immediately made a fire in the stove and made a pot of coffee. By now, the baby had awakened, and she began nursing him.

Carmelo got the look when he walked into the kitchen.

She asked in her cold, tough voice, "What happened? What did you do?"

He lied and said the goat ran away, not mentioning the dogs to put emphasis on her beloved goat. That he and the kids were out for hours searching, and it was late when they returned. The fire was out, so they went to bed. Maria yelled at him, and he knew her temper was at times as bad as his, so he backed off.

Maria herself got sick the next day, and everyone was feeling worse. She bundled up went down the street to her friend, Stella Mancuso's, house and asked her to somehow get a message to her sister Rosa, to come to help care for the family. Stella's husband was going to St. Louis on occasion, looking for a job. He, too, had been working at the mine and was not getting enough work. Maria had given Stella a slip of paper with Rosa's address.

Rosa arrived three days later to find everyone even worse than she expected. She began cooking a big pot of soup with a chicken she bought at the store and stayed the week until everyone was up and feeling better. After the kids were off to school and Carmelo left for work, Rosa sat with Maria and laid into her out about living in the coal mining towns and dealing with all the uncertainties.

"Do you want your boys to grow up and work in the mines? When are you going to realize that there is no future here? Move to St. Louis. My husband is making $0.20 an hour and working weekends in a speakeasy, making an extra $12 a week."

Rosa stayed that night and worked on Carmelo but to no avail. The next morning, Maria and Giuseppina and the baby walked her to the train station.

Maria spent the better part of the day preparing for what she knew would be an argument with Carmelo. Once again, she waited until after dinner and the kids had gone to bed to pursue moving to St. Louis. And as had always been the case, he argued that all he knew how to do was dig coal. His mind was made-up. They were not moving to St. Louis.

The next day, when he went to the mine, his supervisor approached him and asked him and his group to meet at lunch break at the far end of the mine. At noon, they convened where they normally ate lunch, and the supervisor gave them the bad news. The mine had started drying up, and a decision had been made to shut it down. They were being dismissed immediately and were told to pick up their checks in the morning.

The Move to Weaver, Illinois

Once again, Maria was overwhelmed. What else could happen? Carmelo had already made the decision to move to Weaver, the next town.

He said, "Many of the miners from Sicily and a few from Casteltermini are working there." He left nothing to be discussed. There was no argument from Maria. At that moment, all she could think about was the house and the loan at the bank, and how could they satisfy the monthly payment with him out of a job. She knew it was going to drain her meager savings.

Later that week, Carmelo told her, "Make arrangements with Jim Scarpelli to take you and the kids to Weaver and look up the Ferlisis, our *paesani* from Casteltermini. See if you can stay with them for a few days while you look for a house for us."

The first thing out of her mouth was, "And what do you propose we do with the loan on this house?"

He said, "You let me worry about that."

That was enough for her. She was not about to ask. She knew he was scheming, perhaps it was best not to ask.

He then said, "Once you find a house, wait a few days and leave the kids except for Virginia and come back. I will be at the Dinoras. Meet me there."

Why the Dinoras? she thought?

Maria called on Jim Scarpelli to arrange for the trip to Weaver the next day. This time, she asked him the price for the round trip and insisted on paying the $5.00. He showed up the next morning with the coach and two horses, and they were off to Weaver. The kids were excited as they had never ridden in a coach. The ride was easy, much nicer than the last time Maria was in the coach. They had the address of the Ferlisis and were welcomed, as always the case when friends were reunited from their hometown. Almost from the minute they walked in the door, Mrs. Ferlisi started putting food on the table and started cooking the pasta.

Meanwhile back in Marion, the Scoundrel began thinking about that day at the bank when Jimmy D'Angelo explained, "If there's a fire or if the house burns down, the insurance company will pay off the bank." He knew how easy it would be, but how could he do it without any suspicion? He would need an alibi. That would be easy. He could get one of his cronies from the mine to fill that role with him in attendance at a card game. He had to do it late at night. That way, he could use the excuse that he was playing cards, and he had to make sure the fire would burn the entire house to the ground!

Late the next night, he met with his friend, Sam Dinora, and told him of his plan. He asked Sam to send his wife and kids to St. Louis to visit her sister for the weekend to get her out of the house. They could easily say they were up all night playing cards. They set up a card game and invited four other friends over to play cards. During the day, Carmelo set piles of kindling wood and dry straw everywhere in every nook and cranny in the house and loaded the stove with coal, enough to burn all evening and into the morning. He left the draft door open at the bottom of the stove to insure the fire would not die. By setting things like this, he knew it would be a slow process, and the fires would burn across the entire house.

The card game was to start at eight, but the guys would stroll in between eight and eight thirty after they finished dinner. Carmelo always brought ample wine. This particular night, he planned to bring two gallons as he wanted everyone to get drunk! That way, their memories would not be challenged in case they were questioned about his presence or the time of his arrival. About eight, he set all the small fires and left for the game in time to be there as most the players arrived. The wine was passed around. Sam had placed fruit and three different cheeses on the table, and the boys were feasting, smoking cigars, and having a blast. About nine thirty, when Carmelo made an excuse to leave, no one even paid attention. They kept play-ing, drinking, and enjoying the evening. Carmelo ran to the house and could see the fires had started the slow burn as he had planned. He quickly returned to the game.

The game ended around twelve thirty. All but Carmelo, Sam, and one other guy departed in less than five minutes, Giovanni Marconi came running back and stormed through the door, yelling, "*Carmelo, la casa e in flamme!*" (Carmelo, your house is on fire!).

They all ran to the house and found the small fire department there. They were helpless; they could do nothing as there were no fire hydrants, no water pressure in the tank connected to the horse-drawn carriage. The entire house was in flames! As he had planned, Carmelo spent the next two nights at Sam's.

On Monday, Maria arrived at the house and could not believe her eyes. There was nothing left. Virginia started crying, and Maria took her into her arms and tried to comfort her. They walked down the street to the Dinora house and met with Carmelo and Sam. She got the story from them, but she knew this was the work of the Scoundrel!

They went to see Jimmy D'Angelo, who had already heard of the fire. Maria wanted to go to the bank.

Jimmy told them, "There would be an investigation but not to fear anything. Maria was in Weaver, and Carmelo had a perfect alibi."

They went to the bank, and the bank officer also had heard of the fire as had the insurance executive. He had already contacted the insurance company and told them, "An examiner will be coming from Herrin to speak to you tomorrow."

Jimmy told him, "The Reina's will be at my house," and gave the insurance man his address.

Two days later, the examiner came and interviewed Maria and Carmelo with Jimmy as the translator. The insurance company would be paying off the loan at the bank. Maria was presented with a check for her equity in the house in the amount of $1,240. The entire meeting lasted twenty minutes.

Maria asked about the brass beds, "Is it okay for me to clean the beds and keep them?"

He responded at once, "Of course, Mrs. Reina, just take them and anything else you can salvage."

When they returned to the Dinoras, Maria was shocked to find Carmelo put all their personal items and clothes, along with a few books and the medical book in three empty flour sacks.

CHAPTER 6

The Move to Weaver

Weaver, Illinois, 1924

Maria was impressed with Weaver, finally a nice place to live. Weaver was unique with its nice stores, a beautiful park, an incredible public library, and schools. From the day Maria and the children arrived, she was pleased with the amenities. But St. Louis was still uppermost in her mind, and the determination to get there was still a driving force.

As was the case with all the coal mining towns in Southern Illinois, Weaver was a short distance from Marion and just three miles to Herrin. It was founded in 1904, and the mine opened shortly thereafter, but the owner went bankrupt not long after opening it. It was bought later and opened under a new name and it was called The Old Ben Coal Company. A riot by the miners in 1922 really affected the sale of coal from the mine, and steady work was a problem for the miners as a result. The saga continued—the move to another mining town!

Maria had the brass beds moved to the livery stables so she could scrub off smoke and dirt. They survived the damage from the fire, and she intended to take them to Weaver. She had found a nice house there for the family to rent at $12 a month. She asked Mike D'Amico to find someone to move them and asked him to send the guy to the Dinora house to see what in addition to the beds they were taking to Weaver. The day after she cleaned the beds, a large heavyset burly man knocked on the Dinora's door. He introduced himself as Pieter and asked for Maria. He was Polish and spoke no Italian, but fortunately Virginia and Carlo had just arrived from school, and Virginia did the translating. She gave him the address of the new house and showed him the three large sacks with their belongings. He had already seen the brass beds. He could not hide his disappointment. He thought this was going to be a larger move. He was committed to help because Mike had given him the word, "These are nice people," and explained the recent traumas, "First, the baby's hernia operation and then the house burning down."

Mike told him, "Stay clear of the father. He is a rough character. Don't mess with him!"

Two days later, they departed for Weaver. Carmelo road in the wagon with Pieter, the two dogs, and the goat. Always the goat. The rest of the family traveled in style with Jim Scarpelli in the coach.

Maria felt rich with the insurance money in her purse. She made great *melanzana* (eggplant) sandwiches and had plenty of fruit and a gallon of water. They all ate well before they left.

When they arrived at the house, the kids were surprised at how nice it was. While the coal company owned it, it did not resemble any of the company-owned homes in any of the former cities. There were three small but pleasant bedrooms, a nice kitchen with a good-sized pantry. As soon as Virginia saw the pantry, she made a mental note: that's where the goat would sleep, far away from the bedrooms as possible. No more goat sleeping in the kitchen close to her bedroom. No more dealing with the odor.

Once again, there was no indoor plumbing. Water was from a well a block away. While the town was small, it was very pleasant with a short walk down the street to a nice park.

Once they were unpacked, Maria headed for the store owned by the Old Ben Coal Company. She walked into the store and was shocked. It was busy. There were people everywhere, and it was stocked with an incredible variety of domestic and imported foods. She was teaching Virginia how to select the best fruits and vegetables and also how to bargain. When Maria returned, she cooked dinner for the family, Pieter, and Jim Scarpelli, who were spending the night. She made pasta, great meatballs, great *sugo* made with fresh plum tomatoes, heavy on the garlic, and probably the one and only time in her life, Italian bread she bought at the store. The Polish guy ate like he was going to the electric chair, as did Jim Scarpelli! As always, Carmelo served the homemade wine.

The following Monday morning, Carmelo was escorted to the mine with Francesco Ferlisi who vouched for him, and he was hired. He could not believe how deep they had to descend, and that he only had to work nine hours a day. The last surprise was the pay, $0.20 an hour. He could not understand why they paid $0.05 an hour more than the previous company, nor why he had to work only nine hours. He learned a lot that day. First, there were no liquor stores because of prohibition. Also, there were speakeasies; he had never seen one.

Ferlisi told him, "Carmelo, there was a massive strike that had happened in 1924, and a lot of people were hurt, some seriously. Stay away from any union people. The company is tough on workers who even mention the word *union*. You could get fired!"

Carlo had started school in 1924, and unlike Virginia, he fortunately had been speaking English when he began and was doing well. He was a very good-looking boy, and even at that age, he was the talk of the second-grade class among the seven-year-old girls. He had the personality to go with the looks too.

His teacher, Miss Derby, pushed him to read. "Carlo, I want you to go to the library and take out a new book every other week, and let me know what you are reading."

His big sister, Virginia, found the library, and they went together the first week after school. They took out two easy-reading books the librarian suggested, but Carlo's reading was poor, and Virginia had to help him.

Maria was already scheming on how to create a better lifestyle for the family because Carmelo was making only $10.80 a week, cutting the cost of living very close. While the kids were wearing hand-me-downs—as far as their clothes were concerned—from time to time, new shoes were needed. That included work boots for

Carmelo. Maria had to dip into the savings; there seemed to be no end to financial worries.

Giovanni Martino was always on her mind as to possible additional income. She was obsessed with never being satisfied with the status quo of the typical poor immigrant family! She thought, *There must be a better way.*

One night, shortly after the family finished dinner, the girls were helping Maria clean the dishes off the table. Ignazio tried to get out of his high chair and fell to the floor, landing on his head. He had caught the side of his face on the leg of the chair and opened a cut and was bleeding by the time Maria got to him. She panicked when she saw the blood. She immediately put a soft wet cloth on the cut, and the bleeding began to slow. She was concerned about him landing on his head and decided to take him to the hospital. She wrapped him in a blanket, and she and Virginia walked the few blocks to the hospital emergency room.

Ignazio was admitted, and a young doctor took him immediately into a small room. After thirty minutes, the doctor came out and introduced himself, "Hi, I am Dr. Sullivan. I had to put two stitches on the cut. He will be fine, but I believe we should keep him overnight. You are welcome to stay with him, Mrs. Reina. I have given him a sedative so he is going to sleep for a while."

Maria had not prepared for this; she had no money. She and Virginia had to get home to care for the family the next couple of days. After they were escorted to the room, Maria told the nurse to look after the baby, and she and Virginia went back to the house.

She gathered some clothes for her and Ignazio and confronted Carmelo, "I am going to spend the night in the hospital. Look after the kids." She grabbed her purse and some money.

She turned to Virginia. "Here is what you have to do: first, get your brother and sister up in the morning, make breakfast and their lunches, make sure their clothes are clean and pressed, lay them out tonight so you do not have to do it in the morning."

Again, at age nine, Virginia was thrust into taking care of the family. This would not be the last time a nine-year-old Reina would be handed partial responsibility of taking care of the family.

Maria spent the night and early morning with Ignazio in the hospital. After the doctor came in to examine him, Ignazio was released, and they walked home.

Virginia did her job; she was up early, made the coffee and breakfast and sandwiches for Carmelo and her and Carlo, got everyone fed, and got Carlo off to school. She stayed home to care for Giuseppina. (By this time, she was called Josie because Ignazio couldn't pronounce Giuseppina.) Maria walked in to find everything neat and orderly, beds made, dishes washed, and Virginia making bread, as always the young mom. Virginia had excelled in making sure things were in order, not knowing how long her mother would be away.

The move was to be short-lived. Two months after they arrived, with barely enough time to settle in, the miners went on strike. The owners warned them that if they went on strike, the mine would be closed. Once again, Maria had to deal with no income and delved into her savings. Carmelo had no idea how much money she had. If he got his hands on it, he'd be at one of the speakeasies Francesco had taken him to, or he would gamble with it. He had no common sense when it came to money.

Maria was beside herself. This was it. After the kids went to sleep, she sat with Carmelo and said with a determined tone in her voice, "We are moving to St. Louis with or without you! I am sick of trying to make a life in these coal mining towns! I don't want our boys to work in the mines, nor do I want our girls marrying miners! You can't spend the rest of your life worrying about being arrested for stabbing that guy in Casteltermini! Giuseppe Burruano promised he can get you a job working with him with the city of St. Louis."

The Scoundrel knew his time was up digging coal. Maria was set, and there was no changing her mind.

Carmelo was not finished yet. He had some thoughts on moving to Herrin where there was a large mine. He let her have her way for the moment, but there was no way he was going to move to St. Louis without a fight.

Carmelo arrived home on the fifth night after the strike had started to inform Maria that the owners of the company had told the chief foreman to fire all the miners. The mine was to be shut down. That was enough for her after they finished dinner. She looked Carmelo in the eye and said, "We are moving to St. Louis." He saw blood in her eyes!

He replied, "No, we are not. We are moving to Herrin. That's where the other miners are planning to go!"

She responded in a harsh nasty voice that shook the kids, and Carmelo got the look! "We are moving to St. Louis! I say we, me and the kids, and if you want to move to Herrin, go ahead. We are moving with or without you!"

The kids all had their heads down. They had never heard her speak to him in that tone of voice. Virginia was most proud!

Carmelo was so shocked he momentarily was lost for words. Then he sat back, mocking her, and laughed.

He said, "And how do you plan on supporting them? Where are you going to get a job?"

He should never have laughed at Maria, nor should he have embarrassed her in front of the kids. He should have known better. This was no ordinary woman of early twentieth-century America! He knew she had been helping support the family since her arrival, he knew the wine business was her idea, and he knew the weekly trips back and forth to St. Louis was a major contribution to the family's living expenses. Nevertheless, he continued to mock her, not a good idea in front of the children, for her temper boiled over!

Maria jumped up from her chair, gave him the look, and said, "*Dishonorato* [slang Sicilian for no honor], I have been doing things to help support this family since I arrived! Whose idea was it to make the raisin wine? And who has been making the trips to St. Louis and returning every week with the alcohol? You have not worked steadily for the past five years! So don't sit there and laugh at me. You no longer decide where we live. We are moving to St. Louis with or without you!"

Carmelo was in shock. Once again, he knew his dominance was finished. That Maria was now making the decisions! He got up from the table and went to their bedroom and went to bed. He fell asleep immediately between the three glasses of wine and Maria's admonishment. He was finished for the night.

The move

Maria asked Stella Mancuso to help find someone to move them.

Stella said, "We are moving too. Let's see if we can put a deal together and get a good price."

Two days later, Stella knocked at the door with a man who had been recommended to her husband by their bank clerk. They entered the house, and Maria quickly showed them the beds and a few pieces of furniture. They agreed to a price for her share of the moving costs. The man asked for an address in St. Louis. Maria gave her sister Rosa's address, knowing full well it would be no problem to stay there a few days until they could find a place of their own. She thought this would be the last move. Little did she know, the family would move eleven times in the ensuing years between 1926 and 1934.

Carlo and Virginia left for school. Carmelo left for the mine to check in with the miners and discuss the family's move to St. Louis. He learned many were considering making the same move. He also learned there were all kinds of jobs, including in the clay mines, iron-work factories, manufacturers of cigarettes, shoes, and bricks. And the city of St. Louis needed ditchdiggers. This eased his mind, perhaps Maria was right.

That night at the dinner table, to the surprise of the children, there was no dissension. Maria disclosed they were moving in the next two weeks on a Friday. She knew the next argument was coming, about the two beagle hunting dogs and the goat. She wanted to take the goat, but she knew he would be adamant on the dogs. It was one thing to keep the goat in the kitchen in the winter, but the dogs stunk. Unless they rented a house where the dogs could sleep outside, there was to be a problem with the Scoundrel.

Finally the day arrived. Maria was excited but figured while the kids were still sleeping to have it out with Carmelo about the dogs. He was having the usual bread cubes and coffee. She sat down, prepared for the argument, and it ended almost as soon as she brought up the subject.

He told her on no uncertain terms that the dogs were going with them. Period. The end. He would find a place for them to sleep so that they would not have to sleep in the kitchen. That solved the problem; she won again.

The mover showed up about ten thirty and started loading their belongings onto his truck. Maria packed the food for the trip. The kids gathered their things and put them in the bags they were going to carry on the train. As soon as the truck was loaded, they departed by foot to the train station. What a sight: Maria, Carmelo, four kids, two dogs, and a goat boarding the train. This time, the weather worked in their favor. It was a warm sunny day, and the trip was a dream.

Virginia Reina first communion, early photo

CHAPTER 7

Arrival in St. Louis

St. Louis, Missouri, 1925

Maria's mind focused on the fact she had finally achieved what she had been dreaming about for ten years, a chance to get to St. Louis and reunite with the clan and her sister. She knew there was opportunity there. She would find a way to get her independence and be free from Carmelo's inability to earn money and support the family. There was no doubt in her mind she could get into some kind of business, preferably owning a grocery store. She had the insurance money stashed away. She dwelled on the success of the wine business, the alcohol runs, and her connection with Giovani Martino. She knew she could go to him and get into some business that was legitimate!

The train ride to St. Louis was as pleasant as any trip the family had taken.

Once on the train, the kids were very active, running up and down the aisles, except for Virginia, wondering about adapting to a school in a big city. She was nine and already as tall as Maria and way beyond her years. She was caring for her siblings, especially baby Ignazio, and likewise for her baby sister, who was now being called Josie by everyone. She too was very bright and spoke some English but used the Sicilian dialect of Casteltermini with Maria and Carmelo.

They arrived at the same Tower Grove Station in St. Louis that Maria had frequented so many times. They crossed the street and waited for the bus. About twenty minutes went by, and no bus. The kids were getting anxious and needed to use a bathroom. Carmelo took Carlo across the street to a small store and had Carlo ask a clerk if he could use the toilet. At that moment, Carmelo knew there were going to be problems, since he could not speak English. But he was told on the Hill that everybody spoke Italian and/or Sicilian.

Carlo and Carmelo returned in time for the bus and another dilemma.

The driver shouted, "No animals on the bus!"

Virginia asked the driver the directions to the Hill, and he looked at the group as if they had just arrived from Mars. Maria shoved a piece of paper in his face with $2 wrapped in it. Once again, the "badge" worked.

The driver invited them on the bus and turned to Virginia. "Tell your family to move all the way to the rear. Tell your father to hide the dogs and the goat in the last row behind the last seats. Be sure to warn him. If they get loose, and start running around the bus, I am going to ask for you people to exit my bus."

The bus made several stops in the next thirty minutes and later turned down Shaw Avenue, headed west to Edwards, made a left, and ended up making an unauthorized stop at the corner of Edwards and Daggett.

The driver called Virginia to the front of the bus, "Let me see that address again. See that nice brick bungalow? That's where you need to go."

They descended the bus, walked across the street, and knocked on the door. Rosa opened the door and could not believe her eyes when she saw Maria and the family. Shocked and amazed, she hugged her sister in tears!

Giuseppe Burruano arrived an hour later and, to his surprise, greeted the Reinas with open arms. It was a warm reunion, and as always, he opened a gallon of wine and discussed things about the Hill with Carmelo.

"I am working for the city, and they have a major project going on right now and need workers. They are digging a large sewer system circling the entire city, and I know I can get you on." He was a foreman now because he spoke pretty good English and had learned the basic Italian spoken by the northern Italians living on the Hill. He encouraged Carmelo to learn how to speak English.

Giuseppe told him he was involved with some *paesani* making and selling "moonshine," and that he worked on Saturday nights at a "speakeasy." What he didn't tell him was that he was gambling and drinking. Carmelo, always the suspicious one, had been to the speakeasy in Weaver, and he knew what went on in them. There was partying, and most the time, the men were with their girlfriends, never their wives. And they were not there playing chess! He was concerned about Rosa, who still was without children.

Maria and Rosa started working on food for dinner while Virginia started unpacking. Maria, Josie, Virginia, and the baby took the biggest of the two allotted rooms, while Carmelo and Carlo took the room no bigger than a closet, housing a small twin bed. Maria was concerned about their furniture, which was due to arrive in the next couple of days.

At the dinner table later, Giuseppe assured her he would go the next day, Saturday, to The Big Club Hall bar and find someone who knew where they could store the furniture until they found a house. Rosa had made fresh bread that morning, and as always was the case, Maria took charge in the kitchen. She saw an icebox with four maple doors that opened to shelves, one for a block of ice and the other three loaded with food. It was much nicer than those she had seen in the past, and it was loaded with many delicacies. Rosa told Maria she shopped at Giovanni's store, which explained the wide assortment of foods. Maria assumed Giuseppe was doing well. She knew the price on a lot of the items, most too rich for her pocketbook.

The spread on the table just overwhelmed the kids. They had already had some kind of day, the train ride, the experience on the bus, they had watched Maria bribe the driver, the actual ride itself for the first time, and now meats, salamis, and various cold cuts, and meatballs (this was not a holiday). Another first, store-bought pasta that came packaged in a cardboard box and great sesame seed cookies they dunked in their coffee after dinner. And the finale to their pleasant surprise, a large bowl of fresh fruit and three different cheeses! It was a climax they would never forget—but before they went to bed came the thing that topped everything they had ever seen, the *bacasu* (Sicilian made-up word for backhouse or *outhouse*)—was inside! They could not believe they could go to the bathroom inside the house. With smiles on their faces, they were very happy their incredible mother had put her foot down and forced the move to St. Louis.

The next morning, the kids slept in late, as did Carlo and Carmelo. All but Virginia woke up when Ignazio awakened for his early feed, and she and Maria went into the kitchen so as not to wake the others. Maria nursed him, and he fell asleep before he was finished. Maria put him in bed and went into the kitchen and made a pot of coffee and began discussing the next few days with Virginia about getting organized. She explained they would have to stay with Aunt Rosa until Carmelo got a job, but she planned on looking for a place to live that very day. School for her and Carlo was also discussed.

Soon Rosa woke up and came and joined them. Virginia, ever so respectful, got up and went to her and kissed her from one cheek to the other, and Rosa asked her if she wanted to make some pastry with her. Always willing to learn, she agreed, and together they made dough, same as the traditional bread dough, and made shapes like doughnuts. Then they fried them in oil and, after they drained them on wire racks, rolled them in sugar. It was only a short while before the smell of the doughnuts wafted through the house that the rest of the family filed into the kitchen and began munching on the latest surprise for the Reinas with coffee and milk poured out of a bottle.

Later that morning, Giuseppe took Carmelo with him to The Big Club Hall. It had been a bar at the corner of Shaw and Marconi. In those days, it was more of a club than a bar, for prohibition was still in effect. The cops for the second district police were on the take and allowed the penny ante card games and locally made wine and draft beer to be served. The front door was locked, but there was a back door, and with the secret knock, one could enter if the doorman recognized the person knocking. There were quite a few Sicilians and Italians there, but Carmelo did not know anyone. There were four card games going on, two tables all Sicilians and two Italians. Giuseppe started at the Italian tables and introduced Carmelo. They all nodded, but none got up to shake his hand. The day would come when he would get *rispetto* (respect) anytime he walked into any room! Next, they ventured over to the two games in progress with the Sicilians; some were from Palazzo Adriano, some from Palermo, a few from Casteltermini. Again he introduced Carmelo. He did not know any of them. His family in Casteltermini were well-known and respected. Everyone rose to their feet and came over and shook his hand. It would take but a few days for the word to get around that a Reina had arrived on the Hill!

They went to the bar and ordered a beer. Carmelo had no money, and Giuseppe paid for them.

He quietly explained the situation with the Italians, "The Sicilians did not fight with the Italians, but there was an unwritten law they kept to themselves."

He said, "Carmelo, the Italians look down on us. They think we are *classe bassa*, low-class, uneducated." This stuck in Carmelo's mind and registered; he would never forget it.

Giuseppe spoke to a large heavyset young man who had walked in by the name of Salvatore Bommarito regarding the furniture and belongings coming that afternoon. "Salvatore, we need to find some place to store it for a while until the Reinas find a house to rent."

Salvatore said, "Why not go to Spielberg's furniture store? They have a warehouse on Pattison Avenue. Maybe they will allow you to put it there for a while. I know Louie Spielberg. Do you want me to go with you to see him? He is always there on Saturdays." The Spielberg family had opened the store some time in 1916. It was one of four stores owned by Jewish families on the Hill. Phil and Joe Rau owned a high-end, branded apparel store on Shaw Avenue. At the corner of Shaw and Edwards, there was another two-story furniture and appliance store called Fair Mercantile. It was operated by the Paull family. They were fierce competitors of the Spielbergs. At 5103 Shaw was Rosen's Dry Goods Store owned and operated by Saul Rosen. He had opened the store shortly after the end of World War I.

The trio walked down the block to Spielberg's. Carmelo had never seen such a large building; it was a two-story brick facility, a half-block long. They were greeted by a very nice young lady who recognized Salvatore, and assuming all three were Sicilians, she asked in perfect Sicilian dialect, "How may I help you, Salvatore?"

He said, "We need a few minutes with Mr. Spielberg."

The lady made a beeline up the stairs to the second floor, and the men started walking around the store. Carmelo could not believe his eyes; he had never seen so much merchandise in one location anywhere. Everything was displayed very professionally with signage in both English and Italian, with pricing and credit terms. Salvatore was translating some of the signage to Carmelo, who was having trouble trying to imagine a home furnished lavishly with all these things. In a few minutes, Louie Spielberg arrived. He was well dressed in a three-piece suit and tie. He wore glasses, was balding, but was very distinguished, taller than all three of the men before him. He knew Salvatore, shook his hand first, and reached out to Giuseppe as Salvatore was making the introductions and then to Carmelo.

Salvatore explained the Reinas had just arrived the day before from Weaver and were staying with the Burruanos. "Louis, they are expecting a small truck with their beds and personal belongings, no stove or icebox or heavy furniture. They need a place to store it until they can find a house." Spielberg took the bait. "They are going to need to buy a stove, an icebox, and some furniture."

He said in Sicilian dialect, looking directly at Carmelo, "*Signore*, feel free to store your belongings in my warehouse. Salvatore knows where it is. Let me know when the truck arrives today, and I will send one of my people to meet you there, and you can store it until you find a house, and there will be no charge!"

Carmelo was impressed with Salvatore and asked if he could meet them later at the store and then proceed to the warehouse, and he agreed.

Salvatore told them, "Giuseppe knows where I live. Come and get me when the truck arrives, and I will go get the guy from the store to let us in. The warehouse is in the middle of the block on Pattison between Edwards and Macklind. You can't miss it. There is a large sign on the building, wait there for me."

Giuseppe and Carmelo walked back to the house just in time for lunch. Later that day, the furniture truck arrived, the furniture went into storage, and Maria paid the driver. Everything went as planned.

CHAPTER 8

The Clan
Insalacos and the Castellano Rendezvous

St. Louis, Missouri, 1926

One Friday morning, after the kids had their breakfast, Maria informed Rosa she was going grocery shopping at Martino's. Rosa protested! Maria replied, "Rosa, it's one thing for us to intrude and stay here. You are not going to feed us too!" (For her entire life, Maria brainwashed her kids, "Never allow anyone to buy food for you when it is your turn to pay!")

She fed the baby and walked the three blocks to Martino's. It was a warm day, and she was glad to be out of the house; the walk was pleasant. As always the case, she was greeted by Giovanni with the usual respect. He was shocked to see her, and she informed him of the move.

"We are living with my sister, Rosa. Do you know of a nice house I can rent?"

He told her the same thing Rosa had suggested, "Go down the street to Riggio Bank. They will find a place for you. Tell the Riggios you and I are good friends."

She had her burlap sack and began shopping and bought enough food for the week, thinking what a nice convenience it was having an icebox. She even bought two bottles of milk since the kids

100

were enjoying it rather than the goat milk. By the time she finished, there was too much food to put in the bag, and Giovanni put the rest in a box too big for her to carry.

He said, "I will have the delivery boy bring it to your sister's. He knows where she lives."

"Thank you, Giovanni, I'm going to go to Riggio."

She walked into the bank, and a young man asked, "May I help you?"

She replied, "I need to rent a house."

He brought her to a desk and introduced her to a man who immediately rose to shake her hand. She told him the same, "I need to rent a house," and he responded in the same dialect, "Please have a seat." Like the Riggios, he was from Palozzo Adriano. Maria told him they had just arrived from Weaver and were staying with her sister at 5210 Daggett and would love to rent a house nearby.

He opened a large book—it had pages with letters on it—and turned to one with a D. He ran his finger down the page and came to an area and said, "I have a house we will be acquiring soon. The people are moving back to Italy, and we would love to rent it to you. It is only a block away at 5125 Daggett. It's a very nice house with two large bedrooms and a small one, a nice kitchen, a shed which can be used for storage if you need it."

That sparked a thought in Maria's mind, a place for the dogs and the goat.

She asked about the *bacasu*. He said, "Unfortunately it is outside, but very close to the house."

"What about running water in the kitchen?"

He laughed and said, "Of course there is, and a nice stove and an icebox that goes with it."

"When can I see it?"

He said, "I can make arrangements for you to see it whenever you want. Just give me twenty-four hours to go see the people and arrange it."

She replied, "How about tomorrow morning?"

"I can make that happen, but don't you want to know the price?"

She said, "Sure, but I want to speak to Mr. Riggio first about the price."

The young man thought to himself, *This is no ordinary woman.* He got up and went to see Mr. Riggio, and when he returned, he asked Maria to follow him. They went into a very nice private office, she was introduced to Mr. Riggio, and the young man returned to his desk. Maria began her pitch.

"Mr. Riggio, you don't know me. I was sent here by Giovanni Martino. He and I are very good friends."

"Very good friends," that was more than just a referral, and Mr. Riggio got the message. He got up and walked over to the young man Maria had been discussing renting the house and asked what was the price he had quoted and was told he had not quoted a price, "she wanted to see you about the price."

Mr. Riggio smiled and said to himself, "This is a shrewd woman." He returned to his office, facing Maria. "Mrs. Reina, we had planned to lease that house for $15 a month, but because you and Mr. Martino are friends, we will rent it to you for $12 a month. How does that sound?"

Maria said, "Ten dollars sounds better."

He looked at her and laughed and asked, "Mrs. Reina, would you like to come and work here at the bank?"

She laughed back and said, "Mr. Riggio, I have four kids to take care of, but you are just getting to know me. How about the rent? Can you do it for $10?"

He replied, "Mrs. Reina, you are just getting to know me. If it were possible to rent it for $10, I would have given it to you for that price in the first place. I'm sorry, $12 is the best I can do."

She agreed and made a mental note, *This is to be remembered for any dealings with this honorable man in the future.* Before she left, he showed tremendous respect for her and introduced her to his brother and sister-in-law.

Late the next morning, the young man from the bank knocked on Rosa's door and asked for Maria. She could see the house now. Maria agreed and asked Rosa to watch the kids and walked down the street to the house. After a short walk through the house, she went out to the backyard, took a look at the shed and *bacasu*, walked back inside, and asked when she could move in. He said the current tenants would be leaving in two months, and if she wanted to rent it, she would have to come to the bank to sign the lease.

She said, "I will be there this afternoon." He told her she would need the first month's rent and a $12 security deposit. She questioned the security deposit but dropped it. She would discuss it with Mr. Riggio.

That afternoon, she went to the bank. She had $24 in her purse, but they were going to have to drag it out of her to get it. When she walked into the bank, the same young man greeted her as yesterday, and he again asked, "How can I help you?"

She said, "I need to see Mr. Riggio."

He did not hesitate for a moment and brought her to Mr. Riggio's office.

Mr. Riggio got up from his desk and greeted her, "Buongiorno, signora, is everything okay?"

Maria, with a stern voice, said, "Thank you, signore, tutto posto, yesterday, when we discussed the price for renting the house, you told me $12! This morning, when I met with your man at the house, he told me something about an extra month's rent for security, *ma che e* security? Do I have to bring Giovanni Martino here to vouch for me?"

Mr. Riggio smiled and said, "No, Mrs. Reina, that will not be necessary. In your case, we will waive the security deposit. Come with me. He walked her over to the desk where the young man she had met with in the morning was sitting and asked her to sit down. He told his colleague to draw up the lease and waive the security deposit. As he walked away, he said to himself, "This woman has 'coglione' (balls)!"

Maria informed Carmelo of renting a house down the street. He never questioned those decisions; he knew nothing about them and left it up to her. He was grateful for the fact the new house was close, and he could go to work with Giuseppe every morning.

Maria was the first to arise on Sunday. She fed Ignazio and got him back to bed before any of the others awoke and started making bread. It was a bright sunny day in May, a day the group would remember the rest of their lives. She planned to take the Burruanos and the rest of the family to visit Uncle Giuseppe Insalaco and his family. She had not seen him since she left Casteltermini, and that was a brief visit. He was visiting from St. Louis and was there to help organize the coming trip for his wife and children's voyage the following year to America. She could never visit friends or relatives empty-handed. Always the bread, it was a version of the "badge."

Shortly after another festive lunch, they all made the short walk to Shaw Avenue to surprise the Insalacos. It was an incredible entry. Maddalena opened the door and screamed her surprise when she saw Maria, and it echoed throughout the five rooms.

It was Sunday; the entire family was there. Maria was shocked at how her cousins had grown and married. Maria asked for Uncle Giuseppe, and Maddalena broke into tears. Maria knew as soon as she saw the first tear, he had died. Then she too broke into tears, and Maddalena reached her, and they hugged for what seemed like an eternity.

When Maddalena broke away, she said, "He would have wanted us to enjoy this day. There is nothing we can do. We are grateful he came here and worked all those years and brought us to this beautiful country. Everybody come in please."

Maria was in a state of awe. She could not believe she was thousands of miles from Casteltermini here with her aunt, all her cousins, and their kids.

Her cousin Cologera married Mario Carducci; their five children were there. Giuseppina married Pietro Mazzochio; five kids, all were there. Carmella married Gioacchino "Jake" Cunetto, and three children were there. Alfonsa married Crociano VanCardo; four children were there. Francesco married Antoinette Bosnia. Giuseppe Junior married Josie Mignelo.

It is almost too much to believe. Maria and her family, Rosa and Giuseppe totaled eight and Giuseppe's family (forty-eight) squeezed into five rooms. Maria had expected a large crowd, knowing the traditional family gatherings were the norm in Casteltermini. She had been to family get-togethers like this, so she had baked ten loaves of bread and made enough homemade pasta to feed a small army. She had started at five that morning, and thanks to Rosa and Virginia's help, they finished by eleven! Needless to say, she was exhausted. She went into the bedroom shortly thereafter to nurse the baby, fell asleep with him for thirty minutes, got her strength back, and was back in the kitchen, preparing lunch with Rosa.

Giuseppe Burruano brought a gallon of red wine to the party, and the men started on it immediately while the older women started to prepare the feast. All the cousins gathered in different rooms—boys in one area, girls in another—and began what was to become a lifelong friendship, never referring to each other as cousins. They would spend the rest of their lives as if they were brothers and sisters.

It was an amazing group of people. In their adult lives, they never experienced other families having the same love and closeness, not even on the Hill, especially among the Italians. The same closeness would evolve within the rest of the clan. The Castellanos and intermarriages with the Cunettos, the Castellanos, and marriages with the Rumbolos, the Reinas, and the connections between both the first and second generations within the clan lasted throughout their lives. The second-generation kids continued the never-ending ties and, to this day, meet every year for a reunion.

For the better part of two hours, the clan ate from dishes that didn't match, sat on chairs that didn't match, drank from glasses that didn't match, but kings of the day did not eat better. Maddalena made melanzane parmigiana. Rosa breaded the veal and fried it in olive oil. Maria made a huge pot of *sugo* from cans of beautiful Marzano tomatoes for the pasta.

Cologera made the salads, one with lettuce and fresh tomatoes and one with canned tuna, chopped green onions, and a little mayonnaise, which Maria had never tasted.

It was so crowded, some ate standing up, and they were spread out all over the house.

Virginia was questioning the older girls about Shaw School, the public school they attended. It was a beautiful school built in 1907, a brick building that sat on a square block. It was two stories with twenty-one rooms, huge lunchrooms on the basement level, one each for the girls and one for the boys. The library was on the second floor, and while the class rooms were coed, the lunchrooms and the playground separated the girls and boys. Best of all, there was a huge swimming pool on the playground that opened on Memorial Day and closed Labor Day. It was coed. Virginia could not wait to tell Carlo and Maria how excited she was; she had already decided to go there on Monday morning.

They departed at nine thirty and walked back to Rosa's house. As was always the case, everyone had over indulged.

Maria told Rosa she wanted to visit the Castellanos next and, of course, the Rumbolos. She thought about the ensuing Sundays; today's festive reunion was to be repeated. She was finally home!

When they were back at the house, Virginia told Maria she wanted to register at school the next morning with Carlo, and Maria agreed. The next day, bright and early, Maria nursed the baby, made the traditional breakfast for Carlo and Virginia, and asked Rosa to care for Josie and the baby. Then she left with Virginia and Carlo for Shaw School. Giuseppe had left earlier with Carmelo to the City of St. Louis office on Kingshighway, hoping to get Carmelo a job as a laborer.

When Maria and the two kids arrived at the school, they were astonished at the size. They got lost when they entered the building, but a custodian directed them to the principal's office on the second floor. They were escorted into his office; Virginia introduced Maria and Carlo and did most the talking.

After a brief discussion, the principal asked for their birth certificates. Virginia translated the question to Maria, who shook her head, and she told her there were none.

The principal knew enough Italian and picked up on the answer and said, "I cannot admit you without birth certificates and transfers from your school in Marion." He told Virginia, "You will have to go to an Illinois State Office and secure the certificates and come back.

Plus, we are getting close to the end of the school year, perhaps you should come back and start in the fall."

This did not sit well with Virginia; the last thing she wanted to do was lose a year's schooling. They walked home, and she pushed Maria to come up with an answer to the problem. Later they learned the closest State Office was in Johnson City, Illinois. Again, Virginia pleaded, and a couple of weeks later, Maria, Virginia, Carlo, and Josie took the train to Johnson City. After somewhat of a hassle, an Italian clerk filled out all the documents and issued the birth certificates. But the decision was made to start school in the fall, much to the dismay of Virginia.

Later Maria walked to the Riggio Bank on the corner of Shaw and Marconi and opened a bank account and deposited $800.00 of the insurance money. She kept the rest with her savings. Once again, Carmelo knew nothing of what she had socked away, nor the new account. He didn't trust banks, but then he didn't trust anyone.

Carmelo was hired on the spot. St. Louis had begun a major project surrounding the entire outskirts of the city to alleviate a sewage problem during heavy rains. Floods were common, and many streets became impassable. It was called the River des Pere sewage system, and they needed laborers to dig deep channels circling the city that covered over nine miles.

Carmelo was ready; he was wearing his work boots and even brought his own shovel, hoping to get on immediately. Giuseppe spoke on his behalf, and the language barrier was no problem—most the workers had the same problem. Carmelo was assigned to a group of Sicilians and Italians supervised by an Italian who spoke English but very little of the Sicilian dialect. He tolerated the Sicilians but looked down on them. He had little respect for them, thinking they were somewhat illiterate and were ill-mannered.

Carmelo could not believe his starting pay was $0.20 an hour for nine hours a day, but if they worked overtime, they were paid $0.30 an hour. The city was in a hurry to complete the job, so there was to be plenty of extra hours.

At the end of the day, all the laborers were driven back to the office. He met Giuseppe, and they walked home not before they made a stop at The Big Club Hall for a beer. Once again, Carmelo was introduced to more of Giuseppe's friends. Giuseppe paid the $0.20 for the beers. Carmelo was embarrassed and promised to pay the next time.

When they walked in the door, Carmelo asked Maria for a $1. She went to her bedroom and came back with the dollar. Before she gave it to him, she asked why he needed it, which provoked a shout, "I just spent nine hours breaking my back digging a hole bigger than this house for $1.45. Do not treat me like one of those kids, give me the $1!"

Once again, Maria was the victim of his outrage in front of Rosa and Giuseppe, both of whom had witnessed this in the past.

The next morning, after breakfast, Maria took the children to visit her friend, Giuseppina Castellano. They hugged in tears, and Giusippina hugged all the kids. As always, Virginia—ever so respectful—hugged her and kissed both sides of her cheeks and said, "Buongiorno Zia Giusippina." The children would always call all the female relatives and close female friends *zia* (aunt) and the males *zio* (uncle) as a sign of respect.

Giuseppina apologized for not getting Maria a coffee and took everyone into the kitchen. She went to the icebox and poured glasses of milk for the kids and set out a plate of sesame cookies. She poured water from a faucet into a pot to boil for the espresso for Maria. The kids sat once again in awe, first at the icebox, then the milk from a bottle and the water coming from the faucet, even though it was the same at Rosa's. They wondered how the water would get to Zia Castellanos house from Zia Rosa's house and how they would get the milk from the goat's things into the bottle and how come they would never put the goat's milk in a bottle.

They retired back to the living room, and Giuseppina suggested they all come for dinner on Sunday. "The entire family will be here, both my immediate family and Carmelo's brother's family. It will be *una festa.*"

Maria agreed but asked, "Is it okay if Rosa and Giuseppe come with us?"

"*Va bene*, of course."

Maria already planned her contribution and told Giusippina she would bring the bread and the pasta. Giusippina graciously accepted because she had had both on numerous occasions.

On Sunday morning, Maria was up bright and early. It was a blue-sky day and sunny, a glorious beautiful May day. She fed Ignazio, put him back in bed, and started making the bread. While the dough was rising, she made the dough for the pasta, and soon Rosa was there by her side, assisting. They shared a cup of espresso and discussed the house, and Maria told Rosa she would be buying some furniture.

She said, "I have the money, but I do not want Carmelo to know about it, so I am going to tell him I have to borrow it from you and Giuseppe. Please cover that with Giuseppe, then I will give you the money, and later in front of Carmelo, you hand it to me. In a few weeks, I intend on going to Spielberg's and Fair Mercantile to buy the furniture."

This was her life. Nothing was easy, especially when it came to money. She had enough experience with Carmelo, never to disclose what she had socked away.

They returned to the order of the day, preparing for the *festa* at the Castellano's. After making the bread and pasta, Maria took out the veal, flattened the pieces, and made the *modigo* (chopped green onions, bread crumbs, and graded parmigiano cheese). Then she took two eggs and beat them. Rosa then took the veal slices, dipped them in the egg wash, and breaded them. She handed them to Virginia, who had joined them, and fried them in olive oil. The smells soon brought Carmelo, Giuseppe, and the kids to the table. Maria allowed Rosa and Virginia to finish their work while she got the bread and coffee ready for breakfast for the rest of the group. Before long, both Giuseppe and Carmelo requested, "*Un pannini con cotoletta di vitello* (a veal cutlet sandwich)!"

At noon, everyone was nicely dressed for the visit to the party at the Castellano's. The Rumbolos were there with sons Sam and Carlo. Thus, they continued the rendezvous. The house was typical of the homes on the Hill, two to three small bedrooms, a small living room, a nice small-size kitchen, and a separate dining room.

Everyone was there when they arrived. The reunion was joyous. It had been three years since the Castellanos left Marion, and Maria was amazed how the kids had grown, especially how well they spoke English. It took a good twenty minutes for everyone to exchange hugs and greetings. It was a day to remember. They sat outside under a beautiful trellis, lined with grapes growing from vines across the ceiling and down the sides. The sun was shining, and Maria was as happy as she had been when they were last together in Marion.

Carmelo Castellano had passed away in 1923, leaving Giuseppina with five children, Lilly, Francesco, Jimmy, Giuseppe, and Carmella. They had a baby girl who died in a terrible accident at age three. She fell into a hot cauldron of boiling water, a tragic death Giuseppina never got over.

Carmelo's brother, Giuseppe, was there with his wife, Anna, and their children: Francesco, Jimmy, Rose, Caroline, and Josephine. They had been helping support Giuseppina and the children. The kids were like brothers and sisters.

Giuseppe opened the gallon of red wine and started pouring for the men and discussed current things happening on the Hill. Giuseppe Castellano listened intensely, knowing Giuseppe Burruano was involved with the boys who controlled the Hill. They sold the speakeasies moonshine, and controlled gambling.

The food was beyond belief. It went above and beyond the dinner at the Insalaco's. In addition to what Maria and Rosa brought, there was a large bowl of cannellini beans soaked in olive oil, beautifully sliced tomatoes with chopped sweet onions drenched in olive oil, chopped and sautéed broccoli, green beans cooked with enough garlic to ward off Dracula, fried wild rabbit, and *arancini* (rice formed in a ball, then dipped in an egg wash breaded and fried). Maria's pasta was a big hit, as were the veal cutlets. For desert, always the *biscotti al sesame* (sesame cookies). Anna Castellano made two pies, fresh apple, and cherry. It began what was to be memorable feasts that would forever keep the group's fondness for each other well into the nineties. This started as a once-a-month gathering that was indelible in the minds of the first-generation children. They had very little money, but no amount of money could buy what they had!

The interaction and friendships of the clan was the magnet that provided the acceptance by the parents of the first-generation children. Their friendships led to many marriages! Sam Rumbolo married Rose Castellano. Joe Castellano married Lena Cunetto. Carmella Castellano married Carmelo Cunetto. The weddings were classic! The gatherings later were much larger than the earlier days, especially after children started arriving, and it drew the clan even closer. Those children today have an annual reunion; they have managed to keep the second and third generation together, which now spans more than a hundred years!

The first-generation interaction within the clan became even closer after World War II. Since money was more available, they started traveling together, and soon the third generation were getting to know each other, and the same warm feelings and relationships developed.

5125 Daggett, 1926

Maria went to Spielberg's to buy a sofa and a table and chairs for the kitchen and asked to see Louis Spielberg. Maria like Carmelo, was astonished at the selection in the store.

In a matter of minutes, Louis Spielberg arrived. "Buongiorno, signora, how can I help you?" he said in a near perfect Sicilian.

She was overwhelmed. She told him what she was looking to buy. He showed her three sofas at various prices, and the bargaining began. Spielberg was well aware of the tactics and wasted no time. He offered a 20 percent discount, and in a matter of minutes, a deal was reached on one of the sofas. Next, the table and chairs, that, too, didn't take long. Maria had read the price tags which all had credit terms, so she asked about them.

Mr. Spielberg explained, "If you pay it off in twelve months, there's no interest."

She jumped on it, thinking long term about establishing credit. So she took both on the terms he outlined.

Louis said, "Let's move to my office," and asked her to fill out a credit statement, which she was unable to do. So he asked a few simple questions and filled out the application. Maria was embarrassed and made a mental note to bring Virginia from now on when she shopped.

In August, Carmelo came home early from work one day and informed Maria he lost his job. He had been harassed by his boss, pushed to dig more than was humanly possible. The boss had constantly called him "WOP." At first, he didn't understand the term, but finally one day, he asked Giuseppe Burruano, "Cosa e WOP?"

Giuseppe informed him it was a derogatory slang word for someone "without papers" usually thrown at Sicilians. Once again, the boss had pushed Carmelo and was continuously yelling at him, "Come on, wop, dig!" Carmelo hit him right in the mouth, grabbed his shovel, and walked off the job! Once again, financial stress.

Maria thought, *Here we go again.*

Maria went and asked Giovanni Martino if he could help find a job for Carmelo. Giovanni said he could get him a job at the clay mine, and he did.

The following Monday, Carmelo started there at $0.20 an hour, six days a week. Another tie to Martino, and it was not to be the last. Maria was well acquainted with the Sicilian custom. When you ask a favor from someone like Giovanni, best you be prepared to return the favor at some point.

In September, Virginia, Carlo, and Josie started at Shaw School. They walked the seven blocks with Maria the first day, presented their birth certificates to the principal, and were escorted to their classes. They were really amazed at the immense size of the classrooms, the first-floor lunchrooms, the enormous washrooms, and, of course, the library. Carlo's friends, the Rumbolos, and the Castellanos were in the same class, and Virginia and Josie had similar friends of both the Cunettos and the Castellanos in their classes.

Little did they know, these friendships would last a lifetime. It made the first day of school heartwarming.

Late that year, a man by the name of Pasquale Aquisto visited the Reinas on a Sunday with a proposition. He was sent by Giovanni and told them he had a nice house on Bischoff and would let them move in with free rent if they would set up a still-to-make moonshine. He offered to cook himself during the day and suggested Carmelo to cook at night. The Reinas would earn $1 for every gallon they would produce at the end of each month.

After he left, Maria said, "Carmelo, we have to do this. Giovanni has been there for us." There was no discussion. She assumed this was the payback to Giovanni for getting Carmelo the job at the clay mine and did not wait for Carmelo to respond. It was a done deal, but they had to contend with Riggio regarding the lease on the current house, which had five more months on it. This was the Sicilian way! She informed Pasquale they would get back to him after seeing Mr. Riggio.

The next day, she went to see Giovanni and told him about the offer. She knew he knew about it, and Giovanni said, "Don't worry about, Riggio. I will handle that. When do you want to move?"

Maria told him the best would be the first month of the year.

In late December, Maria, Carmelo, and Pasquale met at the house and set up the still. In January, the Reinas moved into the house on Bischoff. It was two doors away from the Castellanos, and because Carmelo was working at the mine, Maria agreed to cook the mash after dinner at night.

The smells were causing concerns in the neighborhood, and Pasquale showed up one day with a small truckload of used tires and began burning them one at a time to dispel the odor from cooking the mash. The first one hundred gallons didn't taste right, and Maria was concerned, but Pasquale assured her that it was okay. "I will still pay you!"

The same problem existed on the next batch, and once again, she was assured of payment. For some reason, the same thing happened throughout the month. They had cooked five hundred gallons, and now Pasquale complained of how much money he had lost.

An argument ensued between him and Maria while Carmelo was at work. He refused to pay her! She knew if Carmelo had been there, he would have gone at it with Pasquale. Pasquale left, as did Maria. She went to see Giovanni Martino, but he was not at the store, so she left a message for him. Late that day, Giovanni sent his son to see her, and she explained the problem.

Maria knew the gang met on Mondays, and the following Monday, she had dinner ready and left it on the table. She told Virginia, "Take care to make sure everyone eats. I will be back in an hour."

She walked to Martino's, knocked on the door, and Giovanni invited her into the store. She discussed the problem. What she didn't know was the group was in the next room, and the door leading to that room was slightly ajar, the gang—including Pasquale and Giuseppe Castellano—were listening.

Maria said, "I want you to arrange a meeting with Pasquale. I intend to accuse him of his promises to pay, and if he denies this, I will spit in his face!"

At that moment, Giuseppe Castellano put his hand on a pistol he had in his jacket. He kept it there, knowing the next move was for Giovanni to bring Maria in the room for the confrontation. He feared Pasquale might attempt to hurt Maria!

As soon as Maria walked into the room, Pasquale got the look from her! Giovanni began to praise Maria to Pasquale. "I have known this woman a long time, and there is no reason for her to lie. So, Pasquale, did you promise her you would pay her?"

Pasquale nodded, and the problem was solved! But it was not over as far as Maria was concerned.

She said, "Excuse me, *Signore* Martino, I paid $100 to move into the house, now I have to move again, and that will cost me another $100!"

Giovanni smiled, walked to the cash register, came back with $200, and told Pasquale to give her $500, which he did, and she left. The rest of the gang could do nothing but show their admiration. Once again, this was no ordinary early twentieth-century woman!

CHAPTER 9

The Moves

1926

Maria summoned Salvatore to help with the move from Bischoff to a house on Marconi. The kids were so used to it now that they didn't even complain. They fully understood all this was related to Maria's trying to deal with the meager earnings of their father.

Shortly after the move, Maria was approached by Carmelo's in-law, John Ingrasci, with another offer to make moonshine.

"Maria, you and Carmelo have experience making alcohol, and I have a very good deal for you. The second floor on my house on Shaw Avenue is vacant right now, and you can quietly make the moonshine up there. No one will bother you with me and my wife downstairs. There will be no rent for you to pay. I will provide all the money and split the profits 85 percent for me and 15 percent for you!"

The nice two flat was located at 5222 Shaw, a half block away. Maria knew he was involved indirectly with Giovanni, but she was not aware to what extent. She also knew sometimes it was a good idea to keep your mouth shut. Carmelo was earning $10.80 a week, and as always, they were barely surviving. She spread the word that she would take in sewing to make ends meet but was not getting any jobs. John mentioned he had a federal agent on the take. "There was no concern about the government. The local police were also on the payroll." To date, this was the most promising deal ever. But what they didn't know was that Giovanni Martino sent a letter asking Carmelo's brother, Luigi, in Casteltermini to help, and Luigi got John Ingrasci involved.

"My brothers and I are doing business with a very nice black man who is dealing in the black neighborhoods. He is good as gold and pays cash when he picks up the alcohol. His name is Crawfish, and he wants as much as we can produce. And Crawfish was willing to put up some money to front the ingredients."

John had made arrangements for them to meet. Later that week, he brought Crawfish to the house, and they concluded the deal.

Maria said, "We will move next month."

Fortunately, they had signed a month-to-month lease on the Marconi house. Carmelo noticed Crawfish was wearing two large diamond rings, one on each hand. A good sign.

Maria woke up one morning having trouble sleeping. It was the middle of July, and the city was experiencing a miserable hot, humid summer. She had that tell-all feeling in her stomach and realized she was probably pregnant, and for sure, she said to herself, "The Scoundrel will no longer sleep in my bed!" She had no idea when it happened but assumed the baby would arrive sometime in late February or early March. Her immediate thought was another mouth to feed and clothe. She was also embarrassed with regard to the children and made every effort to hide her belly in the ensuing months. This made the deal with John Ingrasci even more significant.

The following month, the family moved to the second floor of John's house, the nicest house they had lived in since their arrival in St. Louis. The very next day, John brought all the material for the still, and Maria and Carmelo set it up in a day and a half.

It was routine now. Maria and Carmelo were cooking day and night. Thank God for Virginia; she had taken over the house, making the bread and pasta, cooking dinners, and doing the laundry. There was a basement in the building where she did the laundry. It was cold and damp, but she never complained about the workload. She knew the score. Her parents were striving to get ahead, and she was doing her share. She had her mother's work ethic.

117

For the next six months, business was beyond anything they had hoped for. Crawfish was consuming close to six hundred gallons a month, and the Reinas were finally accumulating some money. Maria was socking it away and carefully making small deposits at Riggio Bank, small because she didn't want to arouse any suspicion.

The month of August brought heavy rains, and then September and October went the other way. It seemed like there was no fall as it got cold early. It was a relief being on the second floor with the summer heat from the still. The weather the past few months was horrible; they had suffered miserably and welcomed the cool breezes brought on by October and November.

In December, Maria confirmed with Virginia that she was having another baby. Virginia had no comment. She knew the Scoundrel had forced himself on her mother. Maria told her, "From now on, I will be sleeping in the front room on the couch!" She ceased sleeping with Carmelo!

On January 9, 1927, a Sunday, Maria and the family had just finished the traditional noon lunch. It was a cold windy day, and they were having coffee. Suddenly, the front door was broken open, and four armed men burst in with pistols drawn!

"Everyone, get down on the floor, face down!" One of the men presented his badge and informed Carmelo he was under arrest. Two of them took him away.

The other two agents stayed and smashed the still and carried away the remaining alcohol for evidence. The children were in a state of shock. Maria was lost for words.

Virginia said, "Mama, those were federal agents," and she warned, "This is serious. These were not local police. You need to get to Giovanni Martino immediately." The store was closed, and she didn't know where he lived. It would have to wait until morning. While she appeared calm, her stomach was churning, and her mind was racing. Carmelo was surely going to lose his job. While she had a decent nest egg put away and money in the bank, she feared the worst, especially with a new baby due in a few weeks. It was a sleepless night. But then she thought of the badge; she had plenty of cash to defend Carmelo.

Monday, bright and early, after she got the kids off to school, she sought the aid of Giovanni Martino. He already knew about the bust.

"Buongiorno, Mrs. Reina, I know why you are here. I heard about what happened yesterday. Please be aware that this is one of those things that rarely happens, and we will help. Do not worry. I will have my attorney post a bond."

Maria knew she was going to have to come up with money since this was not the local police.

Giovanni said, "This is federal, and Carmelo will probably have to go to jail for a while." He assured her it would not be for a long duration.

He asked, "Maria, have you or your husband discussed the business with anyone, friends, or family members? Someone had snitched to the authorities. Otherwise, how would they have known what was going on the second floor of a nice house? Please search your mind and let's find out who had gone to the authorities. We have to take care to insure that person does not do it again."

Maria feared for whoever did it.

Carmelo spent less than twenty-four hours in jail and was released on Monday afternoon. Giovanni's attorney, Vito Agnelli, drove him home. Carmelo asked him for the bill, and he said, "Not now." Carmelo would have to go to court sometime in the next week or two.

Maria was very concerned; she refused to discuss what Giovanni had told her about him ultimately being sent to prison. The biggest concern at this point was his job.

When Carmelo went to work the next day, he no longer had a job, and Maria knew the minute he walked in the door that disaster had struck again.

The next day, in a blinding snowstorm, the kids were drenched when they arrived from school. Maria got them out of the wet clothes and added more coal to the stove. She wrapped them in blankets and got them to chairs so they could sit close to the stove. She made a pot of coffee and handed each a cup. She sliced the fresh bread she had taken out of the oven, drizzled olive oil on the slices, put them in the oven for a few minutes, and served the four of them. It was better than cake!

The snow continued for the next twenty-four hours. On Friday morning, there was a knock on the door, and Maria was shocked to see a federal agent. He politely asked if he could come in. She invited him in and offered him an espresso, and he said, "Yes please."

After she served him, he said, "I have some questions for you and Carmelo."

Carmelo was still sleeping. She said, "Carmelo does not speak English, and mine is not real good."

He said, "I speak Italian. I am sure we can communicate."

Virginia had come in, and Maria asked the agent if he could come back later after she got the kids off to school. They agreed to reconvene at ten.

Maria quickly got the kids fed and off to school. She awakened Carmelo told him about the agent who was coming back at ten. She asked him to keep an eye on Ignazio who was still sleeping. She was going to see Giovanni. She rushed to the store and asked Giovanni, "Can we go into the back room to discuss a problem?" There were three customers in the store. He could see she was in panic mode, took her to the back room, and he made her an espresso, and she explained the situation.

He said, "The guy was there to pump you and Carmelo for information. He was trying to get you to finger higher-ups in the scheme of things and will probably offer some kind of lesser sentence if Carmelo will name the people at the top! He especially is looking to tie it to us. Maria, the federal agent wants and hopes to trace it across state lines to East St. Louis and to Chicago."

Everyone knew Capone and the other three mobsters controlled bootlegging and most illegal activities in Illinois and the surrounding states. Now Maria was really shocked!

Again Giovanni calmed her down. "Tell your husband to play dumb and say he was making the moonshine to sell to the minors at the clay mine. Tell the agent you had just started that month. Carmelo is to keep his mouth shut. He might have to do six months. It will not be that tough."

Maria got the subliminal message, "Keep your mouth shut." That way, no one gets hurt. She also made the decision to quit illegal endeavors!

The agent beat her home by a few minutes and was speaking to Carmelo when she arrived. Carmelo was discussing "his rabbit traps in what used to be the city dump surrounding the Hill."

The agent got down to business as soon as she sat down and explained he wanted information.

Carmelo was quick to answer and said, "The attorney had told me not to discuss the case with anyone," and politely told the agent, "I am not going to answer any questions."

The agent pleaded with them that it was in their best interests to cooperate and give him the names of the higher-ups. He promised he would do everything in his power to get Carmelo a reduced sentence.

Maria decided to perform her poor-family-with-four-kids, soon-to-be-five routine. "My husband works nine hours a day digging in the clay mine and makes $10.80 a week, and he had lost his job that week." She broke down with tears and begged the agent to please try to understand that they had just started the business recently, without discussing how recent just in case he knew when they started it.

He replied, "Mrs. Reina, you broke a federal law. This was not some petty local law. Your husband is in serious trouble and is going to go to jail!" He looked directly at Carmelo, hoping to get a response, instead he got a deadpan look as if to say you don't scare me.

Meanwhile, Carmelo was concerned that the agent was going to start digging into his past in Italy. His worst fear was being extradited back to Casteltermini! He thought, *This never would have happened had they moved to Herrin. Why did I listen to her?*

The tears and her story about him being out of a job worked. The agent abruptly got up, excused himself, and left. He realized he was getting nowhere.

Two weeks later, Carmelo was taken to court by the lawyer. The judge asked how he pleaded, and the lawyer told him to say guilty. Vito spoke on his behalf and explained to the judge that he was an honest man and had no record. He had Maria and the kids in the courtroom and informed the judge that Carmelo was out of work, that his wife was due to have a baby any day, and asked that he release Carmelo to his custody and drop the charges. The prosecuting attorney objected vigorously and demanded the judge to give Carmelo at least a year, at which time Virginia and Josie started crying, and that reached the judge. He asked Vito and the prosecuting attorney to come to the bench and, after a few minutes, told them to return to their respective tables.

The judge asked Carmelo and Vito to stand and promptly sentenced Carmelo to six months at the federal penitentiary in Leavenworth, Kansas. He was to report that same day. Two armed federal agents approached Carmelo immediately, handcuffed him, and led him to the rear of the courtroom, where he was taken outside, placed in the rear seat of an automobile, and whisked away to his new home.

Maria gathered the family and left the courtroom with Vito. He drove them home, and when they arrived, she invited him in for a coffee and to pay him.

He refused and said, "Thank you, Maria. I have to get back to the courthouse. I have another case to try. As for the bill, don't worry about it. Giovanni Martino is taking care of it!"

Maria said, "Wait here for one minute," and she told Virginia in her dialect, "*Vai prendergli una pagnotta* [Go get him a loaf of bread]!"

Carmelo arrived at the federal penitentiary in six hours and was given a physical, led to a shower, given his prison clothes, fed a plate of ham and beans, and escorted to his cell. He was not happy. He said to himself, "Why in the world did I ever agree to move to St. Louis? This was all Maria's fault, and she will hear about it."

Maria was sitting alone with Virginia that night after dinner with a piece of paper and a pencil doing a budget, estimating how much the family would need for the next six months to live.

John Ingrasci came to visit the next day after the trial to express his gratitude to her for Carmelo remaining silent and not implicating him. "Maria, I know this puts a strain on you, and I want to help." He handed her $150 to help cover living expenses while the Scoundrel was incarcerated. "In addition, you can live here and pay no rent."

Maria graciously thanked him, as did Virginia. Maria thought, *This is like a six month vacation!*

After he left, Virginia said, "Mama, this is half of what Papa was earning at the clay mine, and with your savings, we will get through this mess."

She responded, "We need to find someone to take us to Kansas to visit him once in a while. Hopefully Giovanni will find someone with a nice car to drive us," which he did. Maria began making the trip every Sunday and occasionally took along one or two of the kids. Of course, she brought food for a couple of days. She handed the main guard the badge usually a couple of dollars to keep the food refrigerated for the Scoundrel.

Maria was having difficulty with this pregnancy. Her friend, Stella Mancuso, came to visit when she heard about the trial. Maria explained the problem she was having, and Stella said, "You need to see a doctor, and I have a good one. His name is Dr. Wilcox. He will come to the house."

Maria asked, "How do I contact him?"

Stella had a phone number and said, "Perhaps you can go to Martino's. Giovanni has a phone. He can call for you."

They decided to go together while the kids were in school. Maria wrapped Ignazio in a warm blanket for the windy and snowy walk to Martino's. Giovanni agreed to make the call.

A pleasant lady who turned out to be Dr. Wilcox's wife answered the phone and was told the doctor was with a patient. Maria asked if he could come to the house, explaining the problem in her broken English, and adding that with four kids, it was impossible to go to the office. Mrs. Wilcox told her he could visit her late Saturday afternoon.

On Saturday, around two thirty, the doctor arrived and examined Maria in the bedroom. The children were very concerned, knowing how unusual it was for Maria to see a doctor. She received good news from the doctor and was told not to worry, that it was probably due to stress. Maria said to herself, *This doctor has no idea what stress is!* Before he left, she packed a loaf of bread and a bag of her homemade pasta for him, the magic of Maria's bread! Always the bread.

The good news was the relationship with Dr. Wilcox and the Reinas was to last the rest of his life. He became the doctor for the entire family and ultimately took care of the second-generation children.

CHAPTER 10

L'Mano Nero

1927

In late March 1927, John Ingrasci and his brothers, Jim and Pietro, paid a visit to the Baldi brothers, Franco and Antonio. They owned a grocery store at the southwest corner of Wilson and Edwards.

John opened the conversation. "*Buona sera paesani*, we have a proposition for you, so let's not waste any time. We will pay you 10 percent profit for every pound of sugar you can supply us. We own the two houses across the street, and we propose to dig a tunnel from the basement of your store under the street to the basements of both houses at our expense. That way, we can move the sugar so no one will suspect what we are doing."

The meeting was swift and agreed upon in less than twenty minutes. Once again, the potential riches of prohibition reared its greedy head! The brothers had no scruples. The lure of riches about the dangers of bootlegging were of no consequence. Their culture of drinking as a social custom laughed at making it illegal; thus, prohibition was a great opportunity to make money. They were well set up to do this. They owned trucks. They had money for the start-up and were willing to work three shifts around the clock to cook the alcohol, taking only six to eight hours a day to sleep and eat.

The Ingrasci brothers recruited three men who dug the shafts at the clay mines and began the same in the basement of the store.

For the next six weeks, digging by hand fifteen to sixteen hours a day using wheelbarrows, they hauled the dirt to the basement of the store. Then with buckets at night to a truck in an alley behind the store, they completed the tunnels to the two homes.

The brothers had already installed the stills, and the first house started the process of what soon became eight hundred gallons a month. Payment was $10 a gallon! They loaded the moonshine in five-gallon cans and, once a week, hauled it to a large warehouse in Downtown St. Louis. There, sugar and water was cooked and used to color and dilute the alcohol and then bottled in quart bottles. It was sold to the speakeasies in Downtown St. Louis and shipped down the Mississippi River and sold to the towns along the river as far south as New Orleans!

The brothers were good friends with Giovanni Martino and had an agreement not to compete with his business. They were not involved with the Chicago mob, nor were they protected from the authorities, although the downtown police were on their payroll.

At this time, there was an extortion group in New York called "L'Mano nero" (the black hand). They operated mostly in little Italy and preyed on Italian and Sicilian businessman and offered protection by sending a letter simply with a black hand, along with the demand for money. The amount was based on an estimate of how much business was being done by the merchant. This had been going on since the early twenties using organized crime to harm or murder a family member of any merchant who failed to comply. Once the area was under control, they migrated to Cleveland and Detroit. They stayed away from Chicago because of Capone's ties to the Italian and Sicilian neighborhoods.

In August, they made their way to St. Louis. Jake Cunetto's barbershop received a letter, as did the Ingrasci brothers. The demand for Jake was $200 a month, for the brothers, it was $1,000 a month!

Jake called on Maria to cable Luigi Reina in Casteltermini for help. Most of the clan knew he had contacts in New York and Chicago, in addition to St. Louis. The next day, the brothers paid a visit to her with the same plea for help. John's plea was more earnest (his sister was married to Cologero Reina in Casteltermini, Luigi's and Carmelo's brother). He begged Maria for help and offered to pay for it. Since Carmelo was still in jail, the job was in Maria's hands.

Maria took Virginia to a Western Union store to send the cable to Luigi, which took three days to reach Casteltermini and another three days for the return. A phone call was made to the contact that had sent the "Mano Nero" letter on the assumption of setting up a meeting for payment. Once again, John Ingrasci was the spokesman. He told the nameless person, "We would like to meet to discuss payment along with our good friend, Jake Cunetto, at his barbershop on Sunday the twenty-first of August."

It was agreed to meet at six. At five forty-five, the brothers picked up Maria with Pete in the driver's seat packing a pistol in his pocket. John was in the front seat with a machine gun. Maria was in the back seat with Jim. He too had a pistol! They drove to Jake's barbershop, knowing full well the mobsters were already outside watching, aware it could be a setup. Jake was already there.

Pete parked across the street by Calcaterra Funeral Home. Maria exited the car and knocked on the door, and Jake greeted her, "Buona sera, signora." He gave her the traditional cheek-to-cheek hug and asked, *"Vuoi un espresso?"* Seeing a woman walk in, the two mobsters were at the door in a matter of minutes. Jake greeted them with a hand shake, showing respect. They knew the brothers were in the car across the street, but it was already dark, and they could not see inside the car. They gathered at a table in the small kitchen at the back of the shop. Both put their pistols on the table, positioned themselves facing the door.

One asked, "Why aren't the Ingrasci brothers here?"

Maria wasted no time. "This is a cable from my husband's brother in Casteltermini." It was written in Sicilian and Italian and boasted severe retaliation to the families of most of "Mano Nero" members located in the towns of Palermo, Catania, and Marsala, Sicily. It clearly stated if anything happened to Jake Cunetto's family, likewise for the families of the three brothers, the vendetta would take place.

Before they could reply, Maria was looking at them, demanding an apology in a stern voice.

She was defiant and stoic. She said she wanted to invite the brothers in so they could receive the apology. She left the table, went to the car, and had the brothers come in. The two backed down, knowing their plot had been destroyed, and with it, they realized the Hill was well protected. They apologized and asked the powers to forgive them for the threats and call off the proposed vendetta.

When they left, Jake promised Maria and the brothers that their offspring would never have to pay for a haircut. They all thanked Maria for her effort. Once again, her toughness surfaced! Jake and the Ingrasci brothers marveled at Maria, and she graciously accepted their warm thanks.

The Hill, Fairmont Heights, 1927

The population of the Hill was mainly Italians, about 65 percent from Northern Italy, Lombardy, and Tuscany, 30 percent Sicilian from Palozzo Adriano, Palermo, and Casteltermini.

The merchants were divided between the two groups, and they shopped according to their country of origin. In addition, there were the four Jewish merchants: Spielberg's Furniture and Appliances located at Daggett and Marconi; Fair Mercantile, also furniture and appliances located at Shaw and Edwards; the Rau Store, a branded apparel store on Shaw Avenue; and Rosen's Dry Goods at 5103 Shaw.

For the record, there was never an anti-Semitic incident of any kind. The real significant thing was those merchants spoke both dialects of their customers. It was an easy place for immigrants to live because they literally could communicate and shop at every store for their needs. Just about anything anyone wanted to buy was available within walking distance. A small grocery store dotted every neighborhood. So some people never learned to speak English, which included Carmelo.

There was a definite problem between the Sicilians and the Italians. The Sicilians were looked down on by the Italians, and while there were no fights, they pretty much kept to themselves. The sports clubs did compete against each other with no serious incident or fight! Italian boys stayed away from the Sicilian girls and vice versa.

St. Ambrose was the local Catholic Church and was ruled with an iron fist by the pastor, Father Lupo. He insisted on performing all baptisms, marriages, confirmations, and first communions, so he got the gratuities from the parents and grooms.

The leaders of both groups were respected. Louis Berra was the top guy for the Italians, and Jake Cunetto for the Sicilians. He was the "godfather" for the Castelterminiese. The Sicilians were more organized with the Socite d' Casteltermini, which was not for profit and raised money to help Castelterminese immigrants in dire straits of any kind. They also helped family members trying to immigrate to America and assisted them upon arrival to find a home, a job, and make acquaintances.

On March 3, Maria realized the next child was to arrive very soon. Virginia fetched Stella who arrived ready for the delivery with the usual items. It was March, and as always, Maria's earlier projection was right on. It was cold and nasty outside. Stella loaded the stove to warm the house. For the most part, Maria had an easy pregnancy with no serious complications.

Virginia took charge and got the kids ready for school, made their lunches, and they departed. Within an hour after her arrival, Stella delivered a baby boy with no problems. Maria named him Joseph, after her uncle, Joe Insalaco. Carmelo, who had been released from prison, was pleased to have another boy. He thought the baby was named after his brother, Giuseppe.

On April 16, 1927, Rosa finally delivered a healthy little boy and named him Salvatore. He and his cousin Joseph were to become as close as brothers. It was incredible. Their personalities were almost identical. They constantly nagged their respective mothers, wanting to be together.

After Salvatore was born, Maria threw a party for him and Joseph and invited the clan, and another memorable feast was had. What was special about these gatherings was these people were by no means of the imagination well-off. Money was always tight. They always had a good time. The camaraderie was warm. Food was beyond description, perhaps because it was cooked with love from scratch! Every family brought their specialty. There was one common denominator—they didn't know they were poor!

1928

The Reinas moved again. This time to 5300 Shaw and took the second-floor apartment.

This was because they found the rent for $5 a month less than the previous house. A very nice family owned the building and lived on the first floor. The man of the house took a liking to Carlo and, just about every night at six, invited him to meet up the street for an ice cream cone. Carlo would wait outside the ice cream store after dinner. One night, Carlo was late, and the man had departed just a few minutes before Carlo came out the door. As the man crossed the street, a car came speeding around the corner, and two men jumped out with machine guns and murdered him right in front of Carlo's eyes.

This was the roaring twenties. It was one of the wildest times in American history. There was such a vast difference in lifestyle from those that had little compared to the super rich. Those with the vast sums they were earning in the wild stock market were making a mad rush to cram a lifetime of entertainment into a very short period, as if they knew it was to be short-lived.

The stock market crash
October 1929

Maria heard from a friend of the family that Giuseppe Burruano was gambling and owed a considerable amount of money. She asked Carmelo to find out about it as she was worried about Rosa. Carmelo reported a few days later that it was true and said, "He is borrowing money from other people to pay the boys. He is paying heavy interest on the debt. He is drinking a lot too."

Maria told Carmelo, "Tell him I want to see him."

A couple of days later, Giuseppe came to see Maria after work and confessed he was in trouble. Carmelo tried to coax him to quit.

"Giuseppe, you need to sit with the boys and make a deal to pay so much a week. Stop gambling until you get them paid!" What they did not know was Maria had given Rosa $800 so Giuseppe could pay down the debt. Carmelo could never know about it.

Rosa gave him the money that evening and made him promise not to disclose the source and to stop gambling. But it was to no avail. He took the money, paid down the debt, but continued the lifestyle, including Saturday nights at the speakeasy.

Rosa became pregnant that year and had a little boy and named him after her father, Ignazio. But he died when he was only a year old. This poor woman had a dark cloud over her head. The bad luck continued for shortly after the baby passed; Giuseppe lost his job with the city! He turned to the boys and started making moonshine and continued working at the speakeasy on weekends.

That same year, Carmelo lost his job working for the City of St. Louis. He had been doing odd jobs working for various general contractors, and later, he failed to get any kind of work thereafter. It seemed like a never-ending trauma. The financial stress and Carmelo's lack of steady work wiped out the family's savings. They were broke.

Maria Goes to Work
1930

On a hot miserable day in June, Maria walked sixteen blocks to the Lungstress Laundry and Dry Cleaners and applied for work. She was hired for $8, six days a week, nine hours a day! She was shown around the sweatshop and could not believe how hot it was.

Virginia graduated from Shaw School and applied for high school. She was to start in September. Someone told Carmelo it was coed, and that night at the dinner table, he said, "I do not want you to go to school with boys!"

Virginia and Maria went at him. "Pa, you don't understand. I will be in class all day with a teacher there. Please don't do this to me!"

Maria was next; she did not mince any words. "Let her go to school. Someday she will need an education to get a job. What better example than yourself. You can't keep a job! You are limited at what you can do because you have no education!"

He looked at the two of them and said with a firm voice, "No high school."

Virginia was devastated. She told her eighth-grade teacher, who asked her if it was okay to go see her parents. She did and explained to Maria, "Someday your daughter will be looking for a job. She will be competing against girls with a high school education! Please let me come back when your husband is home to discuss this."

Maria said, "He does not speak English. He would not hear of it!"

Virginia started babysitting for neighbors for $0.10 an hour and gave everything she earned to Maria.

A nice house became available at 5132 Wilson and was $12 a month, and they moved again. As always, there was a story. The kids had been on Maria's case to rent a place that had an indoor toilet and a bathtub. And this was what she was looking for—it had both. Still no job for Carmelo.

The depression and serious unemployment had begun. Joblessness reached 8.67 percent.

Banks were failing all over the United States. Fear gripped the country. Well-educated men found themselves out of work. In some cases, they lost everything in the market and lost all their money when the banks failed. By 1931, unemployment rose close to 16 percent, and soon free-soup kitchens and breadlines opened. Men with PhDs were seen selling apples and pencils on the street.

People were actually leaving the country. Some immigrants living in America for years were returning to their country of origin. The effect on the poor was worse, especially the Reinas and most of the clan.

1932

Maria moved into the clothing repair department at Lungstress and got a $2.00 a week raise. She was now earning $10 a week. That same year, in July, upon her sixteenth birthday, Virginia joined the company and started on the nightshift from midnight to 9:00 a.m.

for $8 a week. It was hot that summer, so much so Virginia could not sleep during the day. She took over the household chores, making the bread and pasta, doing the laundry, ironing all the clothes for the family during the day, and caring for Little Joseph.

Carlo graduated from Shaw School and, in September, enrolled at McKinley High School, the first Reina to attend a high school. Maria would give him $0.20 a day for bus fare, but he hitchhiked, even in the rain, and some weeks, he would hand her back $1.

He also got a job delivering newspapers in the mornings and weekends. He made a penny a paper and gave it to Maria every week. The depression marked him for the rest of his life! The Reina children did not have a very happy childhood.

The family was now living at 5339 Daggett, luckily closer to everything, a shorter walk for Maria and Virginia to work, only a half block to the bus stop for Carlo. It was only a block and a half to the public library; all the kids had joined. Ignazio was the most prolific reader in the group. He was so bright that the teachers promoted him to skip two grades in the first four!

On April 4, Giuseppe Burruano was found shot in an alley in the middle of the block of 1800 Hereford, a bullet to the head! The police deemed it a suicide even though there were no fingerprints on the pistol.

That day, Maria took the children to Rosa's house. The police needed someone to identify the body. Rosa asked Carlo, "Will you go to the morgue tomorrow and do that for me?" Carlo obliged, and the next day, he took the bus and made the identification! Another trauma for this nice lady!

There was suspicion by both sides of the family, that Giuseppe was killed by the "boys" for money he owed, but it was never proven. Why were there no fingerprints on the gun? It was believed that the police were on the take to avoid a serious investigation.

Rosa had no money to bury her husband, and Maria appealed to Jake Cunetto to seek help from the Societe d' Casteltermini. The society paid for the funeral and the cemetery plot. Rosa produced an insurance policy she could not read and brought it to Maria, who turned it over to Josie. She read it from cover to cover and learned it was valued at $1,500.

Josie told Rosa, "Zia, I feel the death qualifies for 'double indemnity' if it is deemed an accident or suicide." She said, "We need to contact the company. I will meet and act on your behalf when an adjuster arrives." Josie was only twelve years old! Two months later, Rosa received $3,000!

Rosa was pregnant when Giuseppe died, and on October 29 that year, she gave birth to Giuseppina Burruano (another Josie). She and her brother, Salvatore, were drawn together way beyond the normal brother-sister relationship.

So ended a wild five years with enough tragedies to mark the families for the rest of their lives.

Josie Reina grade school graduation, 1934

Rosa, baby Salvatore (Sam), and Joe Burruano, 1927

CHAPTER 11

1933, 1934, 1935
First Store

1933, Maria at Lungstress

J ack Lungstress called Maria into his office almost the minute she walked in the door. She thought she had done something wrong. He got up from his chair to greet her.

"Good morning, Maria, we are very pleased with your work and Virginia's. You have trained her well. We are promoting you to the head of the seamstress department, and I am raising your pay to $14 a week. We will make the announcement to the other nine men and woman in the department at the end of the day." Next, he said, "We are also promoting Virginia too. We are making her a 'spotter,' and she is getting a raise to $10 a week!"

"Thank you very much, Mr. Lungstress."

It took very little time for Maria to gain the respect of the other nine people in the department, for they knew her work ethic. She demanded and got them to follow her energy in every aspect of the job.

Maria was overwhelmed; that increase would really help. Joseph had started school and needed shoes. While there were always hand-me-downs, sometimes things didn't fit. Carmelo still could not find work. He had all but given up trying to find a job. He was spending every day in the dump, checking his rabbit traps, occasionally selling the rabbits for $0.50, but never giving Maria the money.

Shortly after Maria took charge of the seamstress department, she learned the male tailors were earning $18 to $20 a week. She went to see Jack Lungstress and asked why the difference regarding her pay. He replied, "Maria, those are tailors from Italy who worked at Curlee Clothing Company and were suit makers before the depression started, and I hired them away and had to pay them higher wages to get them to come work here."

Maria was right back at him with that sweet innocent smile. "Mr. Lungstress, this is your company. You can pay what you want to your employees. I just could not understand the difference. I have watched them. They are good tailors, but I am fixing more garments for less pay. I am sorry I bothered you."

She got up to leave, and Jack stopped her. "Hold on, Maria, I want you to be happy. How about if I give you an additional $4 a week, will that make you happy?"

"That would make me very happy. Thank you very much, Mr. Lungstress!"

The depression had taken its toll. Unemployment had reached 20 percent, and President Roosevelt had already started putting it on the front burner. He put a team of economists together to come up with a plan to pull the country out of it. Most people thought it was going to be over in a short period of time. Little did they know, it was to last the rest of the decade.

It was July, and Virginia's birthday was a few days away. Maria went to Martino's after she left work and bought a nice assortment of fruits, vegetables, and ground beef to make meatballs. At six, they gathered at the dinner table, and the family could not believe the spread. She finally announced the promotion but did not disclose Virginia's raise so the Scoundrel wouldn't come after her for gambling money. On Sunday, after lunch, she handed the kids $0.75 and said, "Go to The Family Movie Theatre. There's a nickel for each of you to share candy or popcorn."

1934

In April, Josie's teacher asked her to stay after school for a few minutes. Josie stepped up to her desk and asked, "Did I do something wrong?"

Miss Medes smiled and said, "Of course not, Josie. If the other thirty-six children were as easy to teach as you, I could leave at noon. There would be no reason for me to be here. The reason I asked you to stay is you need to start thinking about high school and make out an application." This was the same teacher who appealed to Maria on behalf of Virginia two years earlier to allow her to go to high school!

Josie said, "I don't think my father will allow it."

Miss Medes said, "Here's the plan, you are not going to make a big issue out of graduation. Do not wear your school ribbons around the house, do not discuss it in front of him! Take this application home, fill it out, bring it back to me, and I will file it for you. Mullanphy High is about the same distance from your house as this school, so you leave each morning at the same time. He will never know you are attending it."

Josie thanked her and walked home. She had not even considered continuing her education.

On Sunday morning, after Carmelo went to check on his traps, Josie approached Maria and Virginia who were having coffee and developed the plan with them.

Maria said, "Let's do it."

Josie said, "What do we do if he finds out?"

Virginia said, "So what if he finds out? What's he going to do about it? We need to stand up to him. It is that time!"

Maria agreed. "I will handle him. Virginia is right; we are no longer going to take any of his *cacca*!"

Josie graduated the head of her class, and there was not a word mentioned about the graduation and no celebration at the house. In September, she started high school but unfortunately only stayed for one semester.

Virginia was coming home from Lungstress and working in a store until midafternoon and was worn out. Maria needed Josie to leave high school to take over the household responsibilities and give Virginia a break. She approached Josie and said, "I am very sorry to ask you a big favor. Can you please quit school and take over the house, make the bread and the pasta, clean the house once a week, and do the laundry?"

Josie agreed, then went into the bedroom, and cried. Maria heard her crying and felt badly about the situation, but she had no choice. She was working nine hours a day, six days a week.

Unemployment reached close to 22 percent, and the country was experiencing the worst economic period in history. Franklin Roosevelt was trying everything to pull the country out of the depression. He instituted bank reforms, which gave the American people confidence in the banks. Social Security retirement was enacted, and relief programs provided people out of work with script to take to grocery stores for food, it had restrictions on what they could purchase with it. Massive work projects were started by the federal government because new construction had high unemployment. The CCC (Civilian Conservation Corps), was introduced to put young males, eighteen to twenty-five, to work. They were put to work in the national parks, planting trees, and creating paths in underdeveloped federal- and state-owned forests. Roosevelt knew the federal government was going to be the driving force to get the country out of the depression, and those moves were helping restore confidence in the country.

Maria's raise and promotion gave her hope for things to come. This was really easing some of the financial strain, coupled with the $2.00 a week extra from Virginia. The depression had not hurt the laundry company's business. Although many smaller laundries and dry cleaners had closed, her company was running three shifts around the clock, six days a week. Virginia was still working the midnight shift there. The pay increase made it all a little easier.

The winter again was brutal. Both Maria and Virginia walked to work from the Hill, sixteen blocks and partway through a weed infested field. When it rained, it was like a swamp. That winter, it snowed every other day, and when it subsided, bitter subzero freezing took its place. There was the Russell bus, but it was $0.10 each way, and a transfer was needed to reach the laundry, which meant standing and waiting for the transfer bus on Vandeventer. They both refused to spend the $1.20 a week for bus fare, so they walked!

Late that fall, Maria learned the owner of the small grocery store down the street at the corner of Daggett and Hereford had died. Her friend, Giuseppina Lorino, told her, "The store is too much work for Josie Dominina, the widow. She has three little kids, and she is trying to sell the store." Giuseppina confided in Maria that the business was not good, and the store's inventory had depleted since the husband passed away.

Maria's instinct was working overtime everyday on her walks to and from the laundry. All she could think about was Giovanni Martino's store and the times she shopped there. Her never-ending dream of owning her own store!

Maybe this was an opportunity. Perhaps she could work something out with Josie Dominina to buy the store. Maria was smart enough to know it might just be a dream, for she had no money. How could you buy a business with no money? But her instincts kicked in, and she'd decided, all the lady could say was no. Maria very rarely shopped there. Out of respect, she always shopped at Martino's, but on Saturday, November 17, she decided to pay Josie a visit at the store.

Josie was somewhat shocked to see her and greeted her respectfully. While she didn't know Maria well, she knew her by reputation. Everybody knew Maria Reina and had tremendous respect for her, among the men and women of the Hill.

Josie greeted her showing that respect by calling her Mrs. Reina, even though Josie was older. "Mrs. Reina what brings this surprise? Are you okay?"

Maria was not about to show any emotion or play any games. There was no one in the store, so she got to the point. "*Buona sera*, Josie, I am fine. I understand you are trying to sell the store?" Before Josie could open her mouth, Maria came right at her. "I would like to buy it!"

Josie was stunned by Maria's aggressive approach, and before she could think, she replied, "Yes, do you have any money?" She too took an aggressive stance!

Now it was Maria's turn who didn't have time to think, and she replied, "I have $25."

Josie laughed, and after a moment of silence, Maria laughed. This broke the serious cloud that hung over the discussion; reality had taken over. Two women in dire straits in the middle of the worst depression in the history of the United States trying to put a deal together with no money! The truth of the matter, it was comical.

Josie had tried to sell the store to several of her customers, and no one had made an offer. Small stores were being boarded up every day. Major stores of every type were constantly running sales on the finest brands in America, and this was killing the small merchants who could not compete. This forced the federal government to pass laws to protect the brands and the small merchants. It allowed the brands to go to the major stores and demand they sell their products at the price labeled on them by the manufacturer, the Fair Trade Acts.

Now if the store put leaders out at cost or below cost to draw people, the manufacturer could go in and close the account. This took a while to work. It was good for the current small merchant, but it was too late for the damage that had been done. Four years of the depression had hurt small business in general, which had always been the backbone in creating new jobs in the country. The depression put a stop on new businesses starting up.

Josie had stopped stocking the store, so the selection of basic merchandise had dwindled to the point where some of her customers were shopping elsewhere. The last thing she wanted was to continue building the inventory, which meant she would have to get more money for the store. Winter was coming, and business always slowed, and she was dreading it. She began exploring in her mind on how to structure a deal with Maria.

But Maria was way ahead of her. "So, Josie, I have a proposal for you. How much do you want for the store?" Once again, Maria's technique was to have her speak first, then she would negotiate.

Josie quickly replied, "I want $1,500 for everything"—pointing to a six-foot refrigerator—"that cost us $1,000."

The price was music to Maria's ears. She replied immediately, "Okay, how about $25 a month. That's $300 a year for five years." In other words, no money down! This was an economic lesson Maria's children used later in business.

Josie did not hesitate for a minute. "Okay, but I want $25 a month for the store rent, including the rooms in the back."

Maria had not seen the rooms in the rear of the store and asked to see them. Josie escorted her to them, walking through the store. Maria was overwhelmed.

There was a small kitchen, two small bedrooms, a small room in the rear which was being used as somewhat of a stockroom, and an indoor toilet, no bathtub. The kitchen had a stove for cooking, an icebox, a sink, and a nice table for dining. There was a small seating area behind the kitchen and room for a sofa.

Maria's mind was racing. She was paying $15 a month rent for the family's current housing, and it had the usual *bacasu*! This meant the rent for the store was only $10 a month. After seeing the rear area, Josie took her back up front and lifted a trapdoor near the refrigerator and showed her the basement. They went down the steps, and Maria was shocked to find an electric washing machine and sheepishly asked, "Are you going to leave the washing machine?"

Josie said, "Will that make the deal?"

Maria was so excited she reached out and gave her a hug and said, "Yes, I will take it!"

Maria walked home and could barely contain herself. But it did not take long for the excitement to drop to reality. Carmelo was due home any minute, and she had to get supper together. She decided to hold back until the family had finished dinner to drop this bomb. She wanted him to drink a couple glasses of wine before breaking the news. Nonetheless, her stomach was in knots all through the preparation and also during dinner. For some reason, there was little or no discussion. Everyone ate quietly like the calm before the storm.

Soon Josie and Virginia carried the dishes to the sink and started washing them. Maria stopped them and asked them to come and sit. The kids knew something serious was about to be dropped. Maria had that look on her face. Carmelo smelled it too! Maria had rehearsed it in her mind and had her pitch ready for the Scoundrel's onslaught.

"Today I met with Josie Dominina and reached an agreement to buy her store effective January 1!"

For a minute, what seemed like an eternity, she waited for the volcano to erupt and the screaming to start.

Carmelo rose from his chair in such a violent movement that the chair thundered to the floor, and the kids prepared themselves for the outburst. He screamed at her, "*Ma sei pazzo?* Are you crazy? We are just starting to get ahead. Do you understand we are in this depression with no end in sight? You are not buying that store. Do you understand? It is not going to happen. Get it out of your head!"

She let him rave for a few minutes until he sat down, believing he had made his point in as much as Maria had not argued. Virginia looked at him; she had reached a point where she was no longer afraid of him, nor did she respect him. She knew her mother had tolerated him all those years and knew he was finished running the family. Mama had taken charge and was making the decisions.

"Pa, let her buy the store. I am working now, and I am giving her my check every week!"

Carmelo once again jumped out of his chair and yelled at her, "You shut up!" He reached down at the table, picked up a knife, and threw it at her. Fortunately, Carlo saw it coming and stuck his hand out and deflected it so it never reached Virginia!

Maria took over and got in his face. Carlo was sixteen and right next to her ready in case he attempted to strike her.

She yelled, "*Dishonorato!* [Sicilian word for dishonored one] You have not worked for four years. You have never had steady work since you brought me to this country! You get it in your head. I make the decisions for this family from now on. You don't tell any of us what to do anymore. I am buying the store, and you can move with us or go find another place to live! Try and see how you make out with no job and no money. Think about that!"

There was dead silence. The children sat stunned with their heads down. Carmelo was lost for words. He realized this was the end of his dictating to his wife and family. Maria was right; there was nowhere for him to go. Little did he know, there was more change in his relationship coming, more dramatic than the preceding twenty minutes!

Maria agreed to meet with Josie Dominina on Friday the twenty-first of December 1934 to sign the purchase agreement. She brought Virginia to read the contract before signing it. It was a one-page document. Josie had gone to the Riggio Bank and had them prepare it. After Virginia read it and verified that it was for five years and was exactly as the two women had agreed, Maria signed both copies! Less than twenty years after her arrival in the United States with the clothes on her back, she became the proud owner of her first official business! And she did it with *no money down*!

She handed Josie fifty dollars for the first payment on the $1,500 selling price and the first month's rent. Josie handed her a set of keys for the building, along with a folder with paperwork for the business, including a vendor list.

Maria asked Josie, "Will you please show me and Virginia how the telephone works?" It was a four-party line, meaning three other families had use of the line, very common in those days. Since there was no dial, you lifted the receiver, told an operator the number you wanted, and the operator made the call.

Virginia and Maria walked down the street to the house like two proud peacocks.

Maria was elated beyond anything that had ever happened to her, second only to the birth of Virginia. All she could think of was only in America can a Sicilian woman with a second-grade education, who could barely speak English and no money, buy a business in the middle of a depression. *Nice country, America!*

1935, The First Store
1928, Hereford

Maria called on Pepe Rumbolo to move the family's limited amount of furniture and personal belongings on December 31. He finished on New Year's Day. It truly was a new year for the Reinas. Maria insisted that Carmelo move into the small room in the back of the living quarters, barely enough room for a single bed, and he

145

sheepishly agreed to do so. The girls would share a room, as was the case for the two older boys. Maria took the couch and slept on it with little Joseph.

The second of January was a cold blustery day. Maria had Virginia watch the store when she returned from work at the laundry, and she walked down the street to Jake Cunetto's barbershop. As always, he greeted her with the utmost respect, and she asked him to please get the word to the Societe d'Casteltermini that another Casteltermiese now owned a business, not to mention a woman! She needed help getting people to the store. She then walked up the block to the Riggio Bank and met with Mr. Riggio and asked to borrow money on the inventory. He agreed to loan her $800, and she opened a checking account. She knew she had to spend a considerable amount of that cash to improve the inventory, and in addition, she needed to establish credit with the list of the vendors.

Maria had been thinking about how she was going to improve the business. The depression did not scare her. What better model was there than the laundry? Her boss never let it bother him. It was operating six days a week, three shifts. Her attitude was why be concerned about the 22 percent unemployed when 78 percent of the people were working, and they had to eat. Giovanni Martino was not worried about the depression! He and his group were still controlling anything going on that was borderline illegal. But his store did well because he had great inventory and product selection.

Virginia was a major help in the store. Maria had her calling all the vendors to notify them she had taken over the store and giving them the Riggio Bank as a reference to establish credit. Virginia marveled at Maria's ability to adapt to owning a business. Little did she know of the journey the ensuing years would bring.

There was a small room about twelve feet by twelve feet adjacent to the store that housed a leased ice cream freezer. It was winter, and no one was buying ice cream, but the kids were eating the ice cream. Late February, Maria had Virginia call the freezer company to remove the freezer.

A few days later, she walked to see Jack Lungstress, her old boss, at the laundry who really admired her. He had begged her to stay on when she told him she was leaving. She asked, "Jack, would you be willing to pick up and deliver laundry and dry cleaning to my store once or twice a week?"

At this time, there were no neighborhood dry cleaning establishments, no strip centers housing one either.

"Mrs. Reina, for you, I will do anything to help. The answer is yes. How about I give you a discount of $0.03 a garment?"

She turned the small area into her new laundry/dry cleaning and sewing room. Maria's mind was always working. She wanted the sewing business to repair torn clothing and replace zippers. On slow days at the store, she had time to make the repairs. She set up a nice table as a counter for her sewing machine.

On a bright warm day in March, she walked the five blocks to Missouri Bakery and met with the Gambero family. She convinced them to start making 6:00 a.m. deliveries of fresh hot Italian bread, pastry, and cookies on consignment every morning. She requested it be in small quantities initially until they determined what sold. She insisted they pick up what didn't sell, and she would pay for what sold.

Josie was making the family bread. Maria asked her to bake a few extra small loaves. Virginia made a nice handmade sign and placed it on the top of the scale. "Sandwiches, ham, $0.15 on homemade bread. Baloney and salami, $0.10." There was no Subway in those days.

By May, a stream of salesman had been calling on the store. Maria had restocked a good amount of basics, and the $800 at the bank was depleted. She exercised good business sense and paid the bills on arrival to establish good credit. This was remarkable inasmuch as most firms were taking sixty to ninety days to pay their bills. She brainwashed the kids. "If you owe money to someone and you promise to pay on a certain day, even if you have borrow the money from someone else, you make sure you live up to that promise."

That year, Rosa married John Ingrasci to the surprise of Maria. His wife had died the previous year.

June: The Traumas

School was out for the summer, and on June 8, Little Joseph and Ignazio were in the dump, playing with a group of friends. There was a large concrete embankment leading down to the River des Peres. It had been raining; the water was deep. Someone accidentally pushed Joseph down the hill, and he landed head first in four feet of water. He could not swim, and he drowned! One of the boys ran into a nearby building to get help, and they were able to drag Joseph from the water. An ambulance arrived, but it was too late. Ignazio had the depressing news to give to Maria and the rest of the family!

Virginia was given the responsibility of calling the Sicilian-owned Miceli Family Funeral Home.

Joseph's body was laid out for just one night. Maria sat with a devastating look on her face and didn't move for six hours. She barely spoke to friends and families who came to pay their respect. The next morning, she had trouble getting herself together to go to the cemetery, but somehow the kids were able to get her moving. She got in an automobile and made it to the burial site at the cemetery. She could not watch as they lowered her baby into the grave.

She pulled herself together two days later and went to the funeral home with Carlo to discuss the bill. She gave Pasquale Miceli the bad news that she had just purchased the store and was out of money.

He was very nice and said, "Maria, do not be concerned. How about if we come see you on Saturdays and take the $400 out in groceries over the next few months?" They shook hands on it.

One night shortly thereafter, Carlo came home late from a dance held at his club, The Gloom Chasers. He walked in the kitchen in the dark, turned the light on, and found Maria sitting in a chair. Her face was all bruised and red, and she started crying. Carlo knew what had happened and raced to the back of the house where the Scoundrel slept. He turned on the light and dragged him out of bed. He was still drunk! He pushed him into a corner in the hall, grabbed his throat, and told him, "You ever touch my mother again, I will kill you. Do you understand me? Answer me! Did you hear what I said?" He got a meek positive reply and threw him down on the floor

148

and walked away. By this time, Josie and Virginia were attending to Maria. Carmelo never touched her again. The fact remains: he had raped her!

The next trauma

One morning, in early July, Maria opened the store and found the light in the refrigerator was off and knew instantly there was a problem. When Virginia walked in from work, she asked her to call an electrician, Salvatore Modica. Virginia made the call and pleaded with him, "Sal, please get here as soon as possible. We need to get it fixed to keep the food from spoiling." He was there in ten minutes!

After checking out the refrigerator, Salvatore approached Maria. "Signora, I have bad news. The compressor is shot, and the estimate with parts and labor is $600!"

Maria was stunned. "What else is going to happen?" She said to him, "I will get back to you. Right now I do not have the money."

Later she made the trip to Riggio Bank and sat with Mr. and Mrs. Riggio who knew about Joseph's accident. They loaned her the money for eighteen months with monthly payments. Again a woman in 1935 borrowing money on her signature!

In August, Maria woke one morning sick to her stomach. She knew what it was. She said to herself, "God, what did I do to deserve to have another baby? How am I going to explain this to my children and friends?" For the next few months, she wore very loosely fitting clothing and hid her belly.

Business was really picking up. Maria's ability to personally greet people was a key. She was a natural salesperson. She was using her recipes as examples to sell younger people who started shopping at the store. These were suggestions for inexpensive Sicilian dishes, using vegetables with various kinds of pasta shapes as opposed to the old standard with tomato sauce. The store was keeping her mind off the disasters that happened and helping her to keep her sanity. There were no drugs to ease any depression. Because she was so strong and had been through so much stress, she just dealt with it.

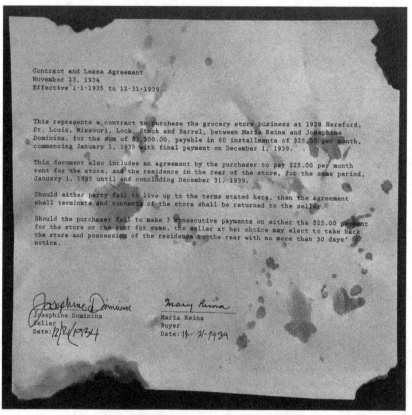

Contract and Lease Agreement
November 23, 1934
Effective 1-1-1935 to 12-31-1939.

This represents a contract to purchase the grocery store business at 1928 Hereford,
St. Louis, Missouri, Lock, Stock and Barrel, between Maria Reina and Josephine
Dominina, for the sum of $1,500.00, payable in 60 installments of $25.00 per month,
commencing January 1, 1935 with final payment on December 1, 1939.

This document also includes an agreement by the purchaser to pay $25.00 per month
rent for the store, and the residence in the rear of the store, for the same period,
January 1, 1935 until and concluding December 31, 1939.

Should either party fail to live up to the terms stated here, then the agreement
shall terminate and contents of the store shall be returned to the seller.

Should the purchaser fail to make 3 consecutive payments on either the $25.00 payment
for the store or the rent for same, the seller at her choice may elect to take back
the store and possession of the residence to the rear with no more than 30 days'
notice.

Josephine Dominina
Seller
Date: 12/2/1934

Mary Reina
Maria Reina
Buyer
Date: 11-21-1934

The first store purchase contract, 1934

GROUP PHOTOS

Left to right Jim and Leona Castellano, Joe & Josie Mocca,
Rose Castellano Rumbolo, Caroline Castellano behind Josie,
Virginia, and Carmella Castellano Cunetto at the Ozarks, 1983

Jake Cunetto the leader of the Castelterminiese, 1944

Jake Cunetto, 1916

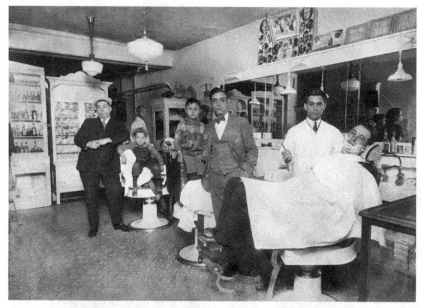

Jake Cunetto shaving the man in the chair, that's
Giuseppe Castellano in the Rear next to the little boy in
the barber chair, believed to be his son Jimmy, 1930

Societe d Castetermini, 1932

Virginia and Josie, 1984

Virginia Reina Maniscalco, 1983

Left to right: Joe Reina, Josie Mocca, Laurie
Reina, Taormina, Sicily, 1992

Left to right: Joe & Josie Mocca, Rose & Sam
Rumbolo, in Casteltermini, Sicily, 1984

Rosa and Maria, "Sharing the Meat Ball", 1976

CHAPTER 12

1936
Joe Reina's Arrival

Maria continues to build the business

On a cold January day, Maria asked Virginia to watch the store and told her, "I am going to the Dirimondi Pasta Factory. I will be back in an hour."

She walked the three and a half blocks in a windy snowstorm, driven to find a solution to what had become a problem with her pasta business.

When she arrived, the newly hired receptionist asked in perfect Sicilian dialect, "How can I help you?"

"I want to see Mr. Dirimondi," she replied in her broken English.

The young lady responded again in Sicilian, "Can I tell him your name?"

Maria replied in English, "He knows me. Tell him Mrs. Reina is here."

The receptionist walked up the eight steps to the owner's office and told her boss of his visitor. He jumped out of his chair and followed her down the steps. She had never seen him show that kind of respect for a visitor. He was a short man in his fifties, about five feet, six inches, balding with the usual comb over. He had the protruding belly from a steady diet of eating his pasta every day for lunch and dinner!

"*Buongiorno, Signora Reina, come stai, tutto bene?*"

"Benissimo, Carlo, ma can we speak English please? I am trying to learn."

"Sure, come up to my office," and when they arrived, he asked, "Can I get you a coffee?"

She said, "Si, un espresso."

He laughed and, in perfect English, responded, "I will be back in a minute." He returned with the coffee. "Allora, what can I do for you?"

She said, "I carry twelve different shapes of pasta from you, and on many occasions, my customers only want to buy a half of a pound, so I break the box. The next thing you know, I have a lot of broken boxes. Once the air hits the box, the pasta dries, and sometimes little bugs get in, and I have to throw it away. The good news is the word of mouth on the Hill has brought new customers to my store because the other stores refuse to break the box."

In those days, preservatives were not being used, so the shelf life of almost all freshly packaged food products had the same problem of spoiling. Maria continued, "I have an idea. Maybe you can help me with bringing more new customers to my store. There are times when a lady comes to the store with $0.20 in her purse and is embarrassed to tell me. She asks for a half pound of linguine, a half pound of ditali, a can of peas, an onion, a hunk of garlic, and a can of tomato paste. She knows to the penny the price of all of it.

"I know she is going to cook pasta with *sugo* one night and pasta with peas the next night. There's no secret here because I do the same thing for my family using the same recipes."

Mr. Dirimondi said, "I have an idea. We package the pastas according to orders, and we always have leftovers. We have been selling the loose pasta to the restaurants at a reduced price, but many of our restaurant customers have closed over the years because of this damn depression! Why don't you start buying the overruns from us? I will sell it to you cheap."

Maria asked, "*Ma che e l' prezzo* [what's the price]?"

He replied, "How about $0.02 a pound?"

She said, "Okay, can I buy it at first in five-pound boxes?"

He said, "Sure Mrs. Reina, for you, anything."

Then she asked, "Now one more thing, you have to promise me you will not give the deal to any of the other stores on the Hill."

He was Sicilian; most the other merchants with grocery stores were Italians. She got her wish.

The next day was Saturday, and her friend, Mrs. Caputa, came to buy groceries for the coming week. Her husband, Tony, was a carpenter. They had immigrated from Palazzo Adriano, Sicily, and were good customers. Maria asked her to have her husband come by. She knew he was always looking for construction work, and she had a job for him. He showed up later that day. She showed him the back side of the counter, where there were large deep empty drawers. She planned to store the twelve shapes of pasta in them.

"Now, Tony, come back to the front. Can you cut holes in the front of the drawers and put small windows in so people can see the pasta shapes?"

He said, "Maria, I can do it, but it will be a mess. Can I come tomorrow to do the job since the store would be closed?" She agreed.

He was there bright and early Sunday morning and did everything and said he would be back to install the glass on Monday afternoon to complete the job.

Maria asked, "L'prezzo, how much do I owe you?"

While he needed the money, he knew she was short of cash. He said, "Just pay me for the glass, $2.50."

Maria said, "No, next week, when your wife comes for the groceries, I will take care to pay for this. You worked all day yesterday, and I appreciate your time."

Thus, once again, Maria's bartering skills surfaced twice in three days, first cutting the deal with Mr. Dirimondi and next dealing with Mr. Caputa.

February: the arrival of Baby Joe

Maria had been hiding her pregnancy from the rest of the kids by wearing loose-fitting clothes. Only Virginia knew!

On February 7, Virginia called Mrs. Wilcox to tell her that the baby was coming that day. When the kids came home from school, Maria gave each of them $0.15 and told them to go to the Columbia Show at seven. She told them to bring a change of clothes in order to spend the night at the Castellano's. Virginia had arranged that with Lilly.

Maria informed Stella Mancuso to prepare for the delivery and to come at six thirty. She went into labor shortly before dinner, and the kids thought she was just having cramps. They had yet to get over the whole idea of going to the movies on a weekday. Right after dinner, Virginia took charge and said, "Let's go!" Stella had walked in and pretended to look after Maria. Virginia told the Scoundrel to leave the house and not to return until late that night.

On the way to the movie theatre, Virginia broke the news to the children. At age forty-three, their mother was having another baby. They were astounded!

Josie asked. "How? She never showed. What is this an immaculate conception?"

Carlo reminded them of that traumatic night he came in and found their mother all banged up in the kitchen! This marked the kids for the rest of their lives.

Dr. Wilcox arrived shortly after Stella and took charge, and the baby arrived a little after nine. The infant was cold and not responding to the doctor's attempt to get him to cry. Dr. Wilcox told Stella to light the oven and get it warm. He wrapped the baby in a light blanket and put him in the warm oven for a little over twenty minutes. Then took him out and slapped him on the butt. The infant started crying.

Maria and Stella sat in a complete state of awe. They wondered what would have happened had this incredible doctor not been there. Surely the baby would have died. Dr. Wilcox would never forget that day, and that baby was handled with very special care by the doctor the rest of his life!

Once he left, Stella moved Maria into the girl's bedroom with the baby and asked about a name. Maria said, "I am naming him after Joseph who drowned last summer." Both ended up in tears!

On February 21, Maria knocked on Giusippina Castellano's door and was greeted by her closest friend with the usual cheek-to-cheek hug. "Come in, Maria, how are you? How is the baby?"

Maria said, "He is fine, and he is the reason why I am here. Are your children here?"

"Yes, they are downstairs, listening to the radio. Let me get them." Soon they came up and greeted Maria, showed their respect by greeting her as Aunt Maria with the same hug their mother had given her. Maria asked the oldest, Lilly, and Jimmy to be godparents to Baby Joe, and Lilly said, "Aunt Maria, we will be honored. Thank you for asking us."

Later as Baby Joe grew, Jimmy was his godfather in the truest sense of the word. He would walk to the Reinas on occasion and take him for ice cream and treated him like a son. There always was tremendous respect between them. Joe idolized Jimmy!

The graduations
1936

Two graduations took place in June, 1936. Ignazio graduated from Shaw School, first in his class. He applied to Southwest High, a new school on Kingshighway, where cousin Vince Cunetto was attending. He and Vince were good friends.

At dinner that night, he made an announcement, "I no longer want to be called Ignazio. I hate that name! I filled out an application for Southwest using the name Jim, after the man who drove me and Mama to the hospital in Herrin when I was operated on for my hernia!"

Carlo graduated from McKinley High the same day. While he was very bright, he didn't study very much yet made decent grades. He was more social and more popular and had more friends than the other children, especially with the girls. Carlo was movie-star handsome. Many said he was the best-looking guy on the Hill! The girls nicknamed him "Ginger," and it stuck throughout his life. His friends at his sports club, The Gloom Chasers, said he could marry any girl he wanted on the Hill!

The fact of the matter was he was very modest and had no display of ego regarding his looks. His personality was heartwarming. Everybody loved Carlo.

The day after he graduated, Carlo went to the Carondelet foundry and applied for a job. It was a delightful sunny morning, and Carlo had his best suit, Arrow shirt, and tie on! A very nice young man by the name Charles Dechecci escorted him in for the interview and introduced him to Burt Nolan.

He was greeted, shook hands, and took charge. "Mr. Nolan, I need a job. My family is in debt. My father has not worked since the depression started, and there are seven of us. My mother has a tiny grocery store on the Hill and does enough business to keep the doors open. "I promise you I will be the hardest working person in your foundry!"

The manager was so astounded at Carlo's aggressive approach. He just sat there, smiled, and said, "Carlo, in all the years in this job, I have never had anyone take over my job and conduct the interview. You have the job. The pay is $10 a week. The hours are eight to forty thirty. You get half an hour for lunch. When can you start?"

Carlo graciously accepted and told him he could start the next day, shook his hand and walked home very proud of himself. He had Maria's self-confidence and inherited her sales ability, of that there was no doubt!

Mr. Nolan called his plant manager into his office and told him, "I just hired a very tough kid. His name is Carlo Reina. He starts tomorrow. I want you to keep an eye on him. He will be one of your best workers!"

Jim (Ignazio), in search of work like his big brother, walked to the Dirimondi spaghetti factory the same day and asked to see the owner. Once again, the receptionist who had greeted Maria asked, "May I help you?"

He said, "My name is Jim Reina. My mother is Maria Reina. We buy our pasta from you for her store."

She reacted as soon as she heard the last name and summoned the boss and escorted him to the office. As soon as he walked into Mr. Dirimondi's office, he stuck his hand out and said, "Mr. Dirimondi, my name is Jim Reina. I believe you know my mother."

"I know and respect your mother very well. She is an incredible woman." After politely greeting him, he asked, "Why the visit?"

Jim said, "Mr. Dirimondi, I know my mother owes you a lot of money, and business is not great at the store. I want to help her. Do you have a job for me?"

Mr Dirimondi asked, "How old are you?"

"I am thirteen, but I am not afraid to work, just give me a try. If you are not happy with the way I work, you can fire me after the first week. Just give me a chance to show what I can do, and you don't have to pay me. Just take it off my mother's bill. I need a job this summer. There are seven of us, and my mother's trying to pay off the store. Please, Mr. Dirimondi"

"You are quite a salesman. I wish you were eighteen. I would hire you to go out and sell my pasta. I'll tell you what, I will give you a job in the loose pasta area, packing the very pasta your mother is buying. I can only pay you $0.20 an hour, and you will have to work nine hours a day, six days a week, but only for the summer. I want you to go to school in the fall. If you want, you can work after school and on Saturdays. How does that sound? You are a natural salesman, Jim!"

"Can I start tomorrow?"

"Yes, we start at 8:00 a.m. Come with me. I will show you around the factory and introduce you to everybody. We eat here every day. We cook pasta, so you do not have to bring a lunch!"

Jim thought to himself, *I understand where that panzia (belly) comes from.*

Jim was so excited he could not wait to get home and tell the family. He told Maria but asked her, "Ma, do not say anything. Let me tell everybody at dinner tonight." That night, he proudly announced his new position at the factory, and he was most proud that he had scooped his older brother when he announced he was making $10.80 a week as opposed to Carlo's $10! Everybody was giving their check to Maria. She thought, *Maybe this depression is finally leaving us.*

Maria said, "You have all been after me to buy a radio. Here is the deal: I went to Spielberg's, and they have a nice radio. It is $60, and I can buy it with $8 down and make payments for a year! I want your help to pay for it. So no going to the movies for the year. I have been giving you $1 a week and in fifty-two weeks that pays for the radio. Is it a deal?"

The kids agreed, and the next day, she brought home a beautiful Zenith wood-framed radio. Maria had the money for the radio, but she wanted them to understand there were no handouts in life. She wanted them to realize they have to pay for their material things!

1937

Maria asked Virginia to call the Heil Packing Company and have them send a salesman to the store. The very next day, a man showed up and was greeted by Maria. She asked, "May I help you?"

He said, "I would like to see the owner of the store."

She was somewhat offended. She said to herself, "I wonder if men will ever be able to accept women as business owners. Just because we do not have 'coglione' does not mean we can't run a business." She said, "I am the owner. Does that shock you?"

He knew already by the tone of her voice to start dancing. "I am very sorry. I apologize. My name is Tom Dimitri, and I am with the Heil Packing Company. My company did not tell me I was meeting a lady."

"Are you Italian?"

He said, "No, we are Greek. Our last name is very hard to pronounce, so we shortened it. How can I be of service to you, Mrs. Reina?"

Maria asked him a lot of questions about different cuts of meat and prices.

She picked his brain as to retail prices and finally said, "Do you know where I can buy a meat block to cut meat and knives?"

He knew a man who could sell her both. "They are used, but he refurbishes them, and they are like new."

She gave him an order for a loin of pork chops, a rack of veal, and ten pounds of sirloin and asked him to deliver it the next week. He told her the man would come in a few days with the cutting block and knives. She said, "If you need credit references, just call the Riggio Bank. They know me."

The salesman left and made up his mind, never to prejudge a new customer. It was an inexpensive lesson. Within a few days, the man with the meat block and the knives showed up. He had been warned. The salesman from the packing house told him, "Don't mess with the lady. She will take one of those knives and cut your balls off with it!" He carried the block in along with the knives. Maria was impressed and asked for the price.

He said, "I need $50 for the block and $15 for the knives."

Maria looked at him and said, "I have $50. Will you take it?"

He quickly said, "Make it $55, and you have a deal."

The next venture and education began, a lady butcher in 1937. The following week, the meat was delivered. Virginia and Maria scanned books to learn about it, and Virginia made a nice sign for the prices. Maria priced everything initially with a very low markup to draw people into the store. At Maria's suggestion, Virginia changed the sign for the sandwiches and added veal cutlet sandwiches and a "free cookie" with every sandwich.

One day, Carlo was having lunch with a group of foundry workers. They were savoring his veal cutlet sandwich. The smell of it was incredible, and a few of them inquired if it were possible for him to bring some for the group.

He told them, "Fellas, these sell in our store for $0.35," and four said, "Bring them the next day!" That led to additional varieties every day. Some days, they bought as many as twenty sandwiches.

Grocery stores didn't carry "pop" at that time. On a cold miserable windy day in November, Marie walked to the Blue Ridge Bottling Company, owned by the Venegoni Family. They bottled

166

soda pop. They agreed to start selling her three different kinds of pop, another product to the mix. Between the growing business and the checks coming in from the children, Maria was building a nice savings account at Riggio Bank and also quite a reputation as a businesswoman, and with that, the respect on the Hill.

That year, Rosa gave birth to her third child. This one with John Ingrasci and named him Carmelo, who later changed it to Hugh.

Another trauma
1938

Baby Joe was walking in the store, always in the arms of customers. One day, a lady was holding him right in front of the open trapdoor. Joe reached for her glasses, she tried to stop him, and he slipped out of her arms and fell down the steps. As he slipped, he grabbed the shelf next to the door, and a bottle of catsup came crashing down with him! It broke, and a lot of it smeared his face, along with a nasty cut. He was bleeding profusely.

The lady screamed, as did Maria, who ran for him and picked him up and took him to the kitchen and started cleaning his face. Virginia put a heavy gauze bandage on him and then called an ambulance. Maria went to Barnes Hospital, where he was admitted, and a very nice doctor put six stitches just to the right of his right eye.

"Mrs. Reina, your son is very lucky. The glass from the bottle cut him, and another inch to the left, we would be removing his eye."

Maria thanked the doctor and had the nurse call a taxi for her and went back to the store. From that day on, she always kept an eye on him anytime he was in the store. For the most part, she would not allow that trapdoor to be open when he was in the store.

Josie went to Maria one day in May and sat down with her. "Ma, I have an idea. We have plenty of pasta here…I can make bread at night, twice a week. I want to go to work. We can hire a lady to clean the house and do the laundry once a week. Please let me do it."

Maria said, "If that is what you want to do, go find a job."

The next day, Josie took the bus downtown and applied for a job at Famous Barr, the nicest department store in the city. She was hired on the spot for $12 a week, plus she got a 20 percent discount on anything she wanted to buy. Needless to say, she gave her checks to Maria. She was a salesperson in the glove department.

The Reina kids inherited Maria's work ethic, her integrity, her love for the family, and more importantly, her entrepreneurial instincts!

Ignazio (Jim Reina) grade school graduation, 1936

CHAPTER 13

1939
The Eviction

There was a serious recession in 1938 in spite of Roosevelt helping the British government with war material. This put more people to work initially, but there were layoffs in the businesses not making war material. Carlo was the victim of the times. He and several coworkers were told business was not good and were laid off. Business at the foundry had declined for two years.

He tried several other factories, but no one was hiring, so he went to work in the store.

Maria told him, "I want you to take over making sandwiches, and I am going to teach you how to cut meat. In addition, I want you to learn to order merchandise, and with your personality, you handle the young ladies who shop." Carlo was more than happy to accept, and he quickly adapted. This was to ultimately be a blessing for a coming disaster.

All the moves Maria had made in the previous four years had brought the business way beyond her wildest dreams. In 1935 the store made just over $600 a week and $31,700 that year. It climbed to $87,300 in 1938! Because the overhead was very low, Maria had accumulated a tidy sum at Riggio Bank.

But it had taken its toll on her, working long hours, taking care of Baby Joe, cooking for the family, losing Joseph, being vigilant after Baby Joe's fall, and raising four other kids! Not to mention, from time to time, dealing with the Scoundrel's temper tantrums. Sometimes she even worked on Sundays, her only day off.

In March, Virginia came home one morning and dropped bad news. She too was laid off. She related, "Jack Lungstress called the entire plant to a meeting and said he was shutting down the entire nightshift. There just was not enough cleaning and laundry coming in."

Maria blamed it all on the depression. Will it ever end? Another setback, it was $20 a week less coming in. Jim continued working after school and Saturdays, and Josie was doing well at Famous. The business at the store was good, so Maria decided Virginia should start working at the store so she herself could take care of the baby.

The weather that winter was horrible. When it snowed a lot, business at the store dropped. When spring came, things picked up. Carlo was doing well in dealing with the salesmen. People on welfare would bring their script for food, and Maria was very easy on them. She basically let them buy what they wanted and ignored the rules on the restrictions. Josie worked out the details to get the money back and filled in the numbers on the form that went to the government once a month.

Maria was also very generous with giving credit to families in need. Some people had continuous bills. They would come on payday, pay it down, and then shop and run it up again.

Josie Dominina would come by the end of every month to collect the $50, and Maria was always ready for her. Josie could see how the business had grown. Most the time, she would arrive on Saturdays which was always busy. Maria's instincts had kicked in. Josie would ask questions, and at first, Maria would share the success. Soon she decided to be more evasive, figuring she had something up her sleeve. Things were fairly normal through the summer and fall. Business continued to be good, but winter would soon arrive, and Maria was scaling back on inventory.

On Saturday, November 7, Josie Dominina waited until close to six to show up for the payment. Carlo was cleaning up the meat block, and Virginia was sweeping the floor.

Maria was in the kitchen, fixing dinner. Jim and Josie had not arrived from work.

Maria came out and greeted Josie as she always did with a pleasant "*Buona serata*, Josie, I have the money for you in the drawer."

Josie said, "We have to have a talk. Can we sit down?"

Maria got the money and invited her to the kitchen and asked, "Would you like an espresso?"

Josie refused and said, "Your lease is up at the end of the year. You are going to have to move!"

Maria was dumbfounded; she could not believe what she just heard. She collected her thoughts and said, "What are you talking about? I bought the store. I have one more payment left. You can't throw me out!"

Josie replied, "You bought the business and signed a lease, and the lease is up. I brought the agreement with me, and it very clearly says it ends December 31, 1939. I want the store back, and you have to be out the thirty-first."

Maria was in a state of shock. This couldn't be happening. Josie got up to leave, and Maria lost it. She let Josie have a vile Sicilian butt chewing, so loud it brought Virginia and Carlo to the kitchen. Carlo had never seen his mother this way. He thought Maria was going to strike Josie; she was right in her face! Virginia saw it too. She grabbed Josie Dominina and escorted her out of the kitchen and out the door.

Jim and Josie arrived almost at the time Josie Dominina was leaving and found Maria, Virginia, and Carlo in the kitchen. They sat down and joined the discussion and were stunned.

Josie, always the calm one, said, "Let's settle down. We need to come up with a plan."

She said, "Ma, we have been through some horrific traumas over the years, and we will get through this. We need to find a vacant store and move. Our customers are very loyal, and they will follow us."

Maria was not focusing on any of the discussion; her mind was racing. There was a store up the street in a large building, perhaps too large. It had been vacant a long time. She thought, *Maybe something's wrong with it. Why would it be vacant for all these years?* She interrupted the conversation, "There's a store on Shaw Avenue. I am going to look at it Monday."

On Monday, she went into the store next to the vacant store, Rosen's Dry Goods. She knew the owner, Saul Rosen. He opened that store in 1918 after World War I and greeted her as always with warm respect, "Good morning, Mrs. Reina, how are you?"

"I am fine, Saul. Tell me about the store next door. Why do you think it has been vacant all these years?"

He replied, "That's a good question. It used to be a bar before prohibition, and it closed in 1920! Then the depression started, and no one was opening businesses, so I am sure that is why it remains vacant. Why do you ask?"

Maria said, "I am interested in renting it. Who is the owner?"

He said, "Anheuser Busch owns it. It is the same size as my store, and there are four rooms upstairs and a nice bathroom. Would you like to see the second floor?"

Maria said, "Yes, please."

They proceeded upstairs. Saul was very interested in her taking the store, figuring she would bring customers to the area, and it could help his business.

After seeing the second floor that Saul was using for inventory storage, Maria left with the name of the man to see at Anheuser Busch, Mr. Braun. The next day, she and Jim took the Russell bus down to Busch and asked to see Mr. Braun in the real estate department. A very nice young man walked them into a beautifully furnished office with a large picture window overlooking the Mississippi River. They were greeted warmly.

Mr. Braun introduced himself first to Maria and shook hands with Jim and asked, "What brings you here to Anheuser Busch?"

Jim started the conversation, "My mother owns a store on the Hill, and the lady who sold her the store in 1934 wants the store back and is throwing her out!"

Mr. Braun asked, "Why is she throwing you out? Have you been paying the rent on time?"

Maria would have no more of this and said, "Mr. Braun, I have never been a day late on the rent and the $25 a month payment for the store. She wants the store back because we have increased the business, and she is a miserable greedy woman! I want to rent your vacant store at the corner of Shaw and Hereford."

His attention now turned to Maria and asked, "What kind of store do you operate?"

Maria said, "I have a nice store that sells groceries and meat."

"I am sure you have a fine store, Mrs. Reina, but we sell beer, and we want a tavern in that location."

Maria replied, "There is a tavern across the street and a block down the street on Shaw and Marconi there's the Big Club Hall bar. You do not want another tavern there?"

Braun was somewhat taken back by this aggressive woman and smiled. He gathered his thoughts. He did not want to offend the lady and calmly said, "I am sorry, Mrs. Reina. I respect your situation, but again, we sell beer—"

And before he could say anything, Maria interrupted him, "I will sell your beer!"

He smiled again. "Mrs. Reina, people want cold beer. How are you going to cool it?"

In those days, there were no refrigerated stores selling cold beer. It was sold primarily in taverns. At dinnertime, the man of the house would send a male child to the corner tavern with a pail to buy cold draft beer.

Once again, Braun collected his thoughts and said, "Mrs. Reina, I like your spunk. Why don't you open a tavern there?"

She looked at Jim and said in her Sicilian dialect, "*Cos e spunk?*"

He replied in English, "Spirit, Ma!"

Braun smiled again. He had never experienced anything like this woman in all his years running the real estate department. He once again refused to rent the store, and respectfully the Reinas left.

Maria was not to be denied, and as soon as they returned, she told Carlo and Virginia the bad news. She told Carlo, "Tomorrow I want you to go find a cooler or large used refrigerator for us to cool beer."

The next day, he started making calls, and after some network-ing, he got the name of a man named Pete Elias, who told him he knew of a man who sold all kinds of refrigeration and had a large warehouse on Manchester.

"Carlo, I can meet you there tomorrow say at one?"

Carlo's friend, Charlie Dichecci (he worked with him at the foundry), drove him to the warehouse. He was amazed at the used merchandise in the place. He was greeted by the owner, Abe Epstein, who showed him a large walk-in cooler.

Carlo was right to the point. "Mr. Epstein, my mother owns a small store, and we are being evicted and moving to a larger store, and we are going to be needing a lot of refrigerated items. I am interested in this cooler. How much is it?"

Epstein took the bait regarding other items and said the cooler was $900! Carlo sat for a moment and said, "I am sorry that is too much."

He told Charlie, "Let's go," and turned to leave.

Epstein was on him, "Wait a minute, how much are you willing to pay?"

Carlo said, "I will give you $500!"

Epstein looked at Pete Elias, he was obviously getting a commission, and Pete jumped into the discussion, "Carlo, he wants $900. You are offering $500. Why don't you guys split it?"

Carlo waited to hear Abe's response. Abe came to $700! Carlo said, "I will give you $650. That's my final offer."

Abe accepted. "I need to confirm with my mother. Can I use your phone?"

Maria answered the phone and gave him permission to buy the cooler, pending a meeting with Mr. Braun at Busch. Carlo explained the situation to Epstein and gave him a $50 deposit on the cooler and proceeded to look around the warehouse. He made a note of all kinds of used store equipment that had accumulated as a result of the depression's business failures.

Maria and Carlo went to see Mr. Braun the next day and told him about the cooler.

Braun was a little suspect of the whole deal. Carlo was ready for him and showed the receipt for the deposit.

"Mr. Braun, the man who owns the warehouse is Abe Epstein. His phone number is right here on the receipt. Please feel free to call him."

Mr. Braun could see Carlo was telling the truth because he looked him right in the eye, and he thought this woman was raising a great bunch of kids.

"Okay, Mrs. Reina, we will rent you the store and the flat upstairs as of January 1, 1940 for $50 a month, is that all right?"

Marie said, "Why do I have to pay $50? Rosen pays you $45?" She said it with a smile on her face that stretched ear to ear, and Braun could not help but laugh, as did Carlo. He was beaming. This was Maria Reina, a woman in 1939, successfully negotiating with the head of real estate for the largest brewery in the United States! Braun agreed. She got the store for $45 a month!

Rosa, Salvatore, Josie, Carmelo (Hugh), 1939

First grocery store, Maria by the refrigerator, Virginia
behind the counter, and baby Joe, 1939

CHAPTER 14

1940
The New Store

5101 Shaw Avenue

The new store at 5101 Shaw Ave, on the Hill, 1940

Once again, Maria called on Pepe Rumbolo about the move to the new store. On a cold miserable day, December 23, Pepe arrived early at the old store. "*Buongiorno*, Maria, I got your message about the move. Unfortunately my truck is loaded with coal. I have asked my friend, Antony Shirrow, to come by to look at the job. He assured me he would do it for a good price."

There was not a lot to move, the shelving was bolted to the wall, and the counter was old, as was the refrigerator—it was staying. Maria took Pepe up to the new store, and he cautioned her. "This a big store, Maria. How do you intend on filling it?"

She replied, "Don't worry about that, *compare*. I will fill it, but I need help with the move."

He said, "I will round up some of the clan, and we will have a team at the old store packing and another at the new store unpacking."

Maria said, "I have asked Tony Caputa to build some shelves, and Sal Modica will be installing the cooler and two used refrigerators. Carlo bought one for meat and one for vegetables. We have to do all that in the next week before we schedule the move."

Pepe started making the moves. First to Jake Cunetto's barbershop, where he enlisted Vince, Jake's son. Then to the Castellanos, where he got a commitment from Jimmy and Joe, and of course, then to his sons, Sam and Carlo, and even his wife, Santa. These plus the Reina children were all that were needed. Maria stayed at the old store while Carlo looked over the delivery of the cooler and refrigerators. He had paid Abe Epstein an additional $900, and it took Sal Modica, the electrician, three days to install them. Meanwhile, Tony Caputa built shelves and a huge island in the center of the store with shelves for self-service. On December 29, half the team was at the old store, packing, and the other half, waiting for the first load to arrive at the new store. Josie made a huge amount of homemade buns for sandwiches, and Virginia fried veal cutlets for them. Everyone ate well when they finally took breaks over the two days. Within forty-eight hours, the Reina's personal things had been moved to the second floor, and the new store move was complete. But the store was half empty. No other store was anything like this. It was the largest store on the Hill.

The Reinas spent their first night at 5101 Shaw on New Year's Eve 1940, but it was a sleepless night for Maria. Most of the $9,000 she had in the bank was gone! Pepe Rumbolo's predictions were echoing in her mind. She knew she was going to spend the rest of her cash to fill the store. "What if her customers failed to follow?"

Virginia had canceled the phone service at the old store.

She called the phone company and ordered a single party line for the new store. It was $6 a month, but at least now calls could be made and received with no interruptions. And they had their own phone number, Mohawk 3037!

Maria opened the store to a throng of people on Tuesday, January 2, 1940. Old customers, new ones, and lots of friends: the Cunettos, some of Uncle Joe Insalaco's family, her sister Rosa with Josie and Sammy, the Rumbolos, and of course, the Castellano's! There was even a surprise, Giovanni Martino! Maria greeted him with a hug and a tear in her eye! She said to him, "You and your store have always been an inspiration to me. I am grateful for all the help you provided for me in the tough years, and I will never forget you!"

Giovanni said, "Mrs. Reina, you earned everything I ever did. You are an incredible woman. I often wondered where you got your work ethic, your drive, and your nerve. You are tougher than most men. This store is a testament to who you are. The best of luck! There is no doubt you will do well. My god, it is twice the size of my store!"

The next day, Maria and Carlo inventoried the store and made a list of what to order. They had stopped ordering over the last month at the old store so as not to have to move inventory.

Marie said, "Carlo, let's be careful on reordering. I do not have a lot of money left. I may have to go to Riggio and borrow some money." He fully understood and was extremely conservative.

One by one, over the next two weeks, the vendors came by to see the new store and were amazed at the size. Maria worked them. She used the same pitch, "I need an extra thirty days to pay for merchandise this year. I have always paid my bill early with your company. Can you arrange it?"

No one denied her request. Some even offered ninety days with a 1 percent discount if paid in sixty. Maria told Josie, "Pay those early and take the discount."

The weather was cold and bitter, but there was not a lot of snow. Spring came early, and that helped business. The word was out on the Hill, and people Maria had never met were shopping at the store. The big surprise was many were Italian. This was the topic of discussion at the dinner table one night.

Maria said, "She was learning the Italian dialects."

In late May, Virginia announced she was going to go to beauty school, the same one the Cunetto girls were attending. Maria hated losing her in the store, but Jim was about to graduate from high school, and he agreed to work in the store.

In June, Maria asked the salesman from Heil Packing, "How much does a quarter round of beef cost?"

Carlo was standing there and looked at her as if she was hallucinating. The salesman said he would have to get back to her.

A few days later, the salesman from Swift Packing company was in the store, and she asked him the same question. He gave her the same answer.

Both salesmen got back to her the following week, and she worked them on the price. She told Carlo, "Why should we pay them to cut the meat? They sell off the fat and charge us a higher price for all the cuts. Find me a meat grinder so we can grind our own meat."

Carlo had learned not to argue with her and once again went to see Abe Epstein. He bought another meat block and a used meat grinder.

The following week on a Thursday, a quarter of a cow was delivered, and Maria and Carlo cut it up. Thank God for the cooler as it easily housed the quarter round of beef! Carlo was once again amazed at his mother. When they figured the costs with these items that they butchered compared to what they had been paying for the same items, they were shocked! Once again, Maria scooped the other stores on the Hill. None of them could offer fresh meat at the new prices.

Jim graduated from Southwest High and went to work full-time in the store. He handled the customer's needs at the front, while Maria and Carlo took care of the meat department. Jim had joined the Knights Athletic Club across the street from the store on

Hereford and knew most the guys. One of his friends was Joe Mocca, a very nice, soft-spoken, well-liked member. They were both good dancers and occasionally participated in dance contests at the Casa Loma Ballroom.

One day, in early May, Joe approached Jim about Josie. "Jim, does your sister Josie have a boyfriend?"

Jim laughed. "Joe, she has never had a date!"

"Do you think your mother would allow me to take her on the club picnic Memorial Day weekend?"

Jim said, "First, let me see if my sister will consent, then I'll ask my mother, as long as I am going, she will allow it." It was agreed at both levels, and Jim had Joe over for pasta one night so he could meet the family. Carlo knew him from attending Shaw School together.

Jim and Joe and Josie and Jim's girlfriend went to the picnic, and Josie really enjoyed herself. Joe later said he knew she was the girl he was going to marry.

He and Josie started the traditional courtship with his parents. Maria had chaperoned the first few dates that summer. Joe asked for a private meeting with Maria and asked, "Signora Reina, I would like your permission to marry Josie."

Maria asked, "Have you asked her?"

Joe said, "I wanted your answer first," and he got a yes. The next evening, by plan, she had him over for dinner, and in front of the entire family, he proposed. They set a date in January.

While this romance was going on, toward the end of summer, Maria received a call from Pasquale Miceli, the funeral director who buried Joseph. He told her of a nephew from Chicago who was in town and asked permission to introduce him to Virginia.

Maria told him, "Let me speak to my daughter first, and I will get back to you."

Virginia was not interested, but out of respect to Pasquale, who buried her baby brother, she agreed to meet the nephew. His name was Martin Maniscalco.

The family was invited to the Miceli's for dinner, and Virginia and Martin hit it off immediately. He was tall and very good looking, and he asked, "Would you like to go out for dinner one night this week?"

She said, "Yes, but it would have to include your aunt and uncle and my mother."

Martin smiled and thought to himself, *The old Sicilian custom*, and he accepted the condition.

Neither Maria nor Virginia had ever gone out to eat in a restaurant. They went to a very famous St. Louis restaurant and could not believe how elaborate it was—or the prices. They both ordered the chicken specialty because it was the least expensive thing on the menu. Everybody had a nice time, and this was the beginning of a second romance for the Reinas.

Carlo had met a very nice Sicilian girl, Lena Salerno, in 1939 and was dating her steadily. They had been talking about getting married. She had been invited to the house on an a few occasions, but no serious plans were made in 1940 because of the store move.

In November, Martin was visiting from Chicago. He called on Maria and asked for her approval to marry Virginia. She asked, "Have you asked her if she will have you?"

He said, "Yes, but she told me I have to have your permission."

Maria said, "If she wants to marry you, then you may marry my daughter." Maria was somewhat reluctant because he had been married before. His wife died of a serous kidney ailment, leaving a nine-year-old, son who was being raised by Martin's parents.

At Christmas dinner, Virginia made the announcement. "Martin and I have agreed to marry next June here in St. Louis."

Business was growing at a much faster pace than they had hoped. People were calling and placing orders in advance and started requesting delivery service. No other store offered delivery service. Another added service and one more draw for the store. Maria's instincts were always at work, coming up with ideas to increase the business. One day, she ordered a leased freezer from a company called Bird's Eye, offering frozen vegetables, another scoop on the other stores on the Hill.

In October, Virginia graduated from beauty school and told Maria she wanted to open a beauty shop. Maria asked, "Do you have a location? There are too many on the Hill, plus the Cunetto girls have one, and I do not want you to compete with them"

Virginia said, "I don't want to compete with them either. A girl in my class from Clayton knows of a vacant store there, but we have no money."

Maria was expecting that. Virginia never asked for anything, always giving Maria whatever she earned. "Virginia, find out how much you need to open the shop. Go with Carlo to buy used equipment, and I will give you the money."

"But, Mama, I know you have spent a lot of money on the store—"

Maria stopped her. "If we have to, I can get the money at Riggio. I want you to have your own business!"

As it turned out, she and Carlo found a beauty salon going out of business. She got what she needed for $1,000 and rented the shop for $20 a month. In sixty days, she opened the shop in one of the wealthiest parts of Clayton and was doing business the first week. Virginia and her friend, Barbara, were partners with the understanding Maria was to be paid back before they split any profits. There was no doubt Virginia had inherited Maria's entrepreneurial instincts!

By the end of the year, the realization surfaced. Josie Dominina had done Maria a big favor. Josie Reina had been keeping records of revenue in 1938 and 1939, and on December 31, she totaled the income for the year. The new store more than doubled the sales for 1939! Maria was not satisfied; she continued to look for ways to increase the business.

She asked Carlo to come up with a plan to buy coffee to make good old-fashioned espresso. He placed a call to Pete Elias, a good friend.

Carlo said, "Pete, do you know anybody in the coffee business where I can buy the green beans?"

Pete responded, "I know a guy, but I have not talked to him for a while. I'll get back to you," which he did the next day.

"Carlo, I contacted the guy, but you would have to buy it in fifty-pound sacks."

"How much for the sack?"

Pete said, "He told me $0.06 a pound, but I know I can get him down. Is it to be an ongoing business? Carlo, you will have to roast it and then grind it. Are you ready for that?"

Carlo said, "That's one-third of what we pay now for the packaged stuff. Let me talk to my mother."

Maria was all over it. She told Carlo to see if Epstein has a used roaster and a machine to grind it and to buy fifty pounds of beans. Within the next two days, he purchased a used roaster that could roast ten pounds and a fairly new grinder.

But now the problem of roasting. The Scoundrel had been sleeping in a small room in the back of the store just behind the trap-door that led to the basement. It had its own entrance from the rear. He had not bothered Maria in any way shape or form and helped around the store on occasion.

Carlo showed him the roaster and explained, "We have to cook the coffee over a fire."

Carmelo left and came back in an hour with an empty fifty-gallon drum, cut the bottom out of it, put a slot on each side at the top to slip the edges of the roaster on it. He mounted it on a stack of bricks he had assembled in a round shape so that it would fit level. This enabled him to build a fire under it. When they tested it, in a matter of fifteen minutes, they had ten pounds of finely roasted coffee.

This was a nice profit maker for the store and later became a major profit source. With Carlo's contacts, Maria was making the store a serious business way beyond her wildest dreams. It had become the busiest grocery store on the Hill!

CHAPTER 15

1941
Two Marriages and World War II

Joe and Josie were married at St. Ambrose Church on a cold nasty day the end of January. The reception was held at the Palma Agusta club. The hall cost $15. The food for the most part came from the grocery store. While Maria did not charge for it, the bill came to $90! Josie and Virginia baked forty loaves of bread. Missouri Bakery made the wedding cake and didn't charge Maria for it. Joe's parents paid for the flowers, and Pepe Rumbolo donated the homemade wine. The store provided the beer. The store was now carrying five brands of beer, a major attraction for customers.

The year started off with very good sales. People from all over the Hill were coming to shop. Maria started another addition, "prepared foods."

She told Carlo, "I don't want to throw anything away. From now on, I am going to take things such as veal or steak that has been in the refrigerator for more than two days and fry it or bake it. I will make fried veal cutlets. From round steak, I will make Bracilole [rolled meat wrapped around hard boiled eggs with bread crumbs and grated cheese tied together, fried, and finished cooking in tomato sauce].

"See if Abe Epstein has a used sausage machine. We can use pork and any small cuts of beef along with some pork trimmings to make Italian sausage. With vegetables, I will make a pot of soup every day. It is better than throwing the stuff out."

Unemployment was no longer a problem. Factories worked overtime, making war material. Woman were doing the jobs once held by men; they didn't have time to cook. So Maria's latest brainstorm took hold.

Carlo went to see Abe and bought a hand-operated sausage machine for $20. He found a recipe for Italian sausage and made the first batch, about ten pounds all from meat that would have had to be thrown out! The sausages sold out the first day. Maria fried it for lunch that day and made sandwiches with her homemade bread and shared it with a few customers. It was a hit.

In June, Martin and Virginia were married at St. Ambrose Church and had the reception at the Palma Augusta. It was a repeat of the Mocca wedding, only a lot of guests from Chicago attended. Virginia and Martin drove to Chicago for their honeymoon.

The Reina children were listening to the news on the radio. They reported to Maria that the United States entering the war was becoming a very serious possibility. Roosevelt had been hammering the Japanese for invading China, where there were a lot of American's working in American businesses. Roosevelt warned the Japanese to get out of China!

The Japanese, like the Germans, had massive armies, strong navies, and air forces. It was widely believed Roosevelt knew the only way to get out of the depression was for the country to go to war. But he realized after World War I, the American people did not want another war.

Maria became very concerned about her boys, as well as her new son-in-laws. The threat of war was on her mind ever since the kids reported the news from Europe. Her baby brother, Ignazio, in Sicily was already in the Italian army, fighting for the Germans.

Virginia's beauty salon was doing well, and Martin had brought his nine-year-old son to live with them. He was working for the city, driving a streetcar.

Josie was still working at Famous Barr, and Joe Mocca had started working at Emerson Electric on the assembly line, making motors for a secret military project.

There was a quiet calm in the fall almost like a tornado was about to strike. Then on December 7, the Japanese bombed Pearl Harbor, and the next day, Roosevelt asked permission from congress to declare war on both Japan and Germany. They had been sending their submarines to torpedo American supply ships crossing the Atlantic.

1942

Jim, Carlo, and Joe Mocca registered for the draft in January. Martin was exempted because he had a son. In February, the others were called to take a physical, but both Carlo and Jim were rejected. Carlo had a double hernia, and Jim had a heart murmur. Joe Mocca passed and would be called for active duty soon.

In March, Josie found out she was pregnant, and when Joe went to the draft board, they gave him a temporary deferment which lasted into 1943.

In early May, the government issued ration books to all American families. Most food and material things were rationed. This was especially true for sugar, coffee, meat, toilet paper, and cooking oils, including olive oil. Chocolate, liquor, and many items were not rationed, but they were going to the war effort and were in short supply.

Families received the books and early on were not budgeting them. They soon found no way of buying daily needs, and a black market surfaced. On some items, the price doubled. Maria called a meeting with the children on this and said to Carlo, "Get with your friend, Pete Elias, and start finding out where we can buy the main items that are being rationed, especially coffee. We have been giving those people a lot of business. It is their turn to help us!"

Carlo started spending 75 percent of his time scouring the market for anything rationed. When none of the stores on the Hill had coffee, Reina's had coffee. The same held true for all the rationed items!

Carlo was cashing in the on all the contacts he had made, using his great personality and sales ability. The word spread that there was a store on the Hill, where you could get just about anything if you had the coupons and the money to pay for it. By the end of the summer, people were coming to Reina's Market from all over the city and from small towns outside the city. Restaurants came to buy those items, and Maria laid down the law. She would tell new customers, "Don't come here for sugar and coffee and other rationed items. We sell vegetables and canned goods and other products!" Business was booming, and the cash was rolling in.

One day, in October, Maria met with Mr. Braun from Anheuser Busch. He had arrived early to collect the rent, and Maria asked, "I heard a relative of mine inquired about buying this building, is that true?"

Braun replied, "We have had a couple inquiries from people interested in purchasing the building, but nothing serious. Why do you ask?"

"If you ever decide to sell it, please give me chance. I would love to own it!"

He thought to himself, *This is some kind of woman.* "Let me see if the company would be interested in selling. I will get back to you next month when I come for the rent."

In November, he told Maria, "The company would be willing to sell the building." He discussed the price and the terms and handed her a term sheet.

Maria once again began scheming on how to make this happen. She was still concerned that Josie Burruano's godfather was rumored to be interested in buying the building. That was not going to happen, not if she had anything to do about it.

As 1942 flew by, business almost doubled the previous year's sales! On Christmas Day, after dinner was served, the table had been cleared, Maria had everyone at the table. She had that look, that confident smile, that I-am-in-charge demeanor. They had seen it before when she announced she was buying Josie Dominina's store. There was a momentary silence. The kids turned and looked at each other, and they thought, *Here we go again.* Maria, looking directly at Carlo, said, "I have made a decision to buy this building!"

Everyone had a look of amazement

Carlo just could not believe what he had heard!

He said, "Ma, are you crazy? Don't you realize when this war is over, we will be right back in the depression! People are working to supply the war. All these women working will be laid off. The business we are doing will go back to the way it was before the war started. Please don't do this!"

Maria said, "I don't care. I have heard people have been inquiring at Busch about buying it, and no one is ever going to throw me out of my store again!"

Carlo was right back at her. "And how much are you going to pay for the building?"

Again, staring him down, she replied, "Eleven thousand dollars!"

All the kids smiled except Carlo. "And how do you propose to pay for it?"

"Busch is going to carry the mortgage for five years with 10 percent for the down payment."

"And where are you going to get $1,100?"

Maria got up from the table, went to the next room where she slept, reached under her bed, and returned with a shoebox and emptied it on the table! Eleven rubber-banded packets spilled. Each contained $100 in fives, tens, and twenties!

There are no words to describe the look on everyone's face.

Carlo collected himself. He was not finished, but he knew he didn't have a chance of changing her mind. "Ma, what are the terms? How long will they carry the loan?"

She replied, "Five years."

This gave him a reprieve. "Now that is ridiculous. There is no way we can pay off $9,900 in five years. Ma, please you have to get more time."

She said, "With the rent from next door plus the $45 a month we are paying, I have figured it out and we can meet the monthly payment. I am not worried about it."

Josie could see Maria was getting aggravated with Carlo and said, "Carlo, let her buy the building. She has made some good decisions over the years. Besides when the war is over, maybe you're right. Some people will not be working, but the soldiers will be coming back and getting married and buying homes and furnishing them. And no matter what, they have to eat."

That was it. Everybody got up from the table, walked around, and gave Maria a hug, even Carlo.

The next day, Maria and Carlo went to meet with Mr. Braun. It had been prearranged. She told him she was there to buy the building. "I have the money, Mr. Braun. Can we start the paperwork today?"

He looked at her and broke bad news. "Mrs. Reina, the federal government in an effort to stem inflation passed a regulation, you now need 20 percent down. We need $2,250!"

Maria's face dropped. "Mr. Braun, it took me two years to save this money. I do not want to spend the next two years waiting and possibly lose the building. Can we work something out where I pay you extra each month until we achieve the other $1,100?"

"I am sorry, Mrs. Reina, that would be breaking the law. It is not possible."

Carlo could see she was about to break down. He said, "Come on, Ma, we will find a way. Thank you, Mr. Braun, we will be back."

Maria was undaunted. All the way home, she was thinking, *Where am I going to get $1,100?* The minute she and Carlo walked in the store, Josie and Jim knew something had gone wrong. They could see it on their faces. Carlo explained what happened.

Maria said, "I will be back."

Josie said, "Ma, where are you going?"

"Riggio!"

Maria, with a determined mindset walked into the bank, and the young man at the front desk knew to get Mr. Riggio.

Maria was on speed control, and Riggio could see it in her eyes and hear it in the tone of her words. She told him what had happened and asked to borrow the $1,100.

He responded, "I am so sorry to hear that. Do you have anything for collateral?"

"Yes, my word!"

Riggio smiled. "I will be back in a minute." He returned with his wife. "Maria, will you please repeat what happened this morning?" She did and closed by again, asking for the $1,100. "I can pay you $50 a month for eighteen months, and I will make one last payment for the interest and final payment!"

Mr. Riggio looked at his wife, got the positive nod, stuck his hand out, and said, "Maria, stay here. I will go have the note prepared, and we will give you the check. Should we make it out to you or Anheuser Busch?"

With a single tear dropping down her eye, she said, "Please make it out to Anheuser Busch."

It was a bright sunny day in December, unusually warm as Maria walked back to the store, beaming!

In less than forty minutes, a woman in 1942 walked out of a bank, having made a loan on her word and her signature. What a great country, America! Maria walked into the store with a smile on her face from one ear to the other, waving the check from Riggio, and the kids once again had that look of pride on their faces. Josie started crying, and Carlo could do nothing but laugh. Jim just stood admiring her.

The next day, Carlo called for Mr. Braun and learned he had left for a brief vacation and would be returning the first week of January.

The year 1942 would be forever indelible on the minds of all the Reinas.

Maria Buys the Building
1943

Carlo had left a message for Mr. Braun at Anheuser-Busch to call him when he returned from vacation. In mid-January, the call came. Carlo explained that Maria had secured the money and wanted to finalize the purchase of the building. Mr. Braun confirmed the deal was still on, and he would get with the legal department and start the process. "It will take sixty days to run the title and get the paper work together. When do you want to come down?"

Carlo answered, "Today."

Braun laughed and said, "How about Monday at nine?"

On Monday, January 18 1943, Maria, with Jim and Carlo, signed a purchase agreement and a note to buy the building at 5101

Shaw Avenue for $11,000, with $2,250 down. The note for the balance was payable in five years, and a scheduled closing sometime in March.

Only in America can an immigrant woman in 1942, in the middle of a World War, with a second-grade education, buy a building after arriving in the country with barely the clothes on her back. This in spite of the traumas she experienced—raising five kids, losing Joseph, and the ordeal of living with a husband who had not worked since 1930. Maria thought she had arrived! The cold, blustery winds of March and rain every other day took its toll on business. Carlo received a call from Mr. Braun's secretary and was asked to come to the Busch office for the closing on the ninth, which brightened the day.

Maria could not sleep the night of the eighth. Was this really happening? That night, she fixed a great dinner. Carlo had gone down to the basement and siphoned wine from his special homemade barrel, which the store was selling to good customers. This was a night to remember, and even Maria had a glass.

The ninth of March was one the family would never forget. Maria and Carlo went to the closing, and everything went according to plan. They were there for less than an hour. Even the weather cooperated. It was a bright sunny day, and once again, a well-deserved happy one for Maria.

Mr. Braun gave her a warm hug and thanked her for the years. "It has been a pleasure dealing with you, Mrs. Reina."

She replied, "Thank you for making this happen, Mr. Braun. I will never forget what you have done for me."

He said, "I did nothing. You made it happen. I, too, will never forget you. You are a remarkable woman! I still can't believe just a short while ago, you walked in here and asked to rent the store, and now you own the building. My sincere congratulations!" Carlo walked out the door and hugged Maria. He was so proud of her and so emotional he could not speak. There were many hugs and kisses when they walked into the store. Some of their best customers happened to be there. Carlo again went to the basement and drew some wine. Everyone in the store celebrated with the family and toasted with a glass of wine. The next day, Maria met with Saul Rosen, and said, "I want you to know yesterday I completed the purchase of the building. I am your new landlord."

He sat there dumbfounded. "Did I just hear you? You bought the building?"

"Yes. I have a copy of your lease which expires in September, so the $45 a month comes to me as of April 1."

He was lost for words. He tried collecting his thoughts, but the shock of this aggressive woman overwhelmed him. All he could say was "Congratulations," but he did not mean a word of it. He was thinking, *How could I let this uneducated woman scoop me? I have been here for almost twenty-five years. With the rent I have paid, I could have bought and paid for this building twice!* On April 1, Saul walked across Shaw Avenue, then crossed Hereford, to the mail box, and mailed the first month's rent check. On May 1, he mailed the check with a letter notifying Maria he would not be renewing his lease, stating he was having trouble buying merchandise for the store due to the War. Most soft goods and apparel companies had converted their entire plants to making products for the military. In reality, he was disgruntled over the fact Maria was his landlord. He figured this would hurt her. Now she would be $45 a month short on her quest to pay for the building. Carlo opened the envelope with the rent check and the letter; he was visibly upset when he handed it to his mother. He said to himself, "I knew this was going to happen." Maria, the consummate optimist, said, "So we will rent it to someone else. We have four months to find a new tenant." Carlo put the word out to friends, and Maria went to Riggio and gave them the news, asking them to help find someone to rent the place. Mr. Riggio said, "Do not be concerned, Mrs. Reina, there are no vacant stores for rent on the 'Hill.' You will find a tenant." Carlo placed a call to Jim Gualdoni, he was in the liquor business, who came to see the space. He sat with Carlo and Maria and asked the price. Carlo started to open his mouth, and Maria kicked him under the table. She said, "So, Jim, do you like the store?"

He said, "Yes. I want the store. How much is the rent?'

Maria said, "We have never been in this position. What do you think is fair?"

Jim said, "I was thinking $75 a month."

Maria came right back at him, "That will be fine, but it is the store and the basement, not the second floor."

Jim Gualdoni gave a positive nod. "I will take it, and you do not have to do anything to it, just have it swept nice and clean for me. I want a five-year lease fixed at $75 a month!"

Carlo added, "We will have Riggio draw up the lease. Can you come by next week and sign it?"

They agreed to a date and he left.

The following week, he came by, signed the lease, and gave Maria $75 in cash for the first month's rent. Once again, Carlo just smiled and said, "Where does she get the 'coglione'?" Saul Rosen started his going out of business sale on August 1 and finished it on the last day of the lease. He was out on schedule and never even said goodbye to the Reinas. Carmelo and Jim cleaned up the place on the first, and Jim Gualdoni moved in the next day. Maria was on top of the second floor immediately. It was a mess, needing paint, a new tile floor in the kitchen and bathroom, and a complete renovation. She called Tony Caputa in to build some cabinets in the kitchen and bathroom, and a painter to paint the entire four rooms. Josie explained to her the government had instituted rent controls. She had read the most a landlord could charge for a four-room apartment was $35. Maria walked down the street to Riggio to give them the news about Gualdoni. As always, she was greeted and ushered to Mr. Riggio's office, and after the handshake, she asked Vincenzo (they were on a first name basis now after twenty years) for help renting the second floor.

He said, "We had a couple in here yesterday, and I have the man's phone number. Do you want me to call him now?"

Maria, always anxious, said, "Yes."

Tom Benich answered the phone, and after Mr. Riggio explained the rental possibility, agreed to bring his wife to see the space on the weekend. Maria offered to pay Vincenzo; he looked at her and smiled, "Just bring me a loaf of your bread next time you bake it." He had it many times. When she got back to the store, she put a loaf in a bag and sent baby Joe, who was seven, to the bank with it. On Saturday, the Benich family looked at the four rooms with their two young daughters. They agreed to sign a three-year lease for $35 a month, and once again, Maria came out on top of the negative letter from Saul Rosen. The monthly income was $110. She followed her plan to use $45 of it toward the Busch notes, and $65 to the note at Riggio. She ultimately paid Riggio in one year! The loan at Busch was for five years, yet she hated paying interest. Some months she paid them as much as an extra payment on the principle! Her plan was to pay the entire mortgage in three years. She followed the same procedure with Riggio. Some months doubling the payment. In September, Josie delivered the first Reina grandchild named Phillip, after Joe's father. By this time, Joe Mocca was in the Army, stationed in Louisiana. There were no issues with the birth. Dr. Wilcox delivered the baby.

Joe and Josie Mocca, 1942

Josie Reina Mocca, 1942

Joe and Josie Mocca wedding photo, 1941

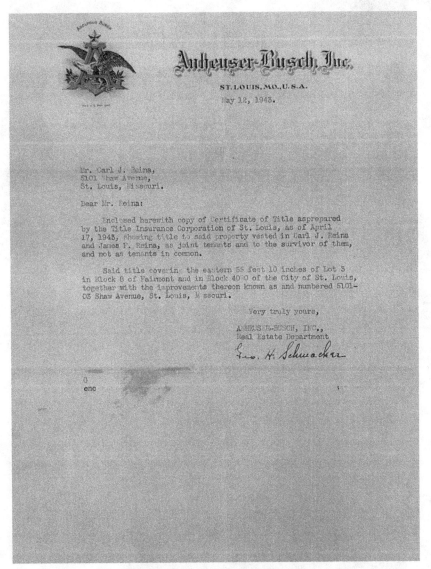

Maria buys the building, 1943

CHAPTER 16

1944
The Payoffs

Business in the store was booming. Every month, Maria was doubling the payments to Riggio on the small loan, same on the loan with Busch! Carlo said to her, "Ma, be careful. I am concerned this war may end soon, and business will slow down!" "Let's not deplete our cash."

Maria was right at him. "Carlo, you worry too much. I hate paying interest, and we are paying 5 percent on both loans."

"Let's not deplete our cash."

She had received letters on occasion from Sicily. In March, a letter from her sister Carmella informed her that her father had passed away. She was in the store and excused herself.

She went back to the small kitchen behind the store and cried. She was overcome with guilt. *Why didn't I go back to see him before the war?*

Josie came back to see what was wrong, and Maria told her what had happened and shared her guilt. Josie, always ready to use logic for any problem, said, "Ma, how could you go? During the twenties, we barely had money to pay the rent! The struggle continued into the thirties. You were the only one working until 1932! Please do not put this guilt on yourself. You know Grandpa understood times were tough here. Come on, let's go for a walk."

Maria said, "Okay, I have go to Riggio to make the payment."

They made the payment to Riggio and continued down Shaw Avenue. It was a warm beautiful day for a walk, and they took the time to visit with Rosa to give her the news. Rosa burst into tears; she too was overcome with guilt for not returning to visit Ignazio.

Maria started having health issues in April. The first necessitated a gallbladder operation. That happened on a Tuesday at which time Dr. Wilcox took out her gallbladder. She was in and out of the hospital in four days and back to work on Saturday.

On a Friday, six weeks later, a severe toothache brought her to the dentist. Dr. Lundergan gave her the bad news: her teeth were all bad, and at age fifty-one, they had to be pulled!

"Doctor, can we start tonight?"

"Yes, you are my only patient this evening." He gave her a shot to ease the pain and took out half of her teeth! She made an appointment for the following Tuesday to remove a few more and the following Friday to take out the rest. Then he fitted her for false teeth. She wrapped a towel around her chin and tied it in a knot over the top of her head so she didn't have to miss a day at the store. She had to go to the bathroom periodically to rinse her mouth because some bleeding occurred.

In September, she walked into Riggio and made the last payment on the $1,100 loan.

Mr. Riggio was not surprised. "Maria, if every client at this bank was like you, I could let a third of the staff go."

She handed him his loaf of bread and thanked him again for his help. As she walked out the door, he once again could only stare and admire her and followed her walking out of the bank! Vincenzo thought to himself, *What a woman!*

On the way back to the store, she said to herself, "One down, one to go, Anheuser Busch is next!" It was a glorious warm day! The day complimented her feelings.

Baby Joe was growing up fast. At Shaw School, his first-grade teacher put him in third grade, as he was so bright, it was useless for him to go to second grade. Now eight, he went to the public library and was reading two books a week in addition to helping in the store, stocking the shelves, and sweeping the floor.

One fine summer day in August, one of Joe's classmates, Tony Milano, approached him with a proposition, "Joe, when the guy who delivers cigarettes to your mom's store comes next time, let's get some out of his truck while he is in the store."

"Tony, I have never stolen anything in my entire life!"

"I will take them out of the truck, and we can go to the alley behind my house. I'll teach you how to smoke." Tony was a year and a half older than Joe.

A week later, the cigarette salesman pulled up in front of the store. Tony and Joe were playing catch with a baseball in the street.

Tony said, "You stand by the door and watch when he goes in with your mom's order, and I will get the cigarettes." In a matter of seconds, the boys were running down the middle of the block through Tony's backyard and into the alley.

They sat in a shady spot, and Tony pulled out a pack of matches and lit the first cigarette and handed it to Joe. He then lit one for himself and inhaled it and explained to Joe how to inhale. Joe tried and gagged and started coughing. Tony laughed.

In less than ten minutes, Joe saw his brother, Jim, driving down the alley in in his 1934 Buick. They had been caught. It was so fast that Joe froze. Jim jumped out of the car and slapped Joe across the face! Jim started dragging Joe down the alley, sometimes kicking him in the butt! Joe was crying, but it didn't faze Jim. They turned the corner of the alley and headed down the street to the store.

When they reached the building, Jim dragged Joe, kicking up the nine steps to the second-floor bedroom. Joe's heart was pounding; he had the fear of God and was scared to death! "Take your pants down and your underwear." Jim took off his belt and began beating him on the butt!

Maria heard the screaming all the way down to the store and came running up the stairs. Carlo was right behind her. She told Jim, "Stop! Leave him alone!"

Jim backed off, and Carlo took Jim into the hall, grabbed him by the shirt collar, and told him, "Don't you ever hit that kid again. If I ever catch you doing it, I am going to kick your butt!"

For the record, Joe never smoked again! Through the years, Jim was constantly on Joe's case, causing great concern for Maria. She was always getting between them. At times, Joe wanted to run away from home, his brother Jim being the big reason.

There was good news on both the European and Pacific war fronts. The war was coming close to an end. At every level, the military was making major advancements.

Carlo, ever so conservative, had taken over all the purchasing for the store, but even though business continued to grow, Maria had to prod him sometimes to order more of certain items. The store continued to do well, and Maria was once again tapping the cash register without discussing her cache with the family.

On May 7, Germany surrendered, and Americans celebrated with joy, never to be forgotten by those old enough to remember. On the Hill, all the main neighborhood streets were blocked off for street parties starting that weekend and lasting throughout the following week. At the corner of Shaw and Hereford, dummies portraying Hitler, Mussolini, and Tojo, the Japanese leader were hung from the electric wire strung across the street.

There were parades in every section of every neighborhood. Bands played on many corners, people danced in the streets, and food tables were bountiful and brought by some of the best cooks on the Hill. The good old "dago," red homemade wine flowed like there was no tomorrow. Entrances were sealed off until Monday, the fourteenth of May! Normal business stopped!

Josie was excited; the war in Europe had ended. Joe Mocca was in Germany, in the engineer branch of the US army, and she thought he would be coming home soon. Not long after the news of the end in Europe, she received a letter from him with bad news. His company had been ordered to board a ship headed for the South Pacific. Destination unknown! She was devastated. Phillip was now three and had only seen his dad briefly when he was a baby and in a few photos.

But Josie, having the patience of a saint, dealt with the situation. Once again, her logical mind prevailed. "He is alive. That is all that matters!" Joe ended up in the Philippines, and fortunately the United

States had captured the islands. The summer was once again hot and humid, offset by the good news of the war ending. On September 2, the Japanese surrendered, bringing a close to World War II.

The celebrations started all over the world again. Japan and most of Europe were war-torn. The people were starving, many homeless, and Maria had received letters from her family and Carmelo's about the problems in Casteltermini. There was no economy, no jobs, and no money.

When the bad news from Casteltermini reached Maria from her family of the sad conditions, she decided to do something about it! She and the family all pitched in and made wood crates to ship food. They packed cans of just about every type, sugar and ground coffee in seal-tight containers, plus packaged cereal and canned milk. This was not to be a one-time donation. It became an ongoing gesture, and none of the kids objected doing the work. Once again, the lesson surfaced, "Take care of your family!"

In September, Mr. Braun arrived for his usual quarterly visit to pick up the mortgage payment.

Maria greeted him, "Good morning, Mr. Braun, how are you? Would you like an espresso?"

He said, "As a matter of fact, I would, Maria. How are you feeling?"

"I am fine, thank you."

Josie went to make three espressos. She could tell Maria had something up her sleeve; she hurried back to the front of the store with the coffee. Josie had cut a check again for $900, which was three times the normal payment. She had given it to Maria before Braun arrived. As they started sipping the coffee, Maria had a brown paper bag with some numbers on it sitting on the counter. "Mr. Braun, here is a check for $900. I figured with it I now owe Busch $2,400, is that correct?"

Braun was not prepared for the question. He opened his briefcase, checked his file on the loan, borrowed a piece of paper, and, in a matter of minutes, said, "Mrs. Reina, I should have known better than to bother looking up the balance. You are correct."

Neither Josie nor Braun had noticed a small grocery bag sitting on the counter. Maria dumped the contents in front of them and said, "Here are twenty-four packets. There is $100 in each! Mr. Braun, this building now belongs to me and my family!"

Josie was beaming! Braun was momentarily speechless. He looked at Josie first, "Were you aware of this?"

With a tear in her eye, she nodded no. He then looked at Maria. "Maria, you never cease to amaze me. You are remarkable. Congratulations!"

CHAPTER 17

1945
The Marriages and Saint Clair

In the summer of 1945, Carlo met a beautiful young lady at The Forest Park Highlands amusement park dance hall. He was with his buddy, Al "Red" Schoendienst, the second baseman for the St. Louis Cardinals baseball team.

Her name was Imojean Baxter. Carlo and Red approached her as she sat with her girlfriend. The girlfriend warned Imojean, "Watch out for the guy on the right. His name is Ginger, and he is a real ladies' man."

Carlo got to the table and said hello, looking straight at Imojean, "Come on, let's dance." While this was somewhat of an unusual approach, Imojean had said to herself, "This is the best looking man I have ever seen in my life. I hope to God he asks me to dance and not my girlfriend!" Because of his approach, she changed her mind and said, "No, thank you."

Red asked the girlfriend to dance. Carlo came back a while later again and asked, "Come on dance with me, I don't bite."

Imojean agreed. She thought, *He is so good looking. Why not?*

For Carlo, it was love at first sight! Imojean hit him with the *bolta* (Sicilian for thunderbolt right to the heart). Carlo introduced himself, and she likewise as soon as they got on the dance floor. After a while, he asked, "How old are you?"

She said, "Nineteen. How old are you?"

"I am twenty-four."

They danced a few more times during the evening. In the ensuing months, they ran into each other on occasion and danced at the Casa Loma Ballroom or at Tune Town dance hall.

In September, Carlo saw her again at the Highlands one night. They danced and talked for a long time, and they agreed to go out on a date. When he came to the house, she invited him in and introduced him to her mother and father. "Mom and Dad, this is Carlo Reina."

Carlo was very pleasant and said to her parents, "I am very pleased to meet you." He could see the look of concern on Ray Baxter's face. He knew what he was thinking: "This guy is too old for my daughter." There was no doubt Carlo was smitten. He knew it, but he was taking it slow, and he didn't want to rush this. He knew this was the woman he was going to marry.

It was miserably hot and humid the night of their next date, and he asked, "Would you like to go to a movie, one that has air-conditioning?"

Imojean agreed, and they sat in the balcony at the Fox Theatre. There were not many people up there, and after they sat down, Carlo put his arm around her, and she removed it with no fanfare. He smiled.

They had exchanged birth dates, and Carlo made a note of hers, September 10.

In late August, Imojean agreed to celebrate her birthday with him. On a beautiful September evening, he brought flowers when he picked her up. They went to dinner at Angelo's on the Hill. He had called the restaurant owner and an old friend. "Hi, Angelo, I need a table tonight. I am bringing my girlfriend for dinner. It is her birthday. Please do something special for her."

Angelo responded, "No problem, Carlo!"

Imojean wore a beautiful black dress. She looked like a model who just stepped out of *Vogue* magazine. Carlo was in a dark navy blue suit. He looked like a movie star! They dined by candlelight and received the royal treatment. Angelo personally served them, and for desert, he made bananas Foster at the table. Imojean was visibly impressed. She left briefly to go to the washroom.

Angelo came to the table and said to Carlo, "Mama Mia, she is a knockout. Where did you find her?"

Carlo responded, "I am going to marry her, Angelo."

The following Saturday, they joined a large group of Carlo's friends at a table at the Casa Loma. She was supposed to be home at eleven, but they were having so much fun that she completely lost track of time. It was one! She told Carlo, "I better call my dad. He is going to give me hell."

Ray Baxter was in bed when the call came and told her, "You get your butt home this minute, young lady, and you are not to see that guy again!"

When they arrived, Carlo insisted on going in to talk to her father. He was in bed, got up, and Carlo apologized profusely. "Mr. Baxter, this was my fault. I am really sorry. Don't blame your daughter. She kept asking me to leave, and I kept saying one more dance. It was all my fault!"

Ray Baxter just stared at him!

"Come on, Mr. Baxter, do you remember when you were our age, dating Mrs. Baxter, and were out having a good time, you just did not want the evening to end, right?"

One of his best-selling jobs. Ray said, "All right, get out of here. You, young lady, go to bed."

In March, Jim went to the ice cream store on Marconi and was served by an attractive Irish young lady. He stayed for a while and had his ice cream in the store and waited until the crowd left and then went up the girl and introduced himself.

She had long strawberry blonde hair and great eyes, and what he could see, a very nice figure!

"My name is Jim Reina. What's yours?"

"My name is Virginia Nelson."

"My pleasure, Virginia, that's my sister's name."

After a brief conversation, he asked, "Do you have a boyfriend?"

She laughed. "I have a few. Why do you ask?" She had a sly grin on her face.

"I am asking because I want to take you out."

"And where do you want to take me?"

"Do you like to dance?"

"I love to dance. Are you a good dancer?"

"I am told I am the best on the Hill."

"You sure are proud of yourself and modest too."

"Okay, come on. Are you going to go dancing with me?"

"Where are you going to take me to dance?"

"Have you ever been to the Casa Loma Ballroom?"

"No, I am only seventeen. I am not supposed to go to nightclubs."

"How old are you, Jim?"

He lied. "I am twenty-one."

"I think you might be too old for me."

He said, "My father married my mother when she was your age, and he was nine years older than her."

She said, "That was then, this is now. I believe my parents would object to us dating."

Jim, already a good salesman and already scheming on how to get her to agree to a date, said, "Look, how about this—let's just go to a movie. I am willing to come to your house, meet your parents, sit with them for a while, and if they object to our going to a movie after meeting me, I promise I will leave quietly. How's that sound?"

"Okay, I am willing to go for that."

He said, "How about this weekend?"

She agreed to Sunday night.

On Sunday, Jim went to the house on West Pine Street and met the Nelsons, the entire family, two sisters, and two brothers, a very nice Irish family.

Jim's personality was very pleasant. The Nelson's were an openhearted family. They offered Jim a beer, and he joined them, even Virginia had one. It took less than an hour to get the nod from Mr. Nelson.

Virginia and Jim were out the door and in the car. "Do you want to go to a movie or shall we go dancing?"

"Let's go dance. I want to see you dance!"

They went to the Casa Loma. No liquor was served, only set-ups. Jim had a bottle of whiskey. It was $0.50 to get in, and Virginia was impressed. Jim knew everyone, and they got the VIP treatment. It was the era of big bands, and they were seated at a table practically on the dance floor. Before they ordered setups to mix their own drinks, they were on the dance floor. It was a jitterbug song. Jim was shocked that she could dance, no match for him, but she was good! Most of the night was spent on the dance floor. She had promised her mom she'd be home by ten, and out of respect, Jim had her home right on time. She shared a room with her sister, Florence, and when they went to bed, she told her older sister about the evening. Florence picked up Virginia's excitement and knew this had turned out to be more than a casual date.

1946

In January, the romance with Carlo and Imojean (by now, she was being called Jean) bloomed. They were in love. Carlo had met the parents quite a few times by now and, one evening, approached Jean's father.

"Ray, I am in love with your daughter, and I would love to have your blessings to marry her!"

Ray Baxter responded immediately, "Carlo, my wife and I are very fond of you, and we have been hoping this day would arrive. You have our blessing!"

They had already set a date for June 9. The plan was to convert the living room at the far end of the second floor over the store as their bedroom. By this time, the secret was out: Carlo was twenty-eight, and Jean was seventeen.

Jean Baxter and Carlo Reina were married on June 9, 1946. Jimmy Castellano was his best man. Brother Jim and Charlie Dichecci were his other groom's men. It was a typical Sicilian wedding. They were married at St. Ambrose Church, and the wedding reception was held at the Swedish Rite Hall. Nothing fancy, but the food was out of this world.

Jimmy Castellano toasted the bride and groom. He looked at Carlo. "Carlo, you are the luckiest guy in the world. You have the most beautiful lady in the City of St. Louis. Jean, I have known Carlo since we were babies, and you too are very lucky. He is and always will be my closest and dearest friend. He is one of a kind. Congratulations to both of you! I know I speak for everyone in this room. We wish you the best of luck for a long lifetime together!"

It was an extremely hot, humid night, but everyone was having a great time and barely noticed the weather. The couple spent the honeymoon evening at the Chase Hotel.

Virginia and Jim were having a great time dating, out almost every night dancing and double dating with some of Jim's buddies from the Knight's club, including Joe and Josie Mocca, who also were great dancers.

In late June, Jim asked Virginia to marry him. Virginia was stunned.

She said, "Jim, I love you, but I don't know if I am ready for marriage. Let me think about it."

Jim went into his best pitch. "What's there to think about? You just said I love you and I love you. We love being with each other. We have been out every night for the past two months, we love to dance, the same food, the same kind of movies, the same kind of people… why not get married? I want to spend the rest of my life with you!"

"What about my parents?"

"Let me handle your parents. I can sell them!"

She laughed. "There's no doubt about that. Let's do it together."

Jim called the Nelson's and invited them to Sala's Restaurant on the Hill for dinner the following Saturday. Jim knew Charlie Sala; he had been in some craps games with him. He called him and asked him to put up a good front for him and the family. "Please give us the VIP treatment, Charlie."

When they arrived, they were given the best table in the house. Charlie was aware of Jim's plans and put them in a very quiet area of the room. He sent over some homemade ravioli as a complimentary appetizer, and once dinner arrived, Jim ordered a bottle of wine. When it arrived, they toasted each other, and Jim thought, *This is it!*

"Mrs. and Mr. Nelson, I would be deeply honored to have your beautiful daughter's hand in marriage."

The Nelson's were moved. Virginia had told Florence about the plan, and she had hinted to them that Jim wanted to marry Virginia.

Still it came as a surprise, and Mr. Nelson asked, "Have you two set a date?"

Virginia took the question and replied, "Yes, this August!"

Mr. Nelson said, "That's only two months from now?" Mrs. Nelson smiled and bluntly asked the question, "Please tell me you are not pregnant!"

Both Virginia and Jim laughed and simultaneously answered no!

Neither Virginia nor Jim wanted anything to do with a big wedding reception. They met with a priest at St. Ambrose, and Jim asked, "Father, we do not want the traditional Sunday morning wedding. We intend on inviting our immediate families and close friends, and then we will have a dinner right after you marry us."

Virginia echoed Jim's plea and asked, "Can we just come here on a Saturday morning and get married?"

The priest said in a pleasant voice, "Of course, we do it all the time."

There was no formal announcement, no official engagement, no wedding invitations, just phone calls to a few friends and relatives on both sides.

On the first Saturday in August, with fewer than fifty people present, Virginia Nelson and Jim Reina were married. The entire group was invited to Sala's dining room for a very nice luncheon. Once again, Missouri Bakery delivered a cake, compliments of Josie and Virginia. A good time was had by all. Carlo gave a very nice toast and welcomed Virginia into the Reina family. Mr. Nelson toasted the bride and groom and likewise welcomed Jim into the Nelson family!

The St. Clair Opportunity

In mid-August, Jim Gualdoni walked from next door and asked Maria if she had a few minutes. She invited him to the kitchen behind the store, made coffee, and waited for him to speak.

"Mrs. Reina, I just purchased a strip of land in St. Clair, just an hour from St. Louis. There's a restaurant, a gas station, a liquor store, and eight cabins on it. It is right on Highway 66. I have learned the federal highway commission has approved widening Highway 66 throughout the state of Missouri, and they will have to buy property along both sides of the road, and that includes my land. I bought it from a widow whose husband died last fall, and the businesses have been closed for almost a year. I need someone to go in, reopen them, and build them back. I can get a lot more for the property if there is a going business and not just the land."

Maria asked, "What's this got to do with me?"

"I was wondering if any of your children would be interested in taking over the businesses. I would not charge them anything, not even rent. There's a beautiful four-bedroom house on the property too. They can make a lot of money!"

Maria asked, "Jim, how long will it be for?"

He said, "I am not sure, probably one to two years."

"When do you want them to start?"

He said, "As soon as possible!"

"Let me speak to my daughters."

At the weekly Sunday luncheon, Maria disclosed the Jim Gualdoni proposal. Josie led the discussion. She was not working, and Husband Joe was making $20 a week, Martin, $15.

Virginia had had an offer to sell the beauty shop for $3,000 and took it. She was helping in the store.

Josie said, "Let's take a drive out there to look at it."

Everyone agreed.

The following Sunday, they met Jim Gualdoni at the site. It was a mess. The cabins needed paint and new bedding and a major cleanup. Jim agreed to pay for material if they would provide the labor.

Josie, always thinking (she had Maria's instincts) said, "Jim, will you do the same for the restaurant, the liquor store, and the gas station? They all need work." She got a yes. The plan was to get there right after Labor Day and start the renovation.

This was a major move as they had to get out of their respective home leases and move their furniture to set up the house. They did not have a lot of money. Virginia put up the cash she had from selling the beauty shop. They agreed not to take salaries the first year. Martin volunteered to take care of the liquor store, Joe for the gas station, Josie and Virginia to run the kitchen, and both of the men would work the restaurant at night. They had no idea how to handle the cabins. They agreed that whenever someone came into the restaurant to rent a cabin, whoever was available would take care of the customer. Within fifteen days, they were ready to open, and they ran an ad in the St. Clair newspaper and called the business "Moke's." Jim Gualdoni paid for everything. They used part of Virginia's money to buy gas for the station. Maria gave them all the food for the restaurant, including ten cases of beer on credit. Jim Gualdoni stocked the liquor store.

On the eighteenth of September, they opened and could not believe that so many people had showed up the first night and filled the restaurant.

Joe, in charge of greeting people, had to turn people away. The menu consisted of all the old Sicilian recipes from the depression, including every pasta dish they had gotten sick of over the years. Josie and Virginia had baked thirty loaves of bread, and they were gone! They had fried 120 meatballs for spaghetti, and meatballs—gone! That night, they rented all eight cabins at $2.50 each! Josie suggested they start charging $3.00 for the cabins, and they agreed. They also agreed to hire some help, someone to clean the cabins and wash dishes. They were exhausted and realized there was no way they could work like this seven days a week.

Business was brisk the rest of the year, the food was great, the service was beyond any of the locals had ever seen, and the money was flowing in way beyond their expectations. Jim Gualdoni had asked them to please keep accurate records of both expenses and revenue, important when he sold the property. Josie took that job. Virginia got all her money back in the first sixty days.

Maria, 1946

"Moke's", St. Clair, 1946

Moke's, St. Clair, 1946

Moke's, St. Clair, 1946

Carlo Reina, 1946

CHAPTER 18

1947
The Breakup

One night in early April, Martin had been drinking a few beers, and Virginia was on him about drinking during working hours. In front of Josie and Joe, he yelled at Virginia, "Don't be telling me what to do. If I want to have a beer, I am going to have a beer! All we do around here is work seven days a week, and I am sick of it!"

This was not the first time they got into a heated argument in front of Josie and Joe.

Josie tried to calm things down, Martin, "We are all working seven days a week, and this may be the last year."

Almost before she finished, he said, "Mind your own business, Josie!"

Joe, normally quiet and calm, raised his voice, "That's enough, Martin!"

Martin left the kitchen, went back out to the restaurant bar, and got another beer.

About nine, they had cleaned up the kitchen and were ready to close. A young couple had finished their dinner and were smooching at the table.

Martin approached them and, in a nasty voice, said, "We are trying to close. Why don't you two rent a cabin? We have a vacant one in the back. Either that or get the hell out of here, so we can close and have dinner!"

The man got up and told Martin, "Why don't you go to hell you rude jerk!"

Joe heard the ruckus in the kitchen and went out and got between Martin and the customer apologized to the man and asked him to leave quietly. He said, "Your dinner is on us."

Martin stormed out of the restaurant, got in the car, and drove up to the house. Virginia, Josie, and Joe closed the restaurant and went back to the kitchen to eat dinner and had a long discussion about Martin.

Josie said, "We have enough stress taking care of this business. We don't need this."

Virginia said, "I am sorry. What do you want me to do? I have had so many talks with him, maybe he and I should pack up and leave. Is that what you want me to do? I will speak to him in the morning before we open."

When they arrived at the house, Martin was sitting at the kitchen table with another beer. He said, "Well, did the three of you have a nice talk about me?"

Joe grabbed Josie and took her to their bedroom, and Virginia laid into him about his behavior. "You have embarrassed me in front of my family! What's wrong with you? Don't you understand, every time you have a couple of beers, you turn into a monster!"

With that, Martin got up from the table and struck her in the face with the back of his hand, and she hit him right back! He came at her and punched her. The blow struck between her nose and her eye, and she went to the floor! He was on top of her swinging at her face, but she was swinging back.

Joe came flying out of the bedroom with a baseball bat and pulled him off her and said, "Martin, leave her alone, or I will break this bat over your head!" Martin jumped up went to the counter, grabbed the car keys, and took off.

Joe and Josie put an ice pack on Virginia's bruised face and took her to the hospital. She was admitted and cared for in the emergency room. After about an hour, the doctor told them he wanted to keep her overnight for observation. She was released the next day.

The following week, Virginia went to see an attorney and filed for divorce.

In early August, Jim Gualdoni came for a visit and informed them that he had made a deal with the federal government to sell the property. The business would be closing the first of October, so their deal was finished. He thanked them for their efforts and handed them a check for $3,000! They had accumulated another $18,000.

Josie asked, "Jim, what about the liquor, the food and beer in the restaurant, and the supplies at the gas station?"

He said, "You have at least two months to dispose of that, make a record of what is left on your last day, and I will reimburse you for everything!"

On October 1, they settled with Jim, and the trio walked away with close to $24,000 and cut it three ways.

1947

Virginia and Martin had started a business in the fall of '47. The plan was to take the large flatbed truck belonging to his father to a poultry farm in Indiana on Thursday mornings. There they would load it with eighty coups of chickens and sixty cases of fresh eggs, deliver half to the parents live poultry store on Hudson Avenue. It was in the neighborhood where Martin grew up. In the rear of the store was a killing station where the neck of the chicken was slit, then dipped in boiling hot water, and run through a machine to remove the feathers.

After unloading half the poultry and eggs, they proceeded to Maxwell Street, an area on the west side of the city. It was loaded with street vendors, selling just about everything at discounted prices and attracting large crowds. On a corner, Virginia bagged and sold eggs, and Martin handled chicken sales using a scale to weigh them. Martin would tie the legs with a heavy piece of twine so the customer could get the chicken home. Prices were three times the price they paid for them, and even at that, they were still cheaper than the grocery stores. This was long before the mass-produced frozen poultry days!

Virginia said to Martin one day as winter was approaching, "Let's start looking for a store. We can't sell on the street this winter." He agreed. They found a store with a flat on the second floor at 4839 South Wentworth. Virginia had her money from the St. Clair deal, but they were short. It was impossible to get a loan as they had no jobs.

Martin told her, "Let's go see my parents," and they borrowed $10,000 from them and bought the building.

1948

Maria was visiting her *compares*, the Rumbolos in early January. She told them she was going to sell the store. "I am tired. I have been working six days a week, long twelve-hour days. Baby Joe is growing up, and I never spend any time with him! I want to go see my daughter in Chicago once in a while, and someday I want to go back to see my family in Sicily."

Pepe Rumbolo asked, "How much do you want for the store?"

Maria responded, "Why do you ask, compare?"

He said, "Ever since my boys came back from the war, they have not made any money. Maybe we could buy the store. Do you want to sell the building too?"

Maria quickly answered, "No, the building is not for sale."

He again asked, "What is it worth? How much do you want for the business?"

"Pepe, it is supporting three families. It could easily support you and Santa and your three boys. It is worth what you are willing to pay and what I am willing to take."

The three of them laughed. Pepe thought, *This woman is so shrewd.* "Maria, let us discuss this with our sons, Sam and Carlo. Meanwhile, you come up with a price and let's meet next Sunday to discuss it."

On Monday, Maria went to see Vincenzo Riggio and discussed the situation. She was deciding how to arrive at a fair price. "Maria, you have a great business, but it is you. You drive the business, you are the main person who makes it work. If you don't mind me asking, how much did the store earn last year?"

She said, "Josie keeps the books. I really can't answer that question."

He said, "Take that number and multiply it by five or six, and that's the price!"

When she returned, she met with Josie and settled on a price.

The following Sunday, Josie, Carlo, and Maria trudged through a wet snow and met with the Rumbolo's. Everyone greeted each other warmly.

Maria spoke, "Compare, you asked for the price. We want $30,000 for the business and $15,000 for the inventory. The rent for the store is $75 a month. We will take 10 percent down and $75 a month for the balance to be paid over a set period of time that works for both of us."

Pepe looked at Santa, and the boys, got a positive nod from the trio, and said, "It's a deal!"

Maria and Santa hugged in tears, the same with Pepe and Maria. Josie and Sam hugged too. His wife, Rose (Castellano), was there. She and Josie hugged in tears. Carlo Rumbolo put his arm around Carlo Reina and exchanged "congratulations."

Maria said, "There is no family on this earth I would rather have the store than my compare. Pepe, I could never repay you for all you did for us over the last twenty years. I have no words to convey my gratitude to you. *Mei pie sinceri grazie* [my sincere thanks]!"

Part of the agreement was either Maria or Carlo or both would help in the store for the first three months, teaching both Sam and Carlo Rumbolo how to cut meat and meeting with the purveyors for ordering merchandise.

Later the following week, Jim needed to find a job. He started reading the want ads in the newspaper immediately and found a job selling appliances with Ralph Smith Appliances on South Kingshighway. He went to work for straight commission. It didn't take him long to learn the business. He started calling people on the Hill and was making sales right from day one.

Carlo had his cronies at a used car lot also on Kingshighway, where he played cards and shot craps. He was good friends with the two owners of the car lot.

On occasion, Carlo bought an older trade in, never paying more than $100. He would clean it up, polish it, run a small ad in the paper, and sell it from the house, usually doubling his money. He did this on the average eight to ten times a month.

Joe and Josie had moved into the second floor over the liqueur store, and Jim and Virginia lived with Maria, and Joe over the grocery store. They had had a baby named Jimmy in September 1947.

In April, Josie asked for the floor at Sunday's luncheon and announced she was pregnant. Everyone gave her warm congratulations. She thanked them and said, "I am due in December or early January."

Jean said, "Well, Josie, I think I may have you beat! I went to the doctor Friday, and I am due in late November or early December!"

Jean was right; she delivered a baby girl on December 11. It was the first for her and Carlo, and they named her Donna Marie.

Chicago

At the end of May, Maria took Joe who was now twelve to Chicago to visit Martin and Virginia. They were picked up at Union Station, and Martin suggested they go out for dinner. The area around the station on Wabash was loaded with beautiful buildings, and Joe was amazed at the high-rises. They went to a restaurant on Randolph, a rare occasion for them.

Virginia and Martin lived on Magnolia and Addison close to Wrigley Field where the Chicago Cubs played. Joe disliked the Cubs. They were major rivals of the St. Louis Cardinals, his favorite baseball team. He was a rabid fan!

Martin asked, "Joe, would you like to go to a Cub's game? We can walk to the ballpark from here."

Joe politely said, "No, I hate the Cubs." Everyone laughed.

The next day, they drove to the north side to visit Martin's family. Martin's younger brother, Anthony, almost fifteen, shook hands with Joe. Anthony was tall and looked much older. He was already driving and had a great personality. Maria warmly greeted Martin's mom and dad with utmost respect. She had not seen them since their children married.

Anthony could see Joe was bored and said, "Joe, would you like to go with me? I am going to visit some of my friends."

"Sure, let's go. Am I dressed okay?" Anthony was dressed in a nice pair of slacks, a very nice shirt, and expensive loafers. He wore what looked to be very expensive aviator sunglasses.

"We are going to the neighborhood hangout. You're fine." It was an all-encompassing small grocery store, ice cream parlor, and sub shop called Ben's. All the guys and girls were really well-dressed, and Joe was somewhat embarrassed.

The group of friends greeted Anthony like he was a rock star!

Anthony introduced Joe, "This is my cousin from St. Louis."

The gang accepted him warmly, especially a boy who appeared to be Anthony's best friend, Jackie LaBrasca.

Joe was in awe of this group of people and their camaraderie. He stayed with the Maniscalcos the next two weeks and got to know the group well. He could not believe the way Anthony dressed. He always looked like he just stepped out of a fashion magazine with his slicked-back hair, wearing the best looking shoes and great sunglasses. Most of the other guys at the hangout emulated him.

The chicken store was a busy place for the weekend, and the cash flowed in. No credit cards in those days, and the Maniscalco's took no checks. It was all green!

On Mondays, Joe went with Anthony to the bank. He had a brown grocery bag full of money, but before going into the bank, he stuck his hand in the bag and helped himself to a few handfuls of the "badge!"

Maria decided after two weeks that it was time to get back to St. Louis, and they were taken back to the train station. After they were seated, Joe asked, "Mom, how come Anthony dresses like a movie star, and all I wear is T-shirts, blue jeans, and Keds?"

"Joe, his parents have a business where they make a lot of money, and they own a lot of buildings they rent, and we don't. I only get the $225 a month rent from the stores. Why don't you go see Sam Rumbolo at the store tomorrow, see if he will give you a job?"

On Monday morning, Joe was at the grocery store at seven and approached Sam and Carlo.

"Good morning, Sam! Hi, Carlo, I need a job. I used to help in the store. I can stock the shelves and sweep the floor, and I can deliver groceries with my wagon."

They both smiled. Carlo asked, "Joe, how old are you now?"

"I am twelve, but almost thirteen."

Sam said, "Okay, but what about school in fall?"

"I can work after school and on Saturdays."

He got the job. His pay was $0.25 an hour. He started saving his money and, from that day forward, never asked Maria for money for clothes.

In April, Jake Cunetto passed away, a sad day for the clan. St. Ambrose Church was filled to capacity, standing room only, seventy cars lined up to go to the cemetery. Afterward, the clan gathered at the Castellano's, but the usual joy of times past was absent. A silent mood prevailed, most aware that the Hill would never be the same! The clan lost its leader. It too would not be the same. The occasional feasts of the past would be a fond memory without Jake in the kitchen.

In July, Maria got a call from her cousin, Frank Insalaco. "Maria, I have some bad news. My brother, Joe, passed away this morning. He had a massive heart attack."

She had not seen Joe for a while. This was the second death in four months. The funeral was exactly the opposite of Jake's. Mostly family attended the wake and Church services, as well as the lunch at the VanCardo's after the cemetery.

In September, Joe was back in school, cutting his hours to twenty at Rumbolo's, $5 a week. He approached Brother Carlo. "Will you do me a favor? Call your buddy, Angelo Oldani, see if I can get a job at his restaurant."

Carlo made the call, and Joe got an interview for a busboy job. Angelo asked, "How old are you, Joe?"

Joe said, "I will be thirteen next month, Angelo, but don't hold that against me. Call Sam Rumbolo. He will tell you how hard I work. I need this job!"

Angelo smiled. "Sold! You get the job."

He began working Tuesdays and Thursdays, six to ten, and Fridays and Saturdays, six to twelve, another twenty hours at $0.25 an hour. In addition, the waitresses shared tips, usually his take was $15 to $18 a week counting tips. Thus, between the store and the restaurant, he worked forty hours and never earned less than $22! He became the best dressed kid on the Hill.

1949

On January 5, on a miserable cold Wednesday afternoon, Josie went into labor. She called the doctor's office and gave Mrs. Wilcox the news. Mrs. Wilcox said, "Head to the hospital, Josie, the doctor is there. Good luck. I'll call and have him paged."

Carlo drove her to St. Mary's hospital while Joe Mocca was at work. Dr. Wilcox was there and delivered a healthy baby boy! Josie named him Joseph after his dad, another Joe in the household.

When Joe got home that afternoon, Jean said, "Joe, go to the hospital. You have another son!" He was so excited he drove fifty miles an hour. When he arrived, he forgot to turn the motor off on the car, and it ran out of gas. He went in found Josie and gave her a big hug and met his son who from day one was called Jojo!

1950

Maria saw a rift between Joe and Virginia and Jim. She tried to keep everything calm and had many talks with them. The four rooms over the store were small, and tempers flared on occasion.

"Mom, Jim and Virginia are constantly on my back. No matter how I try, I am always wrong, and he never gives me a chance to talk. Why do we have to live with them?"

Maria said, "Your brother has a heart of gold. He means well. Let me see what I can do about the situation. Please try to be nice and respect him and his wife."

At the time, Joe and Josie were completing a new home in a fine middle-class neighborhood just a few blocks off the Hill. It was a nice four-room bungalow with a basement and two rooms on the second floor with a private entrance they intended to rent. Toward the end of the year, Maria approached John Porta, the contractor, about building the same house on the vacant land behind the grocery store.

John Porta told Maria, "I can build that house on your lot for $12,000."

"John, I have $6,000 in cash. Let me go to Riggio and see if I can get a loan, which she did and signed a contract to begin construction early the next year."

Joe graduated first in his class at Shaw School the end of January. He applied at Southwest High and was admitted and began classes ten days later. On February 7, Joe's birthday, John Porta broke ground on the new house, and in August, Maria and Joe moved into their new home. Maria had gone to Fair Merchantile and bought all new furniture, including a TV! Maria called the family together for lunch the first Sunday after they moved in. When everyone was seated, she stated, "Let's do this every Sunday." Everyone agreed. The luncheons were more like dinner. They continued on every major holiday.

As had been the norm, everyone brought their specialty: with Josie, it was pastry, the best cream puffs on the planet; Jean, a pie, usually cherry; and Virginia, Jim's wife, deviled eggs. The crowd grew every year, and soon it included Rosa and her family who would stop in on holidays. Carmelo was excluded! Once the store was sold, he moved to the basement under the liquor store and became very independent of the family for a long time.

In June, Jim went to work selling new Fords for Joe Simpkin's, the top Ford dealer in St. Louis. He rose to the top sales position in three months. He had a contact list of people he saved from his job at the appliance store. He also had the list of customers and phone numbers from the grocery store.

Joe finished his first semester at Southwest the first week of June. He left his two jobs and went to work at Sala's Restaurant, washing dishes for $2.50 a night. It was only for the summer. By the fall, he was working various positions and was on call by Charlie Sala, working almost every night, earning $7.50 a night, and some weeks, he made $40. He kept half his pay and gave the rest to Maria, as was the tradition.

1951

Virginia and Jim welcomed their second son on a cold snowy day, January 20. Virginia had a relatively easy pregnancy, and Dr. Wilcox delivered Thomas Charles Reina with no complications.

In February, an Italian used car dealer who bought older trade-ins at Simpkin's approached Jim one day. "Jim, I know a guy by the name of Tony Costello who has serious money and is looking for someone to start a business for him so he can establish a legitimate stature. He came to America illegally many years ago, made a lot of money, and wants to become a citizen."

Jim said, "Why are you approaching me?"

"Because you might know someone who may be interested in doing the deal with him. He will put up all the money. He wants to start a used-car business, put a few cars on a car lot, and allow the people running the business to operate independently with their own cars. He will pay all the expenses for two years!"

"Let me talk to my brother Carlo and see if he is interested. I'll get back to you. Have you got a phone number for this guy? Is he Mafia?" They both laughed.

The brothers decided to go for the deal after meeting with the used-car dealer and Tony Costello, but they had no money.

Jim sold his 1951 Ford for $1,100, and they went to see Maria. She said, "I don't have very much money. It went to build the new house. Let's go to Southwest Bank and see what we can do."

They met with the head of the commercial loan department and got a line of credit for $20,000 using the grocery store building as collateral. The same building Carlo had advised her not to buy!

As had been the case when she bought the first store, they started a business with no "money down!"

They found a lot in the 5800 Block of Easton Avenue in Wellston, a suburb of St. Louis. It was fifty feet by 125 feet with an old CCC building that dated to the depression. In early March, they hung a small sign, "Reina Auto Sales." Carlo purchased twenty cars for their lot and six for Tony for his business. Jim's responsibility was to keep the books for both businesses. Carlo spent the days scouring the new car agencies for used cars, and then at night, he would arrive around five to relieve Jim so he could have dinner. They both would sell at night. Carlo also would buy an occasional car for Tony when they sold one for him.

In the first ninety days, they sold twenty-two cars and showed a nice profit for their end of the business. This was because Tony was paying the overhead, while Jim and Carlo were drawing $100 a week in salary. They sold eight cars for Tony, and it paid a great deal of the expenses. He was pleased, the brothers were smart not to abuse the deal with Tony and kept the overhead low.

In early June, Joe finished school, and at the Sunday luncheon at Maria's, Jim said to him, "Be ready at eight tomorrow morning. You are going to start working at the used car lot."

Joe said, "But I have to work at Sala's."

"Tell Charlie Sala you can only work Friday and Saturday nights."

Joe had learned not to argue with him, saying to himself, "Someday it will be my turn!" He was fifteen and had a driver's license. The next morning, Joe was finishing a bowl of cereal. It was eight o' five, and Jim opened the door and yelled, "Let's go." He didn't even say good morning to Maria who was about to pour a cup of coffee for Joe.

The ride to Wellston was forty minutes, and Joe got both barrels about being late! "From now on, you be in the car at five to eight. Don't make me wait again."

Joe's job was to start every car every morning. Jim taught him how to use a battery charger in the event a car failed to start and how to detail new arrivals.

He also had to wash every car with a brush attached to a hose every day. At the end of the day, on Saturday, Jim handed him his first paycheck, $75! Joe thanked him, drove home, and gave the check to Maria along with a kiss. Then he went to work at Sala's. He was a sous chef at this time, making $14.50 a night.

Joe worked hard in the hot St. Louis sun and dealt with the humidity all summer. Sometimes traveling to pick up cars Carlo had purchased, he would get great advice about life.

"Joe, never burn bridges behind you. You never know when you will have to cross them again. When you are negotiating a deal, always leave a little on the table, put yourself in the other guy's shoes, be fair, and don't get greedy, and you will make the deal. Always go down a two-way street with everyone, and you will be successful in what you do in life. I know you like to make money but don't let it drive you. If you make it big time, never forget where you came from. You will always be a kid form the Hill, even if you're wearing a tuxedo. Remember when you had patches on your jeans!" These daily messages from Carlo became indelible in Joe's mind.

CHAPTER 19

1952
No Money Down

Carlo and Jim inherited Maria's entrepreneurial instincts. Carlo had become a skilled buyer. His warm personality earned him respect among the new car dealers all over the city. Jim was making great strides with the major high interest finance companies and gaining their respect. Their business was doing far better than they expected.

One day, in April, a full-page ad appeared in the *St. Louis Post-Dispatch* newspaper, "No money down," and listed sixty late model autos! The dealer was J. C. Auffenberg. Jim knew the general manager, Jerry Stein, from the Joe Simpkin's days. He had helped Jerry get his job there and trained him. They were great friends. Jim would often help him close deals. Whenever he saw Jerry was about to lose a customer, he would step in and make the deal. He never asked for part of the commission.

Jim and Carlo were astounded when they saw the ad! Jim called Jerry and inquired about the ad.

Stein said, "I can't discuss it on the phone." They agreed to have lunch the next day.

During World War II, the federal government passed many laws to stem inflation. One of them was regulation W, which required a third down payment of the selling price on anything purchased on credit. There was a term limit to pay the loan, originally twelve months later extended to twenty-four. That regulation was still in effect in most states.

Jim, Carlo, and Jerry met for lunch at Sala's. Jerry was dressed in a fine Boyd's Threadneedle Street suit and in a beautiful Arrow collar man shirt, a silk necktie with a colorful handkerchief. His brown Italian calfskin shoes set off the outfit. There was no doubt Jerry had arrived! He was making more money than he ever dreamed of. He was always very respectful of Jim and never forgot the lessons he learned from him at Simpkin's.

Soon after they ordered lunch, Jim was first to speak. "Stein, you owe me. What's the story?"

"I can lose my job if this gets out. Here is how it works. We take the buyer to a small loan company and get him a loan up to $400 [that was the maximum the small loan company could loan for twenty-four months]. Once the credit is approved, he and his wife use their furniture for collateral. They both sign the note. Then he can buy a car with a price tag up to $1,200, and we finance the $800 balance through one of the finance companies. He has to make two payments, and it is as simple as that! We also sell him insurance, and we receive a commission on that from the insurance company. We have a clause in the sales contract that stipulates the finance company insists on the insurance."

Jim and Carlo bought lunch, thanked him, went immediately back to the lot, and came up with their own plan.

Carlo suggested, "Let's take that 1941 Chevy I bought yesterday and run a small ad on it, just a four-line ad at $395. We can't afford a full-page ad. We then take the customer to the small loan company and finance the entire selling price."

Jim ran the ad the very next day. "1941 Chevrolet, $395, no money down, twenty-four payments at $28 a month."

The phone started ringing nonstop! The car sold the same day, and customers were calling and coming in, looking for the car the rest of the week. After telling the customers the Chevy had been sold, they bounced them from one car to another and ended up doing the "switch" as planned. Jim never called the newspaper to cancel the ad. It ran for the next two years! Carlo started buying all pre-World

War II autos, eight and ten at a time, never paying more than $150 for a car. There was one standard selling price $395! The "no money down" philosophy was a reminder that Maria bought the first store that way. They started their company with "no money down," and once again, the term launched what began as a small business to selling sixty to seventy cars a month!

That summer, when school let out, Joe went from being the porter on the lot to selling. He worked from eight in the morning until nine every day, except Saturday. There were two other salesmen working split shifts. Both had regular jobs and families.

Neither were putting in the hours Joe was. They were all working on straight commission.

The first week, Joe sold three cars and earned $288! He earned more than the other two combined. He gave the check to Maria, and she gave him $50 for spending money. His success continued the rest of the month of June.

One night on the drive home, Jim said, "Joe, I am having trouble with the other two salesmen. They say you are grabbing all the customers. They have families to support. Soon you will be back in school, and I need to keep them happy. I want you to allow them to take first choice of customers, those calling and inquiring about the ads we are running and those walking on the lot. So when three people are looking around, let them take the first two, you take the third."

"That's bullshit, Jim! We are supposed to take turns, and we do! I am selling more cars because I am a better salesman than they are! I work twice as many hours as they do. You don't understand. Whenever you or Carlo are away, Jerry goes to the tavern down the street, drinks beers, and plays the pinball machine! The other guy, Bob, sits and reads the sports page most the time and qualifies customers and sends me out to talk to those he believes do not qualify. Bob is not a good closer. How many times have you had to go in and finish the job with his customers? I am not going to do it." At age sixteen, Joe finally stood up to Jim.

Later that week, Carlo had a talk with Joe and was more diplomatic. "Joe, do me a favor. I need your help, please try to step back and allow the other two guys some advantage when it comes to waiting on people. You can sell better than them. Jim and I know that. You will still make a lot of money this summer. Will you do that for me?"

"For you, Carlo, I will do it, but it is not fair. You know I don't take advantage of those guys. They have regular jobs and are making money. This is all I have, and I work on straight commission. They work six hours a day. I am putting in thirteen. I start every car every day, and I pick up many of the cars you buy, which takes me away from the lot to sell!"

Joe did what he promised and still outsold the other two!

In June, the family gathered for Father's Day at Carlo and Jean's new house for the weekly luncheon. They had bought a house as had Virginia and Jim in a beautiful new subdivision and paid cash for it, $15,000! Carlo was so tainted by the depression. He never would have any kind of a loan on anything his entire life. Just before the food was served, Jean made an announcement. She was going to have a baby sometime in February. Virginia smiled as she and Jean had planned and said, "Jim and I are going to have a baby too. Ours is due in March!"

Everyone got up and hugged them. Maria said, "These two will be boys."

On February 17, 1953, Jean delivered a baby boy and named him Carlo after his father. And on March 1, Dr. Wilcox delivered Richard Lee Reina for Virginia and Jim.

1954

In January, Joe graduated from Southwest High and went to work for the brother's full-time. He had learned a lot the previous summers from both of them. Because financing and auto insurance were intertwined with selling an automobile, he became very adept at explaining to customers how the no money down policy worked. He had a knack for getting the customer's confidence by looking the person in the eye when making his pitch. He was always dressed for success, and his confidence and honesty preceded any sales pitch. While the money was good, he hated the hours and had already determined he was not going to be a used-car salesman the rest of his life.

One hot miserable day in August, a man walked on the lot in filthy mud-covered bib overalls, the same mud caked his work boots. Joe, with a white shirt and tie, approached him. It was one hundred degrees and the same degree of humidity.

"Hi, how are you today. My name is Joe. What's your name, sir?"

"My name is Al Jones. I saw your ad in the paper, and I would like to look at some of your cars."

The beads of perspiration were running down Joe's back. His white shirt was already soaked. The customer landed on a nice 1953 navy blue and white four-door Chevrolet. He asked Joe, "Can you crank it up for me?"

Joe got in and started it. It was 120 degrees inside the car.

Next, the man asked, "Can you open up the hood so I can see the motor?" The heat was stifling. The price of the car was placed on the windshield, $1,395. Al asked, "How come there ain't no radio?"

Joe responded, "We can put a radio in for you, or I can sell the car to you for $1,325."

Joe was losing his patience, and he didn't have much in the way of patience to begin with. Al was walking around the car and kicking the tires and checking for scratches. He asked Joe to open the trunk, which he did. "Al, are you ready to buy this car today?"

Al could see Joe was getting irritable and said, "No, I need to talk to my wife first, but can we go for a ride?" The car was parked in a difficult to reach corner facing the street, and in order to back it out, three cars parked behind needed to be moved. All Joe could think of was how hot it would be to get in and move them. "Al, why don't you go home and speak to your wife about the car and come back later, and I will take you for a ride?"

He agreed. "I will be back."

When Joe walked back into the nice air-conditioned office, Jim asked, "Well, what happened? You were with that black guy a long time."

Joe responded, "He doesn't have two nickels to rub together."

"Oh, so what are you, superman? Since when did you get X-ray vision? You could look in his pockets and see he had no money, into his billfold and know it was empty?"

"Jim, he was full of mud and wanted me to move that '53 Chevy, and it is hot out there. Besides he said he had to talk to his wife and said he would be back."

"I see, so you have been selling for such a long time now that you can qualify a customer by the way he is dressed? Did you ever think that maybe he just got off work, that possibly he works construction? Get it in your head. I don't want 'be backs' big shot! I want green backs. Have you ever tried going to the bank and deposit 'be backs?'"

Once again, Joe was humiliated. He could never do anything right in Jim's eyes. He thought, *I pray to God the guy comes back and buys that car.*

About six thirty that evening, Al Jones came walking on the lot. He still was wearing the same bib overalls. The evening had cooled off considerably, and Jim saw him first and alerted Joe. "There's your customer superman, go out there and don't blow it. He is back to buy that car."

Joe greeted him warmly and treated him with an entirely different approach. They moved the other cars and went for a short drive. When they returned, Joe asked, "Al, are you ready to buy this car?"

He received a nod. "Come inside, it is nice and cool, and I will take a credit statement from you," assuming he had seen the no money down ad in the paper and wanted to finance the car.

Al said, "Why do you need a statement?"

"I am paying cash for the car."

When they walked in the office, Jim greeted Al like he was his best friend. Al started reaching in his pockets, even took his boots off at one point, and pulled money out. He peeled off $1,325 in somewhat discolored greenbacks. Joe filled out the bill of sale, and he and Al moved back outside. They shook hands, and he drove off. Once Joe had him on his way, he braced himself for the second lesson he was about to receive from his older brother.

The minute he walked in the door, Jim let him have it! It was like getting hit by a direct bolt of lightning. There was no let up, and that night, the onslaught continued. He got it on the drive all the way home. He decided this was enough. He could no longer work with Jim. When he walked in the door, he told Maria what had happened. She never took sides and said, "Do what you need to do." He went to see Carlo before he left the next morning and gave him the news. He was resigning.

In September, he answered an ad for a job with the New Era Shirt Company located on Washington Boulevard. He entered a building at 1718 Washington and went to the eighth floor and into the showroom.

A gentleman greeted Joe, extended his hand, and said, "Hi, Ray Konold."

"Good morning, my name is Joe Reina. I saw your ad in the paper. I am looking for a job."

"We don't have an ad in the paper. Are you sure you are in the right place?"

"Is this the New Era Shirt Company?"

"No, this is the Arrow Shirt company, but we have an opening. It is a starting position in the office."

They sat down, and Ray explained the history of the firm, the company philosophy about starting at the bottom, and working your way up for every position. After being interviewed by the office manager and two sales managers, he got the job, starting immediately for $208 a month as the mail and file clerk.

At Sunday's luncheon in Maria's basement, Carlo asked about the job, "How much are they paying you?"

Joe was not about to hold back and dropped the number.

Jim responded, "You can make that selling one car a month. You were making more when you were fifteen years old as the porter! What are you thinking?"

Joe didn't respond. Once again, he thought to himself, *Someday it will be my turn.*

1957, Maria's Travels

Joe made major advancements since starting at the Arrow company. He was in charge of the mail and phone order desk for the entire Midwest. His salary had peaked at $250 a month.

In late summer, at the end of the day, he approached Ray Konold. "Ray, I am getting bored. I took this job with the idea in mind that someday, I could get a territory and sell and make some money."

"Joe, we are very happy with your work. You have an incredible work ethic, but you are going to have to get your military responsibility out of the way before we can put you on the road."

There were options for that obligation: two years of active duty, four years in the reserves, or six months active duty and five and a half years in the reserves. Later that month, Joe again met with Ray and informed him he had joined the army reserves and would be going on active duty in April 1958. Joe spent six months in the army and was released in October 1958.

1959

In April, Maria received a call from Vincenzo Riggio. "Buongiorno, Maria, I have people in my office who are interested in buying your house on Hereford. Would you like to meet them?"

"I have not thought about selling, Vincenzo, but if the price is right, I'd consider it. Why don't you send them down to see me?"

When the people arrived, Maria greeted them and was surprised they were from Palozzo Adriano, Mr. Riggio's hometown, and spoke the same dialect. After touring the house, they asked if she had a price in mind, and without hesitation, she said yes, $27,500! They told her, "Let us think about it."

The following Saturday, Vincenzo called her again and informed her that they had agreed to the price, and he was doing the loan for them, and they could close in sixty days.

In June, the deal closed. Maria had already purchased a two flat at 6232 Arsenal for $22,000, a block from Josie's house. Shortly after Maria moved to the new house, she left for Sicily to visit her family, the first time since arriving in the US. She stayed for three months. The move ended the Sunday *festas* in Maria's basement. Josie volunteered to take over, but in the exchange, the family mutually agreed to celebrate holidays, instead of every Sunday.

1960

In January, Joe went to visit Arrow. He was greeted by Bud Colley, the sales manager for the Midwest and southwest. "Hi, Joe Reina, look at you, all grown-up! What have you been up to?" Joe was in a brand-new suit, very well coordinated, even an Arrow shirt and Arrow tie, he had a dress hat on when he walked in the door and was the picture of the Arrow collar man.

"Good morning, Mr. Colley, it's been a while. I finished my military obligation in '58, and I just left school after two semesters at Mizzou. I am ready to go to work for you."

"We have been wondering what happened to you. We are closing this office at the end of the month and moving the warehouse operation to Chicago and the sales office to Dallas. Are you willing to move to Dallas to start training?"

"Bud, I will go wherever you want to send me!"

"Good. Go home, get all your personal things wrapped up, and report to the new Dallas office on the sixteenth."

Joe was in Dallas the twelfth and rented an apartment, signing a month-to-month lease. He reported to the office bright and early Monday morning. He met with Dan Stoll, the Dallas salesman, and Bud Colley and learned that his training program included being on the road with various salesmen every other week.

In April, he was awarded his first territory and transferred to Amarillo, Texas. The former salesman had been fired. There were no records, but he had a computer printout that listed the sixty-five accounts in the territory, which included southwest Kansas, Western Oklahoma, the northern half of New Mexico, a small strip along the state line of Colorado, and, of course, the panhandle of Texas, a nightmare to travel! His monthly draw was $500 a month against commission, plus the company-shared expenses. The former salesman purposely avoided any information on the territory, the names of buyers, or phone numbers and addresses.

For the next six months, Joe stayed on the road and visited every single one of the sixty-five dealers on the printout. In August, he finally rented an apartment and one day took his dry cleaning to a neighborhood shop and met the owner's daughter, Katie Kelly.

Shortly after they met, he started dating Katie, and Joe was smitten in a matter of weeks. "Katie, I love being with you. This relationship is getting to me. I know it has happened quickly, and I am not trying to rush anything, but I need to know, is it just me or are you feeling the same?"

"Joe, I am very fond of you. I love being with you too, but I am not in a hurry to get serious at this point. I am only eighteen, and I enjoy my freedom, so let's just take it one day at a time and let nature take its course. I am not seeing anyone else, nor do I care to. I am happy being with you, and you have no worry about anyone else stepping into my life, so let's just have fun and enjoy each other's company."

By fall, they were seeing each other every evening when he was in town, and the romance blossomed. Katie would grab Joe every time he walked into the cleaners and pull him into the curtained dressing room and hug and kiss him. "I need my Joe Reina fix!"

On Christmas Eve, they went to Eveleno's Italian Bistrot, and Sam Eveleno brought a bottle of champagne to the table following Joe's earlier phone call, and Joe proposed. They married in 1961. They spent their honeymoon in California. Later that year, on November 27, they had their first child, a beautiful baby girl they named Kelly. Joe didn't have a lot of money, and he worked a Maria Reina bargaining deal and paid the doctor's bill, $150 with Arrow samples!

1962

Joe's work ethic and personality quickly earned him the respect and dignity of his accounts, and by the end of the second year in the territory, he rose to the top of the list of the seventeen salesman in Bud Colley's sales group. He was determined to get promoted from Amarillo to a major city. He was spending forty weeks a year on the road and was not spending the kind of quality time he desired with his family. In May, Katie informed Joe she was pregnant. The baby was expected in late November or early December, and on the first day of December 1962, Katie delivered Michael Reina, a handsome little boy!

1964

The Arrow company made major sales management changes. In January, Bud Colley moved to San Francisco as regional sales manager, and Leigh Silliphant took Bud's place as regional in Dallas.

Leigh traveled with Joe the first week of February for five days and watched him perform. At dinner, on Thursday, he said, "Joe, the company is wasting your time and talent in this territory, I am getting you out of here!"

In June, Joe got the call he'd been dreaming of for four years.

"Hi, Joe, it's Leigh, you are being transferred to Chicago as account executive for three of the major stores. Your traveling days are over. Report to Bryan Wardell at the Chicago office a week from Monday!"

Left to right: Donna Maria Reina, Carlo Reina,
Jojo Mocca and Jimmy Reina, 1954

CHAPTER 20

1964
Joe Reina

J oe flew into Midway airport on a warm Saturday in June and was greeted by Virginia and Martin. He and Virginia hugged, her with a single tear running down her cheek. She had trouble containing the joy of seeing her baby brother.

"I am so proud of you. I still cannot believe you are moving here. Of all the big cities in this country for a promotion, thank God they picked Chicago."

"Virginia, I have wanted to live here ever since Mom and I came to visit you in 1948!"

The next day, Joe met with Bryan Wardell and Jerry Lissner, the district sales manager and Joe's new boss.

Bryan took the lead. "Joe, outside of white shirts, we are doing very little business with the three accounts you will be handling, no other furnishings, no sportswear. Your work is cut out for you!" The accounts were discussed at length, buyer's names, and personalities, information about management, and revenue from each of the stores. It was agreed Joe and his family would officially take over after the fourth of July. He returned to Amarillo to work with the two sales-men taking over his territory. In July, the family drove to Chicago and moved into a small two-bedroom house down the street from Virginia. On weekends, Katie and Joe looked at homes to purchase.

They had sticker shock! Home costs by comparison to what they had in Amarillo were four times higher.

Katie was concerned. "How are we ever go to be able to afford living here?"

Joe assured her, "We will be fine. Let's not panic. I will not know my earnings for next year until we get final shipping figures for both my old territory and the new one."

In August, they met a contractor, Lloyd churchman, who came highly recommended. They had purchased a lot in a nice wooded area in the northwest suburbs. The contractor showed them plans of a home he had built in another town. They approved them. He started building a new home for them in October.

Josie and Joe Mocca hosted Thanksgiving in November. Everyone was asked to arrive at two. Katie and Joe and the kids were the first to arrive. Kelly jumped in Josie's arms. "Hi, Aunt Josie, are we having turkey?"

"Yes, Kelly, and many other things."

Michael was next; he gave Josie a hug and a kiss. Joe and Katie exchanged hugs with Joe Mocca. Soon the family groups wandered in, and the feast commenced. Josie was right; the "many other things" consisted of ravioli, an incredible roasted prime rib, a turkey, and all the contributions by the other woman in the family.

1965

Katie and Joe visited the new house under construction every weekend and loved the progress. They started picking finishes with the contractor who had warmed up from the earlier meetings. He was halfway finished with the house and had not asked for any money. Joe had made arrangements for a loan, and everything was in order. But there were a few things that became extras, and there was no way to know the costs until the building was complete. It later necessitated borrowing the money from Virginia and Carlo.

Joe had a very successful holiday season with the three stores and increased the business nearly 20 percent. He was in the branch stores of the three accounts seven days a week from the middle of

November until Christmas Eve, and the department managers showed tremendous respect for him.

At the end of March, after the kids went to bed, Katie and Joe were finishing their wine. Katie said, "Well, Mr. Reina, I have some news to share with you. I went to the doctor today, and you are going to be a father again."

"You have to be kidding! When?"

"I am due sometime in September. Hopefully we will be in the new house by then!"

On September 18, 1965, Katie delivered her and Joe's third child, Kristen, with no complications, and when she came home from the hospital, Kelly and Michael hugged their baby sister and greeted her with joy.

In August, Bryan called Joe into his office. "Joe, I have the pleasure of informing you that you are part of a major plan the company is doing here in the Midwest region. We are reducing the workload for the sales managers and cutting the number of territories they will be handling, and you will be the new district manager for the Chicago area."

Joe was lost for words. He could not believe what he just heard. The Chicago district sales revenue was second only to Manhattan. He got up and shook Bryan's hand.

His heart was racing. He called Katie and some of his fellow salesman friends across the country and announced the news. He called Phil Black who was his former trainee in Amarillo. Phil had worked his way up in the merchandise and design department in New York. He was vice president of merchandising.

"Hi, Phil, I have just been named district manager for Chicago and the Midwest!"

"Congratulations, Joe! Wow! I have an idea I have been thinking about for some time. Would you be willing to become a liaison between the sales department and merchandising? It would require being in New York once a month for a few days and working with my people on product development."

"Of course, but you better clear it with Wardell and Bob Pritchard."

"That will not be a problem. Let me go to work on it."

While Joe was being honored for his hard work and success, things were not going well at home with Katie. They were arguing and having difficulty getting along, and it was affecting the children. They sought the help of a marriage counselor, and the boat stopped rocking for a short while, but by December of 1970, it reached a point where they agreed to divorce, mostly out of respect to the kids.

In April of 1971, they officially split. Joe received joint custody of the children on the weekends, when they were five, eight, and nine. He had them every Friday after school, until eight on Sunday night.

The house was to be sold and the equity to be split evenly, estimated to be about $12,500 each. Katie was awarded 30 percent of Joe's net income. Joe moved out of the house; it was agreed Katie could stay in the house until school was finished the first week of June.

The custody provision with the children began the first weekend in May. After the second weekend with the kids, Joe decided to buy the house. He called Virginia who was living in St. Louis; she had moved there the previous summer. Martin had passed away, and she elected to move back to be close to Maria and the rest of the family.

"Good morning, Virginia, I need a big favor. I have elected to buy Katie's equity in the house, and I need to borrow some money. I am willing to pay you the same interest you are getting at the bank."

"Joe, I have $15,000, and you can have it, and don't even think of paying any interest, I am fine. I am working at General American Insurance with Josie, and I don't need the interest!"

"Virginia, I don't know when I will be able to pay you back, but rest assured you will get your money."

"Don't worry about it."

In June, Joe and the kids went to St. Louis for the weekend. Katie moved out of the house, and on Sunday, Joe and the kids and Maria drove to the house from St. Louis.

He noticed Maria's luggage was very heavy and commented on it when he carried it to the second bedroom. "Mom, what's in this bag?"

She opened it and brought out four loaves of her bread, four bags of frozen ravioli, four bags of homemade pasta, and four jars of home-canned tomato sauce! He and the kids all laughed, they all hugged, and no one noticed the tears in Joe's eyes. Things settled in, the kids as part of the custody agreement spent six weeks with Joe and their grandmother who was seventy-eight, but she had the energy of a fifty-year-old.

1972

Joe was making good money, but his take-home pay after taxes was depleted by the same overhead he had when he and Katie were married. She was getting her monthly checks, leaving nothing for anything extra. In November, two of his Chicago salesmen came to him with a problem.

Jim Giannini said, "We are stuck with over $20,000 worth of samples, and we can't sell them. The company's closeouts and over-run prices are cheaper than our sample prices. If we don't sell them, they will deduct the sample debt from our commissions at the end of December! We will not get a check after working an entire year! We want to have a sample sale starting the day after Thanksgiving. As you know, there are stores on the first floor of my condo building, and one is vacant. We can have the sale there. I have spoken to the building manager, and we can use the store for $100."

Joe responded, "Jim, we have $50 million in sales with the five major stores on State Street, and there will be complaints from the stores about selling Arrow products at discounted prices! I am the one who will have to handle the heat. At this time, there were no Marshall's or any outlet stores in the Midwest. "I am going to New York tomorrow."

Let me speak to Pritchard, and I will discuss it with him." Joe knew Wardell would never allow it. He was black or white, no gray, and this was gray!

Bryan spent a great deal of the winter in California, avoiding the Chicago winters, which was where he was at the time.

Joe went to Bob Pritchard the minute he arrived at the office. He was now staying at Bob's home on his monthly trips to New York.

"Bob, we have a problem with the salesman's sample charges and explained the request by Giannini."

"Joe, go ahead and do it. In fact, since all of the samples are mediums, call Vince Ferretti, tell him to ship you larges and extra larges from the closeouts we have in each category, but I want you to take responsibility for payment and overlook what they do to insure there's no repercussions with the main stores."

Joe joined them and ordered the merchandise to round out the samples. The night before Thanksgiving, the trio went up and down the apartment buildings along Lake Shore Drive and Sheridan Road, putting out circulars announcing the 3-day sale. It was bitter cold. The temperature was slightly above zero! They posted more than two thousand circulars. On Friday, the people were waiting for them to open. They were lined up through the lobby and out the door. It was madness when they allowed them to come in. Jim and the other salesman's wives, Joe, his girlfriend, and three kids worked nonstop until nine thirty, serving customers!

The traffic continued for the next two days. There was one hitch. Joe had ordered two hundred dozen ties, and they were to arrive at the Arrow office on Tuesday but failed to show and finally were delivered at 2:00 p.m., Sunday. He paid $18 a dozen and sold them to one of the large stores on Monday for $24! When the final customer left on Sunday, they totaled the sales and inventoried what was left. Joe took charge of disposing of it. When the sand settled, he sold everything off in the next two days, and they netted a profit of $3,000 each. The two salesmen received their money for their samples.

1973

Joe's financial woes continued with the family living week to week. Katie had taken 90 percent of the furniture, including the washer and dryer. Joe took Kelly to the laundromat on Saturday mornings and taught her what to do while he ran to the grocery store. Kelly knew what went in the dryer and what to fold and put back in the hamper. She took charge and made the beds when they returned while he prepared lunch for her, Kris, and Mike. At age nine, Joe was reminded of Virginia's role for the family at the same age!

In October, Giannini again approached Joe about them having the sale. Joe said, "I am going to go see the other apparel brands on the floor and see if we can get their samples on consignment for the weekend. It will attract more people if we have pants and jackets and more national brands in the circulars we put out."

The '73 sale was colossal, sales more than tripled, and they more than tripled their take.

The snow started falling on and off every day in early December. Joe took a week off and flew to St. Thomas for a well-earned vacation. From there, he flew to St. Louis, and on Christmas Eve, he showed up at Carlo and Jeans house. Jojo, Josie's son, approached him. They had been close since he was a little boy, closer than any of the other grandkids. Jojo spent two summers as an intern working with Joe at Arrow and also helped in December in '68 and '69.

"Uncle Joe, how you doing man? I heard about your big score. That sale sounds so cool!"

Joe smiled. It was obvious Jojo had ingested some "Mary Jane" (weed). Jojo would have been a perfect fit for a Jesus movie as the main character. His beard was nearly down to his waste, and his hair was so long it nearly reached his hips. This was a description of most men in their twenties in the seventies. The description had nothing to do with Jojo's mentality. He was a very bright young man with a master's degree. This was the tail end of the Vietnam war. The protests of the sixties and early seventies had worked, and congress was questioning the military's decisions on handling things and the lack of progress in ending it.

"Let's open a store and feature off price apparel! You have all the connections to buy overruns and closeouts. I can run it."

Joe laughed. "JoJo, you will scare the customers with that beard and hair."

"I will trim my beard and cut my hair. Come on, Uncle Joe, we talked about this when I was a kid!"

Joe could not help but remember Maria's trip to the pasta factory and buying the loose pasta overruns at discounted prices. "Okay,

Jojo, you do that and drive up to Chicago, and I will consider it. Do you have any money?"

"Yes, I have $2,500, I am willing to put in."

It was time for the feast Jean and Carlo always prepared. "Pork bread," jumbo shrimp, ravioli, breaded veal cutlets, and bowls of fruit that were as sweet as sugar.

1974

JoJo was on the phone with Joe right after New Year's Day. "Uncle Joe, I am heading to Chicago this weekend. Let's go find an empty store." He arrived with his girlfriend, Tommy, and Jimmy Reina, and to Joe's surprise, he had cut his hair dramatically, same on the beard.

Bryan Wardell was in California in mid-January, and Joe was in the New York office for his monthly meeting with merchandising. At the end of the day, he and Bob Pritchard were on the train heading to Bob's house, and as usual, they had a drink. When they arrived, Bob's wife, Jackie, gave Joe a hug and a kiss. She had suggested to Bob they go out for dinner. Joe opened his luggage and brought out a loaf of Maria's bread, a jar of her tomato sauce, and a bag of her homemade Ravioli and said, "It is my turn to cook, Jackie."

Bob opened a nice bottle of wine, and after dinner while Jackie was doing the dishes, Joe asked Bob, "Do you remember my nephew, Joe Mocca? He interned with us for a couple of summers?"

"Sure, nice kid, I thought you were going to hire him."

"Bob, he just doesn't feel he is cut out for a career with a big corporation. He wants to come to Chicago and open an outlet store. Would you object to me putting money in the deal and helping him get started?"

Bob was well aware of Joe's financial struggles. He also was very respectful of Joe's dedication to his three kids and spending every weekend with them.

"Joe, help him and let him do it, but open the store in an area that does not conflict with stores we sell in the same neighborhood." Maria's bread and ravioli once again served like the magic of the "badge."

Late that month, Joe got a call. Carmelo, who had been living in a state-sponsored nursing facility, had passed away, and he and Jojo drove to St. Louis for the funeral. Maria, out of respect to the family, attended both the wake and the cemetery for his final resting place. The family all wondered what she was thinking throughout the entire affair.

In early February, Joe and Jojo found a store in Wheeling, Illinois, nowhere near a regular-priced clothing store. It was in a strip center, a short distance from a Sears outlet store. It was 2,500 square feet. The center was on the corner of a major intersection with plenty of parking. They met with the owner of the shopping center and cut a deal on a lease. There was a lingering problem, Bryan Wardell.

On Monday, Bryan was back in town, tan from his three weeks in California, and at his desk with pink slips scattered all over it. Joe walked in. "Good morning, Bryan, what are all those papers?"

"I sold a beach house that belonged to my brother who passed away last year, and I have a tax problem. Those are all stock sales I sold. I lost money on them to offset the gain."

Joe rose from his chair and closed the door. "I am going to show you how to make back all the money you lost and then some!"

"Reina, what are you up to?"

"Bryan, you and I and my nephew, Joe Mocca, are going to open the first branded apparel outlet store in the Midwest!"

"And how do you propose to get it past Pritchard?"

"I already have his blessings. It is a done deal!"

Joe Reina, 1970   Carmelo Reina, 1974

CHAPTER 21

1974
Midwest Outpost

"Bryan, I have found a store in Wheeling. That's perfect!"

"Joe, are you sure Pritchard is agreeable to this?"

"One hundred percent sure!"

"Let's go look at the store, Joe."

The two met with Jojo, Tommy, and Jimmy who had started building tables and renovating old store fixtures they had salvaged from one of Joe's accounts that had closed in Milwaukee.

Bryan, Joe, and Jojo took a break and went for coffee and discussed the business plan. First, they threw around names, and it was decided to call the store Midwest Outpost.

Bryan asked, "Joe, how much money do we need?"

"Bryan, Jojo has $2.500, and I am going to St. Louis on Friday to get $10,000. Can you come up with the same? I'd like to do the partnership, one-third each. Jojo will run the store. I'll be there on weekends, and he is willing to work for $200 a week."

Bryan replied, "I can come up with the ten thousand. When do you plan to open?"

Jojo piped in, "We will be open by mid-March!"

Joe called Maria to say he was coming to St. Louis and needed to go to Southwest Bank. On Friday afternoon, Maria and Joe met with Charlie Henemeyer, and Joe signed a note for $10,000. For the third time, the grocery store building was used start a business with no money down!

The Outpost opened on March 22 and did more business than was expected. But business slowed soon after. The first three months was not producing the sales they had planned; the partners were not discouraged. People were coming from all over the state, having heard of the store by word of mouth. They were told, "Please tell a friend," Jojo's idea.

Joe was experiencing some difficulty getting some of the desired brands to sell to them. They were afraid of their product being discounted.

In May, a young realtor approached Joe and Jojo about an addition to a shopping center in Morton Grove, a suburb north of Chicago. He made a great offer on a lease for 2,500 square feet. The next day, Bryan stopped by, and the three of them discussed the opportunity.

Bryan said, "Joe, if you and Jojo want to do it, you have my blessings. Go for it!"

Joe met with the realtor the following week. "Irv, we are just starting out, and I need a few concessions, first three months' free rent and a construction allowance of $5,000 to build the store. If you can make that happen, we will sign a five-year lease."

The realtor replied, "I know I can make that happen. I will prepare the lease, plan on moving in August 1."

In the early part of spring, Richard "Ricky", Virginia and Jim's son was diagnosed with lymphoma! In August, an operation was performed on his lymph glands under his right arm. He spent many months in and out of the hospital the rest of the year.

Joe and Jojo began buying for the new store immediately as they had only sixty days to get in the merchandise. The timing was perfect; the brands were moving their year-end closeouts. Then in early July, disaster happened, a concrete strike. Jojo got a call from the realtor. The store opening would be delayed at least a month since everything hinged on ending the strike. The one month went to three, and finally the grand opening was pushed to February.

In late July, Jojo called. "Uncle Joe, we are out of room. We need to move some of this inventory. I am going to rent a storage locker, and maybe we can put some in your garage." Soon the locker was jammed as was Joe's garage and basement.

In September, JoJo called again. "Uncle Joe, I have a problem. I am sitting on $70,000 in bills and have $22,000 in the bank!" Joe went to see Bryan with the news.

Bryan said, "Let's not panic. Have Jojo bring the bills and let's start calling people and explain what happened and set up a payment plan."

The store had been averaging between $12,000 and $15,000 a month, and in September, business picked up with a little over $30,000, and in October, over $50,000! Jojo had emptied the locker and was making trips to Joe's house every other day for merchandise!

On the Saturday, before Thanksgiving, Jojo decided to go to St. Louis. "Uncle Joe, I am going home to get young Carlo Reina. We need to get him up here and make him a partner and have him run the Morton Grove store."

Bryan, Joe, and Jojo could not believe what was happening. Jojo, making note of every check people were writing, showed they were coming from all over the state and also from Wisconsin. When December ended, Bryan who had been keeping record of monthly sales shocked Joe and Jojo with the final numbers for the year— $351,796! The store showed a profit of $151,323!

1975

The Morton Grove store opened on time in February as planned, and young Carlo Reina took over as manager. Jojo and Joe each gave him 5 percent of their stock and made him a partner. Business took off from day one. People coming into the store could not believe the prices and merchandise selection. Joe was having much better luck with the brands, and it showed in the selection.

In February, Bryan called Joe and said, "I am in California, and I think Jojo should fly out and meet me and attend the 'Magic' clothing trade show next week." Jojo met him the following week and returned three days later.

"Uncle Joe, we went to Brittania Jeans, and the place was mobbed!"

"They wouldn't even allow us into the show booths. It was by appointment only. You have to get that jean line for us!"

Joe laughed. "Jojo, it is the hottest line in the country. They aren't going to sell us. They don't need an outlet store."

That month, construction started on the Wheeling store renovation, which included taking the adjacent store and doubling the size. The same contractor who built Joe's house did the work. The revenue each month was triple the previous year's numbers.

Jojo had gotten involved with a young lady, Addie Mostek, who began working at the Wheeling store as assistant manager. She was a fireball, great with customers, and the employees. She became a real asset to the firm.

Joe was spending more and more time buying. He had had gotten very close to a sales team in the Merchandise Mart, Jerry Arbetman and Ira Goldberg. They sold the premier jean and sweater lines and had vouched for Joe when there was any question about credibility or the ability to pay for merchandise they sold him for the store.

Joe was at the office late one evening, catching up on paperwork, and the phone rang at seven thirty.

"Hi, is Joe Reina there?"

"This is Joe Reina. Can I help you?"

"Yes, my name is Dan Prentice with Brittania jeans."

Joe nearly dropped the phone! "Hi, Dan, how did you get my name?"

"My boss knows your boss, and we have heard of your store."

"How can I help you, Dan?"

"I have some consumer returns. I need to move."

"You mean worn jeans?"

"Yes, some are really bad, some need a zipper or a button and are not too bad."

"Dan, I don't buy used apparel. How many do you have?"

"Right now, I have 2,800 units."

"How much do you want for them?"

"Three dollars."

"Wow, Dan, we sell our worn shirts for $0.25."

"Sorry, Joe, I can't take that for them."

"What do you have in closeouts? That's what I buy."

"I have some shirts but no sizes, some styles I only have larges, some only mediums."

"That's what I buy. How many do you have and what do you want for them?"

"I have about four hundred dozen, and I will take $6 each."

"I will take the whole four hundred dozen for $4."

"Joe, I will take the $4 if you will take the jeans."

"I will take one thousand pair of the jeans at $2, how is that?"

"Take all the jeans at $1.50, and you have a deal!"

"Done!"

"Dan, here's the address of the store. When can you ship?"

"It'll go out tomorrow."

Joe called the store. "Jojo, I just got Brittania for us!"

"Uncle Joe, you are a miracle man. How the hell did you score that?"

Joe told the story.

In mid-March, Jojo called Joe. "Uncle Joe, the Brittania goods just arrived. Get in your car and come out here."

"Is it bad, Jojo?"

"No, Uncle Joe, you struck gold!"

By the time Joe arrived, Carlo and Jojo had unpacked the jeans and segregated them by defect. Some were bad, some were like new, needed minor repair. There actually were some in poly bags that were new! Someone had spilled glue on the bag. Inside was a brand-new pair of jeans!

Joe called a friend who ran a clothing repair and alterations shop, his name was Benny Scaduto. Benny was from Brooklyn. He had been a tailor at a major suit manufacturer and was a typical New Yorker, talked out of the side of his mouth with the short cigar in it and used both hands to express himself when he talked, with a great funny, lovable personality. He came right over, and a deal was cut, $0.50 for all repairs except zippers, $1.50 to remove the old zipper and replace it. Benny insisted they be segregated in boxes by defect. After he left, Joe, Carlo and Jojo pulled the jeans they did not want to repair and counted 1,500 pair. Joe took six samples from them and left.

The next day, he met with Ira Goldberg and Jerry Arbetman and asked if they could sell them.

"Are you kidding?" Ira said, "Tell us what you need to get for them, and before you are out the door, they will be sold."

Joe's mind worked like Maria's. He remembered Jim Gualdoni's reply to Maria's question when he inquired how much she wanted for the rent of the store that Rosen vacated. "What can you get for them, Ira?"

"We can get $5 a pair with no problem."

"All right, here's your deal, get $5.50, and you get the $0.50. That's your commission."

Jerry called Joe the next day. "He sold the jeans to a Cuban guy named Frank the Mex on Damen Avenue and asked them to be delivered and pick up $8,250 in cash! Please do it tomorrow. Frank wants them for the weekend."

On Monday, Joe called Dan Prentice and asked if he had any more of those worn jeans and got the answer he wanted.

"We have a ton of them, Joe. How many do you want?"

"Ship what you have." He explained what had transpired.

Two weeks later, JoJo called, "Uncle Joe, you better go rent a warehouse. The Brittania shipment just arrived, and we received four hundred cartons, fifty pair in each, twenty thousand pair!"

Midwest Outpost expansion
1975

Joe heeded Jojo's suggestion and rented a warehouse at 65 East Palatine Road. JoJo and Carlo began the process of sorting the Brittania jeans for Benny Scaduto.

Joe said, "Jojo, a guy from North Chicago Laundry is going to look at the jeans Benny repaired and give you a price to wash and press them. He will poly bag every pair and make them look like they just came from the factory in Hong Kong."

Jojo met with the guy and beat him down from $0.75 a pair to $0.50! One Saturday, in late March, Joe walked into the store with the kids and saw one of Jojo's great signs, "Brittania recycled jeans, $14.99!" They were $30 in the regular-priced stores!

Joe had given Dan Prentice the green light to automatically ship all the worn jeans, and they were averaging twenty thousand pair a month. Tables were set up to sort them. People were hired, and an assembly line was set up for processing them. Soon there were too many to use for the stores, and Joe set up a wholesale program with Arbetman and Goldberg. They were selling them for $8 a pair. That year, Joe left Arrow and became a full-time employee of Midwest Outpost.

In May, Joe and Jojo received the call they had been dreading since Ricky's operation. They were told to get to St. Louis. He was not doing well and passed away a few short days after their arrival. The entire family was devastated. Ricky was everyone's favorite! Virginia and Jim were never the same.

1976

Joe and Bryan purchased a very nice town house in Palm Springs right on a golf course at Mission Hills Country Club. The plan was to allow good friends and business associates and family to use it.

It soon became Joe's Shangri-La. He was working six days a week, twelve to fourteen hour days, and traveling the country sourcing product for Midwest and the wholesale company. In New York one day on the west coast the next on buying trips.

1977

On a warm sunny day in April, Midwest opened the third store in Hoffman Estates. At ten thousand square feet, it was double the size of the other two stores and was as nice as any clothing store in Chicago. Joe had used the Brittania brand as a lever to entice the best brands in the country to sell their products to him! Every fine jean line was now sold in the stores. Even the designer men's and ladies' lines were featured, and people were coming from all over the state of Illinois to shop. The previous year's sales topped $2,600,000 for the retail operation and another $2,100,000 for the wholesale.

Joe invited Maria to join him and the kids for Easter break in Palm Springs. Josie and Virginia had been there in 1976 and raved about the town house. They arrived on Good Friday. Carolyn Long, Joe's neighbor, picked them up at the airport. "Hello, Mrs. Reina, I am Carolyn Long. It is a pleasure meeting you. I feel like I know you. I've heard so much about you."

"Thank you, my daughter Josie has spoken about you and your husband."

As they drove through the guardhouse gate, Maria was amazed at the entrance.

She marveled at the landscaping and was astounded when she walked through the house. Joe gave her the five-minute tour. She started to unpack and brought out the usual four bags of frozen ravioli and four jars of her homemade tomato sauce and, of course, a loaf of bread.

"Joe, let's go to the grocery store so I can get flour and a few things for dinner tonight."

Mike and Kris changed into their swim clothes and headed for the pool. Kelly, Maria, and Joe went to the store. Kelly knew her way around, started shopping while Maria and Joe headed for the meat counter.

"Mister, let me see that piece of chuck," the butcher obliged. "Can you weigh it for me?"

After he told her the weight, she said, "I want you to take some of the fat off the top and cut that grizzle out and grind it for me."

"Lady"—pointing to some ground beef shown in the refrigerator—"I ground that up this morning. It is very fresh!"

"Sir, I was a butcher for twelve years. I owned my own grocery store. I used to butcher a quarter round of beef every Thursday, and I know what goes into that ground beef. I know, and you know it is the leftovers of everything you butchered this morning."

"But my meat grinder is clean. I will have to clean it again!"

Maria looked around. "There are no other customers waiting. You have time to clean the meat grinder, so please do this for me." She said it with that same smile she used when she convinced Mr. Braun at Anheuser Busch to lease her the store. The butcher complied.

On a beautiful sunny Sunday, they went to Easter mass at five. Joe pulled the car into the parking lot catty-corner from the church. Maria commented on the name, "Why do they call it St. Louis Church?"

Joe kidded her, "They changed the name because they heard you were coming from St. Louis."

"No," Maria said, "that's not true."

The kids looked at each other and smiled. Joe helped Maria out of the front seat as a dark-orange Volvo station wagon pulled up across the street.

Joe knew the car. "Ma, there's Frank Sinatra."

She responded, "That's his son."

"No, Ma, his son just got out of the back seat with his sisters, and that other lady is his wife, Barbara."

The church was filling up fast, and they were ushered up to a middle pew.

Maria moved inside, then the kids, and Joe was on the aisle. Soon the priest was up saying the Gospel. He addressed the congregation, "We are gathered here to honor the resurrection of our Lord Jesus Christ and a very special parishioner, Dolly Sinatra, who passed away this past February."

Frank Sinatra had sent a private plane for his mother to attend his opening night in Las Vegas in February, and sadly it crashed on takeoff, and she and the two pilots perished.

Frank and Barbara brought the wine up to the altar before communion. The congregation were amazed. Most didn't know he and his family were in the church. Joe moved all the way to the middle of the pew when Maria and the kids returned from communion, and Maria ended up on the aisle.

When the mass ended, the crowd jammed the aisles. Joe lost sight of Maria. He worked his way quickly through the crowd and reached the front of the lobby, and he saw Frank Sinatra walking Maria down the steps. By the time he got down there, she had Frank Sinatra in a corner, and he was laughing. It was obvious Maria reminded him of his mother. She was asking all kinds of family questions.

Joe approached and said, "Come on, Mom, Mr. Sinatra's family is waiting for him."

Frank waved him off. "She's fine. We are having a nice conversation. I am in no hurry."

The following Friday, they went back to Chicago, and on Saturday morning, Joe took Maria to the airport for the return to St. Louis. Jim picked her up and brought her to Josie's where the family was waiting to greet her.

Carlo asked her about the trip, "Ma, how did you like Joe's house? Did you go into the swimming pool?" That brought a laugh.

"We had a good time, we went to St. Louis church for Easter, and I met Frank Sinatra!"

Josie exclaimed, "What?"

Maria, beaming, told the story.

The following week, Josie sat down and wrote a thank you note to Frank Sinatra. In it, she mentioned Maria was celebrating her eighty-fifth birthday November 25. She mailed it. "Frank Sinatra, Rancho Mirage California." She had no street address. She used her own return address.

In mid-November, one day, a dozen beautiful roses arrived at Josie's home for Maria Reina, compliments of Frank Sinatra, along with a great autographed photo. "Happy Birthday, Maria! Love, Frank Sinatra! As he would say, "Now that's class!"

Reina family group photo, 1976

CHAPTER 22

Maria's Retirement

Maria was enjoying life in retirement. She had sold the grocery store building to the Rumbolo's. There no longer was any financial stress.

Carlo had taken her to Las Vegas. She loved to travel and enjoyed simple things like the holiday feasts in Josie and Joe's basement. But she missed her close friends who had passed away.

Joe called her every Sunday morning, and one day, in July, he invited her to visit Chicago.

"Mom, I am planning a trip to California with you and the kids. Are you up for it? I want to take you to San Francisco, then after a few days, we will go up to the wine country. It will remind you of Sicily. After that, we will drive down the coast. I have a surprise for you at the end of the trip."

Maria said, "Let's go."

Josie used to say she always had a piece of luggage packed, ready to go on a trip. Maria flew to Chicago, and Joe and the kids met her flight then moved to another gate and boarded their flight to the west coast. Maria marveled at her son's ability to drive to the hotel and avoid getting lost. Joe knew his way around San Francisco. He had made reservations at the Hyatt Regency, and Maria watched her son, dealing with the bellhops and tipping them. She thought, *He knows how to use the badge.* Kelly shared a room with Kris. Maria had her own room, and Joe and Mike shared a room.

"Mom, get unpacked, I will knock on your door in about twenty minutes, and we will go to the top floor for dinner."

They were seated at a nice round table. Joe asked Maria, "Ma, would you like a glass of wine?"

"Why not."

The kids smiled. "Grandma drinking?"

Mike asked, "Grandma, have you noticed anything unusual about this restaurant?"

"No, Mike, but I think this wine is making me dizzy. My head is spinning."

"No, Ma, this restaurant is slowly moving in a circle. It rotates!"

"No, it doesn't! You are kidding me?"

Mike said again, "Look, Grandma, see that building on your left? Watch, it will disappear in a few minutes."

Maria could not believe what she was seeing. She couldn't wait to see more of San Francisco. Joe took them all over, and she was overjoyed, and she knew this would be the trip of a lifetime. They visited and walked around North Beach, which reminded her of the Hill. The best thing was the weather. It was in the eighties and perfect the entire three days. On the fourth day, they drove to St. Helena and moved into a very nice condominium. After they settled in and unpacked, they went to the Robert Mondavi Vineyard. Again, the weather cooperated. It was a warm beautiful sunny day.

Maria had a discussion with one of the vineyard workers, a young lady. "I used to make and sell wine."

"Really? What was the brand name?"

Maria smiled. "We had no name. It was during prohibition, and we sold it to the coal miner's my husband worked with for $0.50 a gallon." Everyone laughed.

Later they had dinner at a very fine Italian restaurant. The minute they walked in the door, they heard, "Good evening, Mr. Reina, welcome back." Maria was impressed, but not surprised.

The next day, they visited yet another vineyard.

Kelly suggested, "Dad, let's take Grandma to McDonald's for lunch."

They did since she had never been to one. She ordered a cheese burger, fries, and a milkshake.

They left the wine country and drove to Carmel. The weather was near perfect, sunshine and no rain. The plan was to spend two nights. Joe took them on a tour around the city and the twenty-five-mile drive along the Pebble Beach golf course. Joe said, "Mike, someday we will come here to play Pebble Beach."

From Carmel, they continued south and spent one night in Santa Barbara and then the surprise, Disneyland. It was the first time for the kids, and in reality, it was like having four kids. Maria was beside herself. She said to Joe, "How much money did they spend for this? I can't believe it." She was up for everything. The best were the bumper cars. She had never driven an automobile, but she was driving like an extra in a crash on a movie set, purposely bumping into the kids, trying to dodge them and in uproarious laughter!

Once again, the weather was in the eighties. Maria commented that the weather here in California reminded her of Sicily. "Joe, you need to go there and visit your cousins." The best were the photos with her with Mickey, Minnie, and Pluto. It was three days of bliss. Maria's favorite time were on the dodgem cars. She insisted on going back on them again. Later at the airport, Joe put her and the children on a flight back to Chicago. Jojo and Carlo were picking them up and staying with her and the kids. Joe was heading to Hawaii with his girlfriend, Cathy Berlinger, she had set up the Disneyland portion of the trip.

Maria put her arms around Joe and said, "Thank you for this. You are the most generous person I know. I will never forget this trip. I am very proud of you."

1979

Midwest opened the fourth store in March, and two more were planned for next year. The two new stores were late opening and the shortfall of cash flow due to the late openings, plus cost of construction forced the retail division to borrow $350,000 from Standard

Chartered Bank. Midwest Outpost did $5,600,000, and the whole-sale division did $6,100,000 that year.

The wholesale division line of credit at the bank had grown from $100,000 to $1.5 million, and Joe was importing goods from all over Asia.

1980

Joe had invested money with two friends in an apartment complex in downtown Barrington, a wealthy suburb northwest of Chicago. It was primarily to be used as a tax hedge against the money he was earning.

In March, at the bank, discussing the loans for the two businesses, Joe was warned by Tim Noonen, the bank manager "Joe, be careful the prime rate, which is 8 percent today, could go as high as fifteen to sixteen by the end of the year! You are paying 10 percent now, but you could be paying 18 percent by fall!" Joe was not the least concerned.

On a nasty windy day in March, Bryan Wardell had a private meeting with Joe and informed him, "My cancer is back, Joe. They are going to take out my other kidney, my bladder, and my prostate, and I will be on chemotherapy for quite a while. I will not be able to work. It is time for me to retire. I would like to sell my stock. Will you please get with your nephews and put a plan together?"

"Wow, Bryan, I am sorry to hear this. I will get with the boys and be back to you tomorrow!" Joe put the deal together for $140,000 for Bryan, $40,000 in cash, and ten payments of $10,000 a month.

The prime rate was climbing every other month, having an effect on business all over the country. Inflation had begun raising its ugly head in 1979. In 1980, it was running as high as 14 percent! Unemployment was rising too, and all this was causing a slow down for all businesses.

Many discount stores were popping up. Marshall's opened three stores within a few blocks of three Midwest stores. There were twenty-eight different companies selling off price apparel in Metro Chicago and the suburbs!

The stores failed to meet projected sales figures for back to school the first time since they started their expansion. That coupled with higher interest rates at the bank, and $10,000 a month to Bryan was causing financial problems for Midwest Outpost.

Joe had moved into Bryan's Midwest Outpost position and loaned money from the wholesale company's line of credit to pay the bills on time.

He called a meeting with Jojo and Carlo. "We can't keep doing what we are doing. We have to start cutting expenses right now—today! We are paying 18 percent interest on the loans at the bank, and I am at the limit on the $1.5m line and can't borrow any more. I have put a plan together that will hopefully get us through the economic mess, perhaps we can survive."

In the ensuing months, twenty-three people were dismissed. The trio took a severe pay cut. Joe had ordered major cutbacks on purchasing. Jojo went back to managing a store as did Carlo. While all this helped, it was not the answer. Business was off by wide margins as was profit due to heavy markdowns. The stores dropped 36 percent in same store sales in the fourth quarter, and the $350,000 debt at the bank remained the same as did the $1.5 million for the wholesale division.

1981

In January, Joe met with the accountants to discuss the final profit and lost statements. The two businesses barely showed a profit. He went back to the office and met with Carlo and Jojo, and they discussed the year-end numbers. The bank debt for both operations remained the same. They decided to close two stores, take the money from the going out of business sales, and pay down the bank loan.

Jojo said, "Uncle Joe, let's wait until spring when the weather breaks. It's too cold to have the sales now."

They agreed.

Later the bad news continued. The prime rate went to 20 percent, and now they were paying 22 percent, close to $34,000 a month in interest! The government declared the country was in a recession. In March, Joe was invited to a cocktail party at the bank. Tim Noonan was transferring to the Standard Chartered Bank in Singapore. At the party, he met Tim's replacement, Jeff Williams, who was transferring from the bank in Miami.

Tim made the introduction, "Jeff, this is Joe Reina. He's been with the bank since 1975 and runs a very interesting clothing business."

Jeff had a limp handshake, did not smile, and Joe's intuition kicked in. He said to himself, "This guy will be a problem. I am sure he hated the idea of leaving the sunshine of Miami."

The economy was booming in Florida with the influx of people from all over Mexico, Central and South America flying into the city and buying anything they could get their hands on. They were carrying their buys back to their country and doubling the price they paid, due to 30 to 40 percent inflation.

Joe thought, *This guy can't be happy being transferred to the Rust Belt.*

In May, Joe received a call from Jeff, requesting an audience, and the next day, he went to the meeting. Jeff greeted him with the same limp handshake. "Joe, I have reviewed your year-end profit and lost statements for last year. Your companies did not make any money. We are concerned about your ability to withstand this recession."

"Jeff, it is not easy to make money paying 22 percent interest. We paid your interest without fail every month. We did not lose any money!"

"Everyone pays their interest every month, or they are no longer clients of the bank. You are at your limit on both loans, and it has been that way for over a year."

Joe explained they had cut the overhead to the bone, and they were planning on closing two stores. "Jeff"—pointing his finger at Joe in a very stern voice—"I want you be back here in one week with a plan on how you are going to pay these loans down substantially!"

Joe got up from the chair, looked at Jeff, and said, "Don't you ever point your finger at me again. If you do, I am going to break it off and give you some Sicilian philosophy that will remain a memory for the rest of your life!" He left and drove back to the office, shaking.

The going out of business sales started the following week. Jojo placed large full-page ads in the local papers. The crowds were huge the first five days and slowed the last twenty-five. Joe marched into the bank at the end of the month and paid the Midwest loan down $105,000! While it took some of the sting out of the Midwest loan, it did not help with the other loan. Midwest was unable to pay down what was now a debt to the wholesale company in the amount $190,000!

Once again, on a miserable hot, humid day in October, Joe met with Jojo. "I have an idea. Let's take half of the warehouse and have a warehouse sale Thanksgiving weekend. I am going to give you a $15,000 budget for advertising, buy as many radio stations as you can, and run a full-page ad in the suburban newspaper the day before Thanksgiving. Let's see if we can drum up some business so I can get this damn bank off my back."

They ran a very successful sale. People were waiting outside the door at 7:00 a.m., even though the ads all stated an 8:00 a.m. opening!

When the sales totaled Monday, Joe took a bag of cash to the bank, $60,000 was for Midwest and $141,000 for the wholesale company. Again there was a meeting with Carlo and Jojo. "I want you to continue with the radio advertising. We are going to run the warehouse sale throughout the month of December." Joe went to the bank every Monday and paid down the loans. The week after Christmas, Joe went to the bank with the previous week's sales, and the loans were down to $120,000 for the stores and $1,090,000 for the wholesale company.

1982

Joe lost a great friend when Bryan Wardell passed away in early January. He was selected as a pallbearer. After the mass ended, he and the other pallbearers lifted the coffin and carried Bryan from the front of the church to the hearse. Few noticed the tears running down his cheeks. It was a sad day.

Monday after New Year's, Joe and Jojo drove to Rockford, Illinois, a nice city ninety miles from Chicago. They searched the business districts and found no apparel discount stores. Then they tried to find a large vacant building to run a warehouse-type sale. They found a VFW building and rented it for two weeks. Jojo put an advertising budget together of $25,000! He bought the six and ten news for all three networks and ran a full-page ad in the local newspaper.

The sale broke the second week of January. Sales were robust the first five days then slowed, but they ended up doing a little over $150,000. The weather cooperated nicely. Once again, Joe was at the bank and paid down the loans.

In February, Joe again met with Jojo to discuss a plan. "Let's take the warehouse sales across the country."

Jojo looked at his uncle and could only smile. "Uncle Joe, do you ever sleep, or do you sit up all night and come up with these brainstorms?"

"Jojo, I have outlined small cities like Rockford where the discounters have not penetrated. Advertising is inexpensive. Let's follow what we did in Rockford, only run the sale Wednesday through Sunday. Then take inventory for what is needed to start the next sale. Pack up and move on to the next city and get it there on Tuesday. Meanwhile, we load the other truck at our warehouse for what's needed and send it to the next location. I know we can get the bank paid off in the next six months. The towns I have planned are Memphis and Nashville, Shreveport and Galveston, Amarillo and Albuquerque, Des Moines and Mason City. If necessary, Norfolk and Charleston as the final options. These cities are located close to each other, making it convenient to move a short distance to start the next sale."

"I have formed two groups. You and Carlo will head up one group, and I am going to get my sister Virginia to go with me to head up the other group. The two large trucks will haul the merchandise from the warehouse to each location."

Joe met with his assistant, Casandra Savard, and laid down the locations for each sale. She headed up the plan to find locations, rented tables, and made arrangements within the cities for license fees. Between March and August, the sales created enough cash flow to pay off the Midwest loan completely and reduce the wholesale company's loan to $200,000! There still was the $180,000 due the wholesale company from the stores. They paid off $1,650,000!

Business was horrible. Major companies were going out of business. Ronald Reagan was president, and he was trying everything to get the economy to rebound. But it was not working. When he took over as president, inflation had been running at 14 percent, unemployment very close to same, the prime interest rate was 20 percent.

Midwest closed two more stores and paid some of the bill to the wholesale company, but the handwriting was on the wall. Joe met again with Carlo and Jojo who had by now reduced their salaries to $40,000 a year. "It's that time, guys, there's too much competition for us. There's no way to compete, we need an exit strategy for the next twelve months to shut it down."

Jojo said, "It's no fun anymore Uncle Joe, Carlo and I have been talking about it. I am sick of Chicago weather, and I have been talking to your son, Mike, I think I'm going to Phoenix."

Carlo said, "I miss my mom and dad and the rest of the family. I am going back to St. Louis."

The store ran sales on and off every month; the Morton Grove store closed at the end of June. The last day of the going-out-of-business sale for the Hoffman Estates store was New Year's Day 1984. Joe hugged Jojo. "We had a great ride, Jojo!"

"I love you a lot, Uncle Joe, thanks for giving me the shot!"

"Thank you, Jojo, you bailed me out of corporate life!"

Maria at Disneyland, 1978

Frank Sinatra, 1977

Joe Reina and Jojo Mocca last day of
Midwest Outpost, January 1, 1984

CHAPTER 23

Life Goes On

Joe went to St. Louis to see Maria and the family. Virginia hosted the family gathering since Josie was in Palm Springs.

Carlo asked, "So, Joe, what are you going to do now that the stores are closed?"

"I am not sure, Carlo. I am going to Palm Springs for a couple of weeks. Meanwhile, a guy who used to work for me is in Italy, trying to get the rights to distribute a sandal for the country."

Jim piped in, "You don't know anything about shoes, Joe, be careful. This economy is still a mess."

It was Maria's turn. "He didn't know anything about the blue jean business, and he did okay." Maria the Perennial Optimist!

Joe always slept on the couch. It was old and not very comfortable. When Maria got up and made the coffee, he was right beside her and gave her a hug and a kiss on the cheek. "Mom, when I get back to Chicago, I am going to buy you a couch and a new chair. I have a friend who can help me get them wholesale."

"No, Joe, don't spend the money. From now on, I will sleep on the couch, you sleep in the bedroom."

Joe laughed. "Yeah right."

When he returned, he called Laurie Canalle who worked for his architect friend. He had met her in 1980 when she used her pass to take him to the Merchandise Mart to buy furniture. He liked her style sense and design talent.

They met in the lobby, and Laurie took him to the fifteenth floor to a fine Italian furniture manufacturer. Joe bought a beautiful Italian sofa and chair, and Laurie helped him pick the fabric. It took all of twenty minutes. It was close to lunchtime, and they went for a quick bite in the building.

"Thanks for taking the time to help me today, Laurie. I appreciate this. My mom is eighty-nine, and when I visit her, I sleep on the couch in her living room. It is so old, there is not much padding left. I think it came over on the Mayflower!

"It's my pleasure, Mr. Reina, I love coming to this building. It's no problem."

"Okay, enough of the Mr. Reina. Everyone calls me Joe."

"Okay, Joe, sorry."

They talked a lot about Italy. It was sparked because of the sofa he just purchased was being made there. "Have you been to Italy?"

She said, "No, someday." They finished lunch, and they went their separate ways.

1987

In January, Ron Calabrese, Joe's partner in the Barrington apartment project, invited him to look at a large vacant seven-hundred-thousand-square-foot building in Bellwood, a Western suburb of Chicago. It was raining so hard when he arrived that he refused to enter. He told Ron, "I am wearing an expensive pair of shoes, and I am not about to ruin them, walking around this building. What are you thinking of doing with this monster?"

"We can buy it cheap. It's been vacant for eight years. They used to make auto parts for the big three GM, Ford, and Chrysler, but the unions ran them out of town."

"Ron, I am not interested. But I have an architect friend who did something like this on a much smaller scale, and Lloyd Churchman might be interested. Let me call him." Joe made the calls, and gave them Ron's name and phone number, and left the next day to play golf in Palm Springs.

At the end of February, he got calls from the contractor and architect, both asking if he was in the deal. His answer was a firm no! In early March, Joe received a call from Ron who invited him to a meeting at the architect's office. When Joe arrived, the architect unveiled early sketches of the renovation of the building. They showed major demolition of the facility, reducing it to 550,000 square feet. A ten-acre vacant lot provided parking for employees of the former factory. It was shown with very nice landscaping, and Joe was impressed. Ron said he had had discussions with the US post office in town who were interested in leasing it for their trucks for five years. The architect showed possible ways of subdividing the building into smaller segments to be rented for all types of businesses. He had done a study of the surrounding suburbs. There was nothing like it anywhere in the entire area west of Chicago. Next, he presented the financial plans, which called for acquisition and renovation costs totaling $10,000,000!

Joe asked, "Where do you propose getting $10,000,000? How much cash will you need to acquire the property? That's a lot of money to borrow on a vacant building." Ron said, "That's where you come in. We want you to handle the financing and all the administration."

Joe smiled. "Ron, my money is tied up. I am sorry, but I can't be part of this. First, it will be very time-consuming, and I don't know that I have the time.

"Joe, we want you in the project." This time, it was the architect. "Ron and Churchman [the contractor] are willing to put up the down payment to acquire the building. My office will do all the drawings at no initial cost, Ron will do the leasing, and we want you to handle financing and administration. We are willing to give you 20 percent. You don't need to put in any money out of pocket!"

Joe could not help but reflect on Maria acquiring the first grocery store, Reina Auto Sales and Midwest Outpost, all with no money down! There was nothing more to think about. He looked around the table and said, "Deal, I'm in."

1989

Joe called a meeting at the architect's office. "I have secured an acquisition loan for the building, $2.8 million, using the $500,000 from Ron and Churchman for the down payment. We have eighteen months to get some serious leasing before I can go for the construction and final loan." Ron came with some great news. He had signed a lease for five years with the post office for the parking lot for $250,000 a year!

In the ensuing weeks, Churchman was doing demolition, and Ron was showing and leasing space daily, and in the first ninety days, he signed five leases totaling 160,000 square feet!

Joe worked with Laurie Canalle on several office designs for tenants in the building. His relationship with Laurie had blossomed. They were working closely on the development of the building and occasionally would have lunch or dinner.

1990

The project was a huge success. Joe worked with a large national firm, Sanford Ink, in the pen business located across the street. After three months of negotiating, he leased them 239,000 feet! The lease included moving their corporate headquarters into the building. He and Laurie worked with their corporate executives on the office design. Once that lease was signed, Joe met with the local AFL/CIO pension fund executives and arranged for a $10,000,000 loan for the building.

In the middle of the summer, Joe called Laurie, "Hi, can you to go to the Merchandise mart with me, I need to buy some furniture for my daughter, Kelly."

"No problem, Joe, when do you want to go?" "How about tomorrow?"

They agreed to meet at ten. It took Joe less than twenty minutes to make his purchases. Laurie couldn't believe how fast he made a decision.

"How about some lunch?"

Laurie said, "Sure, where would you like to go?"

They went to Carlucci for some good Italian food.

Working on the tenant improvement designs, they were seeing each other just about every day.

Sometimes they would grab fast food in between appointments with clients or have food delivered to the office. Work on the building had really intensified. Ron and Joe were leasing the spaces faster than Churchman could complete the tenant improvements.

In September, Joe needed to be in Italy for a couple of meetings. He and Laurie were enjoying dinner at the Greek Islands, and he asked Laurie, "Do you have a passport?"

"Yes, why do you ask?"

"I have two meetings scheduled in Italy. I am leaving in two weeks."

"Are you inviting me to join you?"

"Sounds to me you just invited yourself!"

"I'm sorry. Let's start over. Yes, I have a passport, why do you ask?"

They both laughed. They flew to Rome and spent the night and had dinner at Babette's. Laurie was overwhelmed. She could not believe she was strolling the streets of Rome. Joe turned on the charm. The weather was delightful.

Laurie asked, "Where do we go from here?"

"We are taking a train to Naples in the morning. It'll take about two and a half hours, then from there, it's about an hour to Positano."

The next morning, at breakfast, Joe asked, "Laurie, did you sleep well last night?"

"No, I did not, perhaps it's jet lag. I'll catch a few winks on the train." Joe had arranged for a driver to pick them up and take them to Positano. Laurie was amazed at the scenic drive along the beautiful Tyrrhenian Sea. The sun was shining, and it glistened across the water. They were very excited. This was quite a welcome pace from the day-to-day pressure they had been experiencing in Bellwood with the big project and the newest one in Broadview.

Laurie commented, "This weather is incredible, nice day you ordered, Mr. Reina!"

"I thought I asked you to call me Joe!" Again they both laughed.

"Joe, I don't have any idea how I can ever repay you for this. It already has exceeded anything I ever imagined!"

"Laurie, you don't need to repay me. I am enjoying to too."

"Wait until you get to Positano. You will not believe it!"

They arrived and checked into the Sirenuse Hotel, and they both were amazed at the view when the bellman opened the drapes in the room. Later they went down to the beach for lunch at Chez Black for pizza. Afterward they visited art galleries, and Joe purchased a beautiful oil of Positano, looking up from the beach. They went to Ravallo the next day, had a great lunch there, and just enjoyed the rest of the trip relaxing poolside at the famed Sirenuse.

The driver picked them on the fifth day and drove them back to the train station for the train back to Rome, where they stayed the next two nights. They went to the Vatican, and later after lunch, Joe took Laurie on his favorite walk, first to the Fountain of Trevi, down to the Piazza d' Pantheon, visited the Pantheon, then the short walk to the Piazza Navona. After strolling over to the fountain created by Bernini, Joe explained about the rivalry of Borromini, the architect who designed the church opposite the fountain with the statute with his outstretched hand. Bernini told his rival, Borromini, "My statute will be here long after your church falls, and he will catch it!"

On Monday, they took the train to Assisi where Joe had a two-day meeting, and then they proceeded to Florence. The plan was to spend two nights. Joe had the concierge at the hotel make a reservation the night they arrived at Enoteca Pinchiorri, one of the finest restaurants in all of Italy.

The evening was warm and perfect for walking, just as it had been in Rome. They dressed casually, California style. When they walked in the door, the maitre d' greeted them, "Buona sera, signore Reina, nice to see you again." "Buona sera, signora. Welcome to Enoteca. "Nice to see you, Luigi, *come stai, tutto bene?*"

Laurie was in a state of awe. She thought, *This is too much! He is recognized at the hotels in Rome and Positano and now in this fancy restaurant in Florence.*

They were seated at a table away from the crowd. Joe ordered a bottle of Cabreo, their favorite white wine, and after the first glass was poured, he toasted, "To you, Laurie."

"I have a question, as you know I have been a committed bachelor for nineteen years, I promised myself when I divorced, never to remarry until my children were educated and out of the house. I did not want a woman to move in and get into a conflict with the kids and in turn with me. So would you be interested in changing that status?"

Laurie laughed. "That has to be the all-time great proposal, and the answer is yes. When do you want to do this?"

"Let's do it in the spring. First, I want you to come to St. Louis and meet my family, and I want to meet yours."

They concluded the trip with a couple of days on Lake Como and finished the last night in Milan before they flew back to Chicago.

Thanksgiving

Joe and Laurie arrived at Maria's House on Wednesday morning. Virginia, who was living on the second floor, answered the bell and greeted them.

"Joe!" She hugged her baby brother like he was some kind of God.

"Virginia, this is Laurie."

Laurie hugged her and said, "Virginia, Joe speaks of you with the same love and admiration as he does of your mother!"

"Come in please. Mom is downstairs in the basement, getting the dough ready to bake for tomorrow." She walked them through the small dining room to the steps leading down to the basement. "Ma, you have company."

Laurie went first, and Maria was waiting for her. "Hi, Mrs. Reina, I'm Laurie," she said as she threw her arms around her.

"I am so happy to meet you, Laurie! Joe has told me very nice things about you. Are you Italian?"

"I am 75 percent Greek and 25 percent Sicilian."

"Well, that's good. Welcome to my house. I am making buns for the dinner tomorrow. Would like to help?"

"I would love to."

Joe decided to let the two of them get to know each other and went upstairs to visit with Virginia.

Later, Laurie shared part of the conversation she had with Maria. "I asked her how many loaves of bread do you think you have baked in your life? She answered, 'It would be easier to count the hairs on my head!'"

The next day, as the family members arrived, Joe introduced Laurie, and when the usual spread was put out, Laurie told Joe, "My mother and grandmother are great cooks, and I thought I would never see anything like their Thanksgiving dinners, but this is epic! Years later, Tommy Reina's daughter, Susan, summed up Josie and Joe's Thanksgiving feasts with a beautiful story, *Turkey and Dressing Optional!*

Laurie Reina, 1990

Turkey and Dressing Optional

"Variety is said to be the spice of life. Growing up Italian will teach you that lesson quickly.

"I did not have a bland American childhood. My infancy was scented with garlic and olive oil. Peanut butter and jelly sandwiches were unknown in my childhood lunchbox, and I did not have Easy Mac until I was twelve. What I did have that not many of my playground peers could boast was an elaborate family structured around the dinner tables.

"My family was different from that of my friends in retrospect. They were not familiar with the benefits of being the daughter of an Italian family. As far back as I can remember, my entire family was as close as a three-blade razor! With this, I grew up pronouncing words I could not spell to save my life. I never had a Nintendo. I had a swing set and playmates that spanned three generations. My childhood was spent in an unassuming basement in South St. Louis, and it made me who I will be forever.

"My most potent memories are Thanksgiving meals in my aunt Josie's basement.

"I spent countless Thanksgivings never knowing ravioli wasn't a part of the typical dinner menu. Football was not the game that we played. Octogenarians don't tackle.

"The basement was a tribute to immigrant culture. Its centerpiece was a hardened wooden support beam etched with the penciled in height of five decades' worth of children.

"Our walls were plastered with the wallpaper of family gatherings captured by camera and the paintings of my Uncle Joe. The children, ranging from four to thirty-nine, played in the nook of mismatched couches while the adults discussed the depression era of street gangs and distilleries. Dogs had free range of the floor as it was meant to be.

"Laughing was a prerequisite for attending any family function, as well as having an appetite. The best way to bring people together in an Italian family is through their stomachs. We have limitless first-rate cooks in our family, enough to open a chain of restaurants a mile long. All activity subsided when dinner was served buffet style to the throngs of my hungry family. We prepared our plates, standing room only with the delicate pastas and the buttery homegrown vegetables that were available. Sitting at the table was optional, and many of the older generation opted for a TV tray and their favorite armchair.

"Chewing with your mouth closed was not the etiquette of this meal. In fact, it was inadvisable. As a child, you were not in control of your meal. Portions were added to your plate as deemed necessary by the older generations. Mothers competed through their children's appetites. It was raucous! After dinner came the inevitable cleanup. I have been on dishwashing duty every meal since I graduated pre-school. It is my favorite chore. Through conversation and soap suds, we get the silverware sparkling.

"At the end of the event, we all waddle upstairs and off to our respective homes, laden with the smell of fine foods, arms loaded with leftovers, and hearts full of memories.

"My childhood has technically ended. Through the migration of my family throughout the United States, the basement has been packed into boxes, and the mementos have been shared equally. Scrabble tournaments on the lap of my grandmother will never happen again, but who is to say I will never pass that memory on? My family gave me something that can't be found anywhere else in the world. They gave me unconditional love. Family is not defined by the Norman Rockwell painting. It's shown through quirky memories that change your life without you noticing."

Christmas

A month later, on Christmas morning, Joe was with Laurie, and he called Virginia and Maria to wish them Merry Christmas. Laurie spoke to Maria, "Merry Christmas, Mrs. Reina."

"Please call me, Mom, Laurie."

"Okay, Mom, have a nice day with the family. We will see you at the wedding in April."

"I doubt I will be there."

Laurie said, "Why not?"

There was no reply. Maria handed the phone to Virginia who wished Laurie Merry Christmas.

1991

On Friday, March 22, Maria woke up her usual time, around 5:00 a.m. She had had a bad night. Virginia came down and found her sitting in her favorite chair, staring at the wall, and asked, "Ma, do want coffee?"

Maria said, "No, I don't feel good."

"What's the matter? Let me call the doctor."

"No, I will be okay."

After she had coffee, Virginia went upstairs and called Jean and Carlo, who jumped in their car and came to the house. They convinced Maria who had gotten worse to go to St. Mary's Hospital.

On Sunday, Joe received the dreaded call he knew would come someday. It was Josie. "Joe, you better come home. Mom is in the hospital. She has congestive heart disease. She may only have twenty-four hours to live."

It was too late to catch a flight, so he flew Monday and arrived at the hospital late morning the twenty-fifth. When he walked into the room, he saw the whole family, including Cousin Josie Burruano Vitale. As soon as Joe walked in the room, everyone left to allow him time alone with Maria.

She was under oxygen, her eyes were closed, he sat there, and in a few minutes, he went over his entire lifetime with her. He remembered the trips, all the way back to 1948, and the first visit to see Virginia in Chicago. The good times in Palm Springs and the fun at Disney. "Thank God, I took the time to take her on those trips." At that minute, she opened her eyes, looked at him and smiled that unmistakable warm friendly smile that had charmed so many. Then she closed her eyes and passed away.

Joe walked out of the room, crying, and everyone knew she had passed. They all went back in, except Josie Burruano Vitale, who went up to Joe and put her arm around him and said, "Joe, God just took away one of your great loves and has replaced her with Laurie!"

The tears stopped.

EPILOGUE

A year after my mother passed, I was in St. Louis in July, visiting my family to celebrate my sister Virginia's birthday. Sitting in Josie's basement Friday afternoon, we began telling stories about Maria. Both Virginia and Josie were born in that miserable first house.

Almost immediately I said, "We need to write this down or our kids and grandkids will never know of this. The three of us filled more than fifty legal pages with our memories! We continued early Saturday morning until Sunday night stopping only to eat. From time to time, my sisters got into mini arguments over some of the details.

From the notes later, we put together an outline, hoping someone in the family would write the book. It went to three family members and into a file in my office. Over the years, I would be in a discussion with friends and family members, who either knew my mother or had met her. I heard the same suggestion, "You have to write a book about your mother!" My comment was always the same, "I am not a writer, nor do I have the time. Perhaps someday!"

So the outline remained in a file where it sat for twenty-eight years until last September 2019.

In the summer of 2019, on three different occasions, Maria's name came up in a discussion with three people, and all three said, "Joe, you have to write the book."

On the third of September, I dug out the outline and began writing and almost immediately got confused.

My wife, Laurie, went online and began sending me topics about writing and suggested I make a time line that correlated with the original outline, which I did. I became obsessed, waking at three thirty in the morning sometimes to write on my iPad seven days a week, stopping only to eat and or occasionally to go for a walk! On November 25, in the late afternoon, I went into the kitchen and told Laurie I just finished the final chapter, the first draft of the book.

She said, "Do you know what today is? It's your mother's birthday!"

My brothers, sisters, and I inherited my mother's entrepreneurial instincts and, for the most part, her drive, work ethic, generosity, integrity, honesty, and care for the family. Carlo was the most conservative, understandably so, after the sting of the depression. Josie had the most patience and the logical mind. Jim was probably the brightest and could think as fast, if not faster, than all of us. Virginia was the glue early on that kept the group focused as a family, and she was street-smart just like Mom. Like Josie, Virginia did not have a high school education, but she had incredible common sense.

The one common denominator among Virginia, Josie, and myself was the library and the number of books we read. Does anyone go to the library for the love of reading anymore? Amazon seems to have taken that obligation for this society with Kindle and Audible books.

Carlo inherited Mom's easy sales talent, whereas Jim was a force in selling, relentless. I had the benefit of exposure to their talents and possess a combination of their sales ability. My mother was a great sales person, and I inherited her soft sell, "Get to know me, learn to like me, then buy from me."

Jim made millionaires out of just about everyone he worked for, but after Reina Auto Sales, he just could not find success when he tried his own ventures.

Mom once said he has a heart of gold! At age seventy-five, it surfaced. He opened a mission for the needy in a tough black neighborhood, and later it became a food pantry. He found success by dedicating himself, sometimes seven days a week, twelve to fourteen hours a day.

His sales ability enabled him to get the major grocery chains involved, and they provided food for his food pantry. In addition, he was able to get major contractors on the Hill to renovate the old building. Each day, a large group of kids would arrive after school, and he and his volunteer crew fed them. They were allowed to stay until their parents arrived to pick them up, thus, avoiding having to pay for day care. The mission was supported solely from donations. Again, he was great on selling his concept to friends and acquaintances to send him money on a monthly plan, me being one of them. He was not shy about calling and asking bluntly, "Where's the check?"

Carlo was the "capo," the family leader, the one everyone—including all the grandkids—loved and respected. What was not to love? He had it all, looks and personality coupled with Mom's warmth and, like Josie, patience and perseverance. He was the father I never had. He played catch with me in the backyard in the spring and summer and threw a football with me in the fall. He bought me my first bicycle and my first car, a 1937 Chevrolet for $100. He treated me like a son, as did his wife, Jean. She treated me like her baby brother. Never once do I remember her giving me any grief. I love her like a sister.

Carlo passed away in May 2005. I miss Carlo more than words can describe, same goes for all of them. Josie was by far the closest to me. She was more like a second mother, and she was my go-to when I had a concern. She always had time for anyone with a problem. I have never met anyone who could hear a problem and provide the solution almost before hearing its conclusion. Her personal concerns were set aside, regardless who was sitting with her discussing a bad situation. From the heart, she would absorb the concern as if it were hers and, in a matter of minutes, would come up with logical options to ease the pain of the person. I can personally attest to it. When I bought my town house in Palm Springs, I gave her a key. I gave her and Joe carte blanche to use it whenever it was available. I made her understand it was her second home. From 1976 until 2004, she and Joe were there every year, sometimes twice a year. She invited Sam and Rose Rumbolo, Jimmy and Leona Castellano, Carmella and Mel Cunetto to join her and Joe for a couple of weeks.

Jojo, her son, once thanked me for the time I allowed her use of the place. I said, "Jojo, she had to leave high school to take care of me and change my diapers. She was always there for me anytime I needed help or a shoulder to cry on."

In 1963, Josie went to work for General American Insurance for $60 a week as a file clerk and ended up running the national claims division. She reached such a high level of authority that the CEO asked her to rewrite the company's claims manual. She convinced the firm to allow treatment payment for alcohol addiction. That forced the entire insurance industry to add addiction as a sickness in their policies.

She was earning serious money, and when she retired at age sixty-two, more than three hundred people honored her at her retirement party. She passed away in 2005, one of the worst days of my life. To this day, I still grieve for her. There are two photos of her on my desk, and I look at her every day.

I would be remiss here if I failed to thank my nephew, Jojo Mocca, and my nephew, Carlo Reina. Midwest Outpost would never have achieved the success it did if it were not for them. Jojo was my right arm. He had Josie's patience and her calmness, and he became my sounding board, my go-to person. And he holds that position today. We had our problems on occasion. The best relationships get tested, and the strong ones survive! Today it is stronger than ever!

Virginia, on the other hand, took a different role. She had worked hard all her life, and when Martin passed, she moved back to St. Louis to take life easy and relax. She went to work with Josie initially to have health insurance, but Josie pushed her, and she moved up the ladder too. She made a name for herself, not to the extent as Josie had, but she ended up making a good income, and she retired at sixty-two. Virginia's biggest contribution was taking care of Maria. In 1972, she moved to the second floor of Maria's two flat and was there every day to have breakfast, lunch, and dinner with her. While Virginia still enjoyed her friendships and spent time traveling, she took care of Mom until the day she died.

I used to call Virginia every Sunday morning after my mother passed. We both looked forward to those discussions; there was no doubt in my mind that I was the son she never had. She passed away at age ninety-three in 2009. When she died, she left a considerable amount of money to every one of her nephews and nieces. Nine of them split $171,000!

Jim only lived to be eighty-three, and he had passed away in 2006. I had visited with him in the fall of 2005, and he was not doing well. He had become very religious, and he knew he was dying. He confided in me that he was ready to join his son, Ricky, who had passed away at the young age of twenty-one.

I have been told to include myself in the book, regarding my support of my siblings in many ways, always there when called upon by them. I have chosen not to include it.

This book is about Maria Reina, who was fifty years ahead of the feminist movement and about her achievements, her dedication to our family, and her small but important contribution to society. She did not have a selfish bone in her body, she never wanted for anything, and her only demand and need was respect. She was generous to a fault. Once shortly after she opened the first store, a paesano from Casteltermini visited her at the store. Her name was Martorano, whose husband was seriously ill and out of work. She had just left Father Lupo from St. Ambrose Church, where he had reached in his pocket and given her a dime. She had informed him she had no food to feed her family. Mom filled two large grocery bags with enough food to feed her family for two weeks. Shortly after opening the second store, every year on St. Joseph's Day, March 19, Maria had a large altar built in the back room behind the store, loaded with cooked food dedicated to her patron saint.

My brothers went to an orphan home and brought a dozen kids for dinner. When it was time to take them back, Maria loaded them with bags of food from the altar to take to the home. When World War II broke out, she brought six soldiers to the table to join the orphans! There are too many stories to print about her giving back after she made it.

I loved my mother with every ounce of my body, respected her with my heart and soul, and I miss her and my siblings more than words can describe.

ABOUT THE AUTHOR

Joe Reina was born in St. Louis, Missouri, on February 7, 1936. He grew up on the "Hill," attended Shaw grade school and Southwest high school. He went to work for the Arrow Shirt company in September 1954 and took night classes at St. Louis University.

Later, he became a salesman for the Arrow Shirt company and was named sales manager for the firm in Chicago in 1970. He took classes at night for three years at Northwestern University.

Joe's business career kept him involved in the apparel industry throughout most of his adult life, which involved international travel and enabled him to explore a good part of the world.

That exposure helped satisfy his desire to experience the pleasure of meeting and sharing those experiences with his family and friends.

Early, while in Chicago, in an effort to hedge against excessive income tax, he ventured into real estate.

He inherited the entrepreneurial traits and fortitude of his spirited mother. They were the motivation for him to write this book about her and her experiences in her journey from Casteltermini Sicily to America.

Joe is retired and lives with his wife, Laurie, in Dana Point, California.

CPSIA information can be obtained
at www.ICGtesting.com
Printed in the USA
FSHW011422200121
77746FS